A Permanent Beginning

A Permanent Beginning

R. Nachman of Braslav
and Jewish Literary Modernity

YITZHAK LEWIS

Cover image: Experiment made at Annonay, June 4, 1783, by the Montgolfier brothers (1868)

Published by State University of New York Press, Albany

© 2020 State University of New York

All rights reserved

No part of this book may be used or reproduced in any manner whatsoever without written permission. No part of this book may be stored in a retrieval system or transmitted in any form or by any means including electronic, electrostatic, magnetic tape, mechanical, photocopying, recording, or otherwise without the prior permission in writing of the publisher.

For information, contact State University of New York Press, Albany, NY
www.sunypress.edu

Library of Congress Cataloging-in-Publication Data

Names: Lewis, Yitzhak, 1981– author.
Title: A permanent beginning : R. Nachman of Braslav and Jewish literary modernity / Yitzhak Lewis.
Description: Albany : State University of New York Press, [2020] | Includes bibliographical references and index.
Identifiers: LCCN 2019013092 | ISBN 9781438477671 (hardcover : alk. paper) | ISBN 9781438477664 (pbk. : alk. paper) | ISBN 9781438477688 (ebook : alk. paper)
Subjects: LCSH: Naḥman, of Bratslav, 1772–1810. | Jewish literature—History and criticism. | Judaism and literature. | Rabbis—Ukraine—Biography. | Hasidim—Ukraine—Biography. | Jews—Europe, Eastern—History—18th century. | Jews—Europe, Eastern—History—19th century. | Ukraine—Biography.
Classification: LCC BM755.N25 L49 2020 | DDC 296.8/332092—dc23
LC record available at https://lccn.loc.gov/2019013092

10 9 8 7 6 5 4 3 2 1

To A.
and to N., K., and R.
with love

Contents

Acknowledgments ix

Introduction: What Is Jewish Literary Modernity? 1

PART I
POLITICAL-AESTHETIC QUESTIONS

Chapter 1 Positioning R. Nachman 21

Chapter 2 Representing Difference 37

Chapter 3 The Secret of Our Wisdom 59

PART II
QUESTIONS OF SOCIAL AND INTELLECTUAL HISTORY

Chapter 4 Was R. Nachman an Innovation Such as the World Had Never Seen? 75

Chapter 5 Was R. Nachman a "Jewish Intellectual"? 91

PART III
LITERARY QUESTIONS

Chapter 6 Was R. Nachman the Messiah? 117

Chapter 7 Poetics of Intransitivity 137

Conclusion: Reading outside Modernity 161

Notes 167

Bibliography 211

Index 223

Acknowledgments

Writing often appears to be a solipsistic activity. Nothing could be further from the truth. There are many mentors, teachers, friends, and colleagues who have labored with me on this project. Their thoughts and feedback have been integral parts of shaping this book. I cannot purport to offer an account of the "origins" of this project. It found its many beginnings in the multiple conversations I have been privileged to have with all those whose support and insights I am delighted to acknowledge.

I am grateful to my graduate school advisors at Columbia University: Dan Miron, Gil Anidjar, Graciela Montaldo, and Edna Aizenberg (z"l), whose boundless support and rigorous critique have made me a better reader and, hopefully, a better writer. I am thankful for the long-standing support from Sudipta Kaviraj, Hamid Dabashi, and Alan Mintz (z"l). The mentorship of Miryam Segal and Hannan Hever has given me guidance in the process and confidence to stay the course. Susan Last-Stone taught this student of literature how to read law and why it's important. All of these people were invaluable to me as a young scholar finding his way in the ethereal world of the mind and the practical world of academia.

I benefited from the brilliant mind and open heart of my friend and collaborator Yuval Kremnitzer at Columbia University's Jewish Studies Graduate Student Association (JiGSA). Co-organizers and participants Kali Handelman, Elik Elhanan, Suzy Schneider-Reich, and Roni Henig were all invaluable in the process of giving articulation to my thoughts, as were Owen Cornwall, Casey Primel, Omar Farahat, Sahar Ullah, Aditi Surie von Czechowski, Foad Torshizi,

Andrew Ollett, and Wendell Marsh, my friends and colleagues from the department of Middle Eastern, South Asian and African Studies (MESAAS) graduate student colloquium.

The support I received from the Institute for Israel and Jewish Studies at Columbia over many years was integral to the exploration and production of this project. I thank Elisheva Carlebach, Jeremy Dauber, Dana Kresel, Sheridan Gayer, and Annela Levitov for their continued generosity. I am also grateful for the support from the department of Middle Eastern, South Asian and African Studies. I thank Naama Harel, Illan Gonen, Jessica Rechtschaffer, Michael Fishman, and Charles Jester for their friendship and support. I am grateful for the masterful editorial support I received from Simon Cook and Kali Handelman. Likewise, it has been a pleasure working with Rafael Chaiken at SUNY Press. I would like to thank the anonymous reviewers who read and commented on drafts of the manuscript. Their attentive reading and insightful suggestions helped me refine my argument and improve its presentation. It was during the summers in the Scholem reading room at the National Library of Israel that much of this book came together. A special thanks to Zvi Leshem, head of the Gershom Scholem collection, for his support and suggestions.

Last, this book would not have been possible without the patient encouragement I received from my family. I give my thanks and love to my parents for their sympathetic ear and continued support; to my children for their inspirational, inquisitive spirit; and, of course, to my wife, without whom none of this would be.

Introduction

What Is Jewish Literary Modernity?

This is a book about Jews "fitting in," about the modern challenge of figuring out what it means to "fit in." Most important, it is a book in which I discuss a few stories about this challenge. Giving this challenge a narrative form has long been a concern for modern Jewish literature. But this story doesn't begin with "modern Jewish literature." In this book, I will go back to the earliest moments of Jewish modernization in Eastern Europe—the hostilities between Hasidim and their orthodox opponents (the Mitnagdim), the collapse of the Polish-Lithuanian Commonwealth, the appearance of Jewish Enlightenment scholars (Maskilim) in Eastern Europe. In the age of empires and revolutions, we will find, the stakes of fitting in were being defined epistemologically and aesthetically before they were ever defined politically. "Fitting in" was the stuff of literature.

Every student of modern Jewish literature is familiar with the period between 1881 and 1905 in Eastern Europe. This was a period of great instability in the Russian empire. It stretches from the assassination of Tsar Alexander II in 1881 to the 1905 revolution, from the pogroms that accompanied Alexander III's accession in 1882 to the Kishinev pogrom of 1903. Two of the most recognizable texts of the time were responses to these pogroms. Leon Pinsker's 1882 pamphlet on "auto-emancipation" and Haim Nachman Bialik's 1903 long poem "The City of Slaughter." This period was characterized by a series of violent assaults on the Jewish inhabitants of the Pale of Settlement.[1] At the same time, these were the years in which the voice of a new Hebrew and Yiddish literature emerged in the works of writers such as Sholem Yankev Abramovitsh, and Bialik. During this period, tensions embedded in the foundation of the Pale of Settlement, tensions that had defined the contours of its social and political fabric for nearly a century, began to form tears in this fabric, foreshadowing the disintegration of the Pale. One certain result was a great instability in the lives of the Jews of the Pale, which changed the way this generation represented itself and its environment in writing. The concomitant shifts in the literary expression of this generation have been discussed extensively in the field of Eastern European Jewish literature. In fact, the conventional historiography of the field sees precisely *these* shifts as *constitutive* of the object of study called "modern Jewish literature." Yet this conventional historiography is incomplete. While it considers the disintegration of the Pale of Settlement to be a catalyst (if not generator) of a new mode of Jewish literary expression, it does not pause to ask: What social structure was disintegrating?[2] And, more importantly for a *literary* historiography: What literary mode of representation was being undercut in order to generate an aesthetic that can be recognized as "modern" in Jewish letters?

Discussions of modernity often circle back to the discursive construction of a break from tradition that typifies and even constitutes the text as modern.[3] Such discourse was central to the emerging Eastern European categories of modern Hebrew and Yiddish literatures as well.[4] In the 1906 preface to his German translation of *The Tales of Rabbi Nachman*, Martin Buber introduces the teller of the tales thus: "Rabbi Nachman of Bratzlav, who was born in 1772 and died in 1810, is perhaps the last Jewish mystic. He stands at the end of an unbroken tradition, whose beginning we do not know."[5]

Tradition as an unbroken chain that is now broken is the problematic through which Buber will express his ideas about Jewish modernity and renewal. This tradition has an end, at which point its final figure stands *as* the end. Buber's depiction suggests that R. Nachman[6] stands at the end of a transmission, at the edge of a break from which no return is possible for Buber and his readers.[7]

For Buber, the importance of positioning R. Nachman as "the last," who stands at "the end," stems from his efforts to present the storyteller as a point from which a cultural renewal of Judaism can begin. As Martina Urban explains, Buber's focus on R. Nachman dovetails with his wider effort "to foster a model for the new or rather renewed Jewish consciousness envisioned by cultural Zionism [. . .] and, concomitantly, [. . .] the creation of a distinctive Jewish modernism,"[8] a renewal that has its precondition in a backward glance. For Buber, recognizing the gap between himself and R. Nachman is the constitutive moment of a Jewish modernity. Buber, of course, stands on the other side of the break, identifying R. Nachman as a point of departure for a new Jewish consciousness—namely, the consciousness of having broken from tradition.

This seminal idea of a break with the past—a break that constitutes modern literature—has been critiqued as the construction of a past from which, and in opposition to which, modernity can be seen to emerge. But outside this more or less constructed juxtaposition with the present, neither the historiography nor its critique ever pauses to ask about the possibility of a future-oriented gaze *of* this past toward "our side" of such a break. And this lack of interest is rather odd given that what one imagines is being departed *from* is as definitive of the departure as the imagined destination. If we are indeed on a distant shore of history, looking back at the far shore from which we have departed, and to which we can no longer return, my initial question would be: What is, or rather, what was the view from that far shore?

In approaching this question an initial historical observation is in order. The consolidation of the Pale of Settlement occurred in the years between the first partition of the Polish-Lithuanian Commonwealth in 1772 and Napoleon's final defeat in 1815. This period begins the year R. Nachman was born and extends a mere five years after his death. This too was a tumultuous time in the lives of Eastern European Jews. No less so than the last decades of the nineteenth century. Indeed, the constitution of the Pale of Settlement was already replete with those very fault-lines along which the social, political and—crucially for our purposes—the aesthetic order would be ripped up at the close of the nineteenth century.

This historical observation leads into the historiographical argument about "modern literature" within which the present book is framed. As an introduction to reading R. Nachman, I will offer a series of interventions into the conventional historiography and its assumptions, beginning with the following argument. It is evident that Tsar Alexander III's "Temporary Regulations Regarding the Jews" (also known as the "May Laws") of 1882 heralded the disintegration of the *sociopolitical* order outlined by Tsar Alexander I in his 1804 "Statute Concerning the Organization of the Jews." Equally, the shifts in literary representation occurring at the time of Alexander III herald the disintegration of the *aesthetic* order established during the early years of the Pale of Settlement by the literary voices of that earlier generation. In other words, the object of study called "Modern Jewish Literature" is far better defined by an aesthetic turn away from the "local" modes of literary representation that characterized the formation of the Pale of Settlement at the turn of the eighteenth century, than it is by a break in the chain of hitherto unbroken tradition extending from this earlier period back into some imagined origin.

From the perspective of Hebrew and Yiddish literary studies, what I am suggesting is not new. Several scholars have already undermined the narrative of an "emergence" of modern Jewish literature around 1882, in part by introducing its relation to Hasidic writing in the mid-nineteenth century.[9] Building on such studies, I would like to push the discussion back to the literary production of the very first decade of the nineteenth century. More precisely, I would like to frame the discussion between two historical moments. On one end is the accession of Alexander I, amidst the formation of the Pale of Settlement. On the other end is the moment Napoleon lost the war and the European borders and power structures of the nineteenth century solidified. Furthermore, I would like to add to the discussions of early nineteenth-century Jewish literature by relating developments in the realm of literary production more directly to the broader historical context of the turn of the eighteenth century in Eastern Europe.

From the perspective of the history of ideas, my emphasis on the turn of the eighteenth century is not new either. Nor is my assertion that social and political challenges importantly informed, and even shaped, the development of the Hasidic movement. This argument has already been made by scholars such as Ben-Zion Dinur and Immanuel Etkes.[10] More broadly, the fact that the turn was a formative moment for European Jewry—on a socio-political and also on a theological level—is by no means a new observation. There is plenty of work on the many dimensions of this moment—from studies by scholars such as Israel Bartal and Ada Rapoport-Albert to more recent works by Gershon Hundert and Glen Dynner.[11] Nor is it a new observation that the management and resolution of this crisis, of this largescale encounter with Enlightenment ideologies and modernization policies, would shape the next century of European Jewish life, intellectually, politically, theologically, and beyond. In literary terms as well, Marc Caplan has argued that, in both historical periods at hand,

> storytelling is a response to the recurring crisis in Jewish autonomy that these historical circumstances engender, both personally and in the larger culture of the nineteenth century; such crises can be understood politically as the relationship of Jewish power structures with the empires in which they were embedded, or in social and religious terms as the relationship between specifically Jewish sectarian and ideological movements. These crises were as much a problem of narration, representation and idiom as of politics or culture.[12]

However, I feel a certain discomfort with uncritically referring to the social and aesthetic shifts in either of these historical periods (1772–1815 and 1881–1905) in terms of a crisis. A "crisis" certainly implies a social and historical moment. But it is not only that. We must employ a critical conceptualization of the moment at hand. And that is the next point of my intervention: A social crisis is not fully a "crisis" unless it is also, at one and the same instance, a crisis of representation, an undercutting of the ability to signify. A critical conceptualization of crisis would recognize that such a moment is not only a catastrophe in the sense of a "bad" occurrence. More profoundly, it is a moment that undoes the presumed, natural social structure and *simultaneously* undermines the ability to represent this undoing *as* an undoing. Such a conceptualization would make the designation of a crisis both impossible and yet wholly historical at the same time and in the same language.

Yet the fine work that has been done to date on the formation of the Pale of Settlement does not question the *representation* of this moment as a crisis by those who experienced and reported on it. This book offers the missing account of an aesthetic formation, a mode of representation that would be formative of a "crisis." In this introduction, I want to underline that representations of crisis are accompanied by crises of representation. We need to interrogate the possibilities and implications of representing the turn of the eighteenth century as a crisis. This is where R. Nachman of Braslav comes in. He was one of the most prominent thinkers and writers of his time who addressed himself to the consolidation of the Pale of Settlement, both in the context of the socio-political crisis it produced for the Jewish community and in terms of a concomitant aesthetic crisis of representation. Consequently, I will dedicate the bulk of the discussion that follows to reading several accounts by R. Nachman of the particular challenges that emerge in the *aesthetic* construction of this so called "crisis of modernity."

Late nineteenth-century Eastern European Jewish literature inaugurated Hebrew and Yiddish modernism, as well as other forms of representation a student of literature would identify as "modern." However, the preoccupation with a distinctively Jewish literary modernity, characteristic of the field of Jewish literary studies, does not emerge in this context of early national movements, and does not appear as the voice of a political minority. This preoccupation is equally operative, and with as much force, in the earlier context of empire, on the stage of late eighteenth-century imperial expansions. It is expressed in the voice of an emerging form of social and political subjectivity. The context is that of a radical reshaping of the public sphere—indeed, according to some, the very invention of the public sphere.[13]

The partitions of the Polish-Lithuanian Commonwealth at the end of the eighteenth century, and the subsequent constitution of the Pale of Settlement, had a seminal impact on the place of Judaism in broader society, and on the representation of Judaism in letters. This moment marks a greater tectonic shift in representational strategies than even the 1882–1905 pogroms. And yet the effects of the 1882 May Laws, the Dreyfus Affair, and the early twentieth-century pogroms (which Bialik's formative aforementioned poem responded to) are by now self-evident to researchers of Hebrew and Yiddish letters as constitutive of a literary "modernity." These events certainly mark the collapse of an order. But it is the incubation and formation of that order—geographically, socially, aesthetically—against which those later shifts in literary representation developed, and yet has remained outside the scope of literary historiography.

What would be gained by bringing the writing of the early years of the Pale of Settlement into the discussion of modern Jewish literature? Would this offer a "correction" to the historiography at hand? In other words, am I merely relocating the constitutive break that inaugurates modern Jewish literature into the early nineteenth century? To be clear, the answer to the latter is: No. My intention is not to offer a correction to the historiography of Hebrew and Yiddish literatures, locating their constitutive break at an earlier moment. Rather, by problematizing the very notions of "break" and "tradition," my aim is to call into question one of the underlying assumptions of literary scholarship, namely the role and dynamic of rupture and continuity, of tradition and its breaks, at least with respect to the study of Hebrew and Yiddish letters. The conventional historiography (of which Buber is only one proponent) offers an a-historical and essentialist notion of tradition, against which it sets up the modernity of "our" writing as a break. In this conceptualization, "modern writing" becomes a vantage-point from which to generate questions about tradition that can only be glimpsed from "our side" of the break. It is precisely this frame and the questions it generates that obfuscate R. Nachman's oeuvre, rendering it inaccessible (or even irrelevant) to a "modern" reader on the near shore.

The modern break with tradition itself draws on a rich tradition of breaks—even as it privileges "its" break as constitutive, over and against other previous breaks that are subsumed by its a-historical and essentializing tendencies toward the concept of tradition. The condition of diaspora (much like that of "writing"), with its ongoing adjustment to different political circumstances, neighboring communities, and social and religious standards, has importantly assumed tradition to be a local and historical question: What is it to be Jewish here and now? This last observation leads to my subsequent point of intervention. If the turn of the nineteenth century constitutes itself as "modern" through a discursively constructed break from the "far shore" of tradition—by which is meant, as I have just argued, the social and representational structures of the turn of the eighteenth century—what is, or, rather, what was the view from that far shore? To pose this question is to take a local and historical view of

R. Nachman's place along that long series of breaks and starts that is constitutive and incessantly reconstitutive of the Jewish textual "tradition" (or any textual "tradition" for that matter).

Fascinatingly (though perhaps predictably), the view that R. Nachman sees from his "shore" is quite similar to the "modern" view from our shore. He too sees himself looking forward and back from a "far shore," glimpsing a departure that will be constitutive of a future he will not have access to. A century later, we will understand the departure from this future as constituting our own present modernity. R. Nachman is a particularly revealing case study of a previous moment of "rupture" since he is, to some extent, stranded on the far shore, unable to return and yet unable to depart. He clearly recognized "tradition" as synthesizing the fits and starts of a dynamic of rupture and continuity, for example, in such statements as: "I will take you by a new way—a way that has never before existed. It is indeed an ancient way. And yet it is completely new" (such statements will be discussed in greater detail in chapter 4).[14] Another example is his exploration of the Spanish Expulsion as a defining moment in the constitution of a tradition from which he sees himself departing (we will discuss this in greater detail in chapter 2 when we read his story "The Tale of a King Who Decreed Conversion"). And yet he also recognizes his own intransitive position on the shore from which one must depart. It is a position he stylizes through what I will call (in the final chapter of this study) a "poetics of intransitivity."

R. Nachman's view is from beyond the pale of Jewish literary historiography, from within the emergent Pale of Settlement, and from the far shore of modernity's constitutively imagined break. It is the view of a beginning that takes place in part by excluding those whose writing is generating it. This beginning from which one cannot "return" and yet cannot proceed is a "permanent beginning,"[15] which is the origin of the title of the present study, *A Permanent Beginning: R. Nachman of Braslav and Jewish Literary Modernity*.

Why R. Nachman?

Why is R. Nachman of particular interest for a *literary* consideration of the turn of the eighteenth century? In the first years of the nineteenth century, Tsar Alexander I, who had recently acceded to the throne, passed legislation designed to resolve much of the social tumult that had divided the region over the preceding three decades. His 1804 "Statute Concerning the Organization of the Jews" attempted to reorganize the Jewish community of what in the previous decade had been termed the "Pale of Settlement." (Details of this legislation will be discussed extensively in chapter 1.) What is particularly pertinent for us is that R. Nachman's emergence as a Hasidic leader corresponds to Alexander I's emergence as an "enlightened despot." Significantly, R. Nachman devotes much thought and writing to the tsar's new laws, which include, among many other regulations and policies, a mandatory modern dress code for Jewish public officials, curricular mandates for Jewish schools, and—perhaps his most notable decree—an aggressive modernization plan for the Jewish labor force. This latter plan would result in the forced urbanization of about half a million Jews. While it is not likely that R. Nachman read the text of the tsar's statute, neither was he unique in responding to it. The majority of Eastern European Jewry was anxious about the changes it entailed (this will be covered at length in chapter 1). What is unique in R. Nachman's response is his appreciation of the aesthetic dimension this new legislation encompasses and its challenges to the representation of Jewish difference. It is amidst this broad reshuffling of social structures that R. Nachman begins teaching and telling his tales.

What sets R. Nachman apart from his contemporaries is both circumstantial and of the essence. As Yakov Travis states clearly, "more is known about the life of R. Nachman than any other [Hasidic leader] in the first generations of Eastern European Hasidism."[16] The vast efforts of Braslav Hasidim to preserve the most (seemingly) mundane details of their leader's life allow us to paint a full and fascinating portrait of a Hasidic thinker and creative genius at the very moment his world was changing unrecognizably. Most relevant to our present topic is the fact that R. Nachman chooses to engage with these changes through narrative fictions. Several of the more than 160 stories he told were written down by his disciple and scribe Nathan Sternhartz (1780–1844).[17] R. Nathan tells of his practice of reviewing drafts of the tales with R. Nachman. Together, they selected the thirteen that would be published.[18] R. Nachman died in 1810 before reaching his fortieth year of life, but R. Nathan finished the work, and the tales were published posthumously in 1815—in a bilingual Hebrew-Yiddish edition, as R. Nachman had requested.[19]

Researchers agree that the tales are as much an impressive catalogue of folkloric elements that R. Nachman had collected as they are of Kabbalistic symbols and myths. This observation is often made hand in hand with a mention of the Grimm brothers.[20] Those who look to the Kabbalistic symbols in the tales take the Lurianic mythical universe as their major point of reference.[21] However, as will be argued in chapter 6, Kabbalistic readings of the tales pay insufficient attention to the manner in which, as Zvi Mark puts it, R. Nachman "uses the kabbalistic language as a tool to analyze current European issue[s], which the tales deal with."[22] As Mark goes on to explain:

> R. Nachman's literary works were created in the context of a familiarity with world literature, within the limits of its extant translation into Hebrew and Yiddish. And no less important, they must be read as literature that was created with constant attention to "news of the world" and out of a critical necessity to know what was occurring in the wider world at every moment.[23]

This is no less true with regard to the folkloric elements. In *Prokim fun der yidisher literatur-geshikhte*, Chone Shmeruk addresses the association of R. Nachman's tales with the Grimm brothers' folkloristic project.[24] The appearance of Yiddish-language writing in the Hasidic context was nearly simultaneous with the first moments of the Grimms' publishing career in 1812. In particular, the publication of the book *Shivchei HaBesht* in 1815, which clearly drew on folkloristic elements and genres in constructing a hagiography of Yisra'el Baal Shem Tov as the "founder" of Hasidism, has drawn the attention of folklorists.[25] However, Shmeruk continues, this synchronicity has created the impression that all early Yiddish-language Hasidic publications were of a similar "folk" genre when, in fact, the tales of R. Nachman are clearly not.[26] Instead, attention should be given to the manner in which folkloric elements serve to develop in narrative form a set of speculative questions about the organization and reorganization of society. In this regard—and growing out of the tradition of Hasidic storytelling that dates back at least to the *baal shem tov* (if not the nomadic preachers before him)—R. Nachman's tales might be mentioned more suitably alongside such works as Jonathan Swift's *Gulliver's Travels* (1726) than those of the Grimm brothers.[27]

As mentioned, R. Nachman was an avid consumer of what he called "news of the world." In fact, many of his teachings, tales, and exchanges with students are framed by the news of the day. R. Nachman's interests spanned politics, medicine, technology, literature, and more. In one moment, he expounds on the term *poesia*,[28] while, in another, he describes a flying machine capable of reaching Jerusalem in a matter of minutes. It is pertinent that, beyond living through some of the major European revolutions, R. Nachman lived through some important technological advances. The last two decades of the nineteenth century were socially and politically tumultuous, and they also saw great leaps in science and technology. For example, in the span of just two or three years, beginning in 1783, great advances in aviation were accomplished. These years saw the first manned flight of a hot air balloon (in the presence of Louis XVI and Benjamin Franklin) and the successful crossing of the English Channel in a balloon. By the mid-1790s, balloons were being deployed in military campaigns as well, and the first years of the nineteenth century also saw the successful testing of the parachute.[29] These feats of human flight captured the imagination of many, and R. Nachman was no exception.

R. Nachman's great-grandson Shimshon Barsky (1874–1935) reports R. Nachman sharing his vision for the days of the Messiah: "There will be many machines, and there will be such a machine that flies in the air, and a Jew who is perturbed before [morning] prayers, will sit in the machine and fly to Jerusalem before prayers, to ask the messiah for advice how to pray properly, and will make it back [in time] to pray in his own home."[30] R. Barsky further relates the response of R. Naftali (R. Nachman's close friend and disciple), who responded that "if he ever heard of such a machine he would go dancing through the marketplace" for the joy of knowing he was witnessing the days of the Messiah."[31]

Such fantastical technological developments are more in line with the speculative and fanciful episodes of *Gulliver's Travels* than with any folkloric narrative tradition "recovered" by the Grimm brothers. R. Nachman was certainly not unique in imagining the possibilities of such technological developments. Human flight had fascinated many over the course of millennia. But the link he creates in his imagination between this historical circumstance and his set of expectations regarding the days of the Messiah is his own. This speaks to the relation between his imaginative expression and the historical moment in which he wrote. Beyond his interest in "news of the world," it is R. Nachman's penchant for molding this news and his commentary on it into fictional narrative form that make him a storyteller of particular interest for the student of modern Hebrew and Yiddish literature. In this book, I offer a thick description of the relation between text and context (for lack of a better dichotomy) in R. Nachman's writing and thought—in historical and intellectual-historical terms, in theological and ideological terms, in literary and aesthetic terms. The fuller and thicker our appreciation of this relation, the more we will see the literary-aesthetic questions come to the foreground of R. Nachman's concerns.

In my preoccupation with bringing together questions about R. Nachman's historiographical "position" and an appreciation of his literary contribution to that historiography, I follow most closely the work of Yiddishists such as David Roskies and Marc Caplan. Roskies contends with Buber's identification of R. Nachman as "the last," arguing instead that he was "the first Jewish religious figure to place storytelling at the center of his creative life [. . .] Thus, [Roskies continues] modern Yiddish storytelling was born."[32] In R. Nachman's tales, Roskies claims, modern Yiddish storytelling emerged as "the blueprint for creative renewal. [R. Nachman] did not want to create a seamless narrative out of disparate traditions— he ripped out all the seams and started over."[33] In determining whether R. Nachman was the last or the first, however, one may lose sight of the historiographical dynamism of his "position." I will strive to keep this dynamism in full view throughout this book.

Caplan's reading of R. Nachman, in turn, is part of his effort to offer a "theory of peripheral literature as an integral component in global modernism."[34] Following Roskies's identification of the "birth of Yiddish storytelling," Caplan asserts that "the defining focus of Yiddish in this theory [of peripheral literature] is the anticipatory role played by a *belated* modernity in creating an *anticipatory* modernism."[35] He thus argues that R. Nachman's tales "can be considered modernist, even if Reb Nakhman cannot be considered a Modernist. Modernism in this reformulation thus functions coincidentally with modernization."[36] Though R. Nachman is deeply interested in the particularities and uniqueness of his contemporary moment, I do not see R. Nachman's tales as modernist. His "coincidence" with modernization processes leads him in a different literary-aesthetic direction in my own argument. However, the challenge of "positioning" him within a literary-historiography of Yiddish and Hebrew letters is a shared and guiding concern for the beginnings of my own project. The interpretive difference I maintain from the fine scholarship just referenced lies in my understanding of the sense in which R. Nachman is a "beginning," "anticipatory," and so on. In the coming pages, I propose a different appreciation of the possibility or impossibility of a beginning-departure in literary-aesthetic terms.

Having stressed the ties between R. Nachman's writing and his historical moment, a cautionary remark is in order about the impression that "more is known about the life of R. Nachman than any other *tsaddik* in the first generations of Eastern European Hasidism."[37] Our extensive knowledge of R. Nachman's life is due in part to the fact that there have been more rejections of him and his writing than of any other Hasidic leader of the first generations of the movement. This rejection began during his lifetime with attacks by Arye Leib of Shpole;[38] it persisted after his death in attacks aimed at R. Nathan Sternhartz by Moshe of Savran;[39] and it continued into the twentieth century in the works of historians such as Simon Dubnow, who does not mince his words: "All the tales of R. Nachman are, in my opinion, words of hallucination out of the religious fever of a man sick in body and spirit, and for naught have the new researchers bothered to follow the path of Braslav Hasidim and seek an inkling of sense in this pile of nonsense."[40]

Given such caustic rejection, we must address the question of R. Nachman's place among the Hasidic textual and intellectual production of his day. How central or important was R. Nachman really? Was he a marginal radical or a central figure? Considering the above quotation by a respected historian of Eastern European

Jewry, this question relates to (even implicates) a set of ideological historical biases that we must avoid.

R. Nachman is very much a central character of his time, as also of the decades (if not centuries) that followed. Casting him as an outlier is inaccurate, and arguments made by Jewish Enlightenment scholars (Maskilim) that he was shunned by the Hasidic movement are to be taken with due skepticism. R. Nachman was very much a part of the movement and was connected to its intellectual and political elites. He was the great-grandson of the *baal shem tov*, the "founder" of Hasidism. His uncle and early supporter, Ephraim of Sudilkov, was the grandson of the *baal shem tov*. And Levi Yitzhak of Berditchev, a pillar of late eighteenth-century Hasidism, was his supporter.

Furthermore, documentation of ideological resistance to R. Nachman (as opposed to the internal Hasidic turf wars, which is what we seem to witness in the case of Arye Leib of Shpole) that did actually derive from various traditionalist Hasidic leaders, including his own uncle Baruch of Medzhybizh, must also be taken with a critical pinch of salt. These Hasidic voices of resistance were subsequently amplified by Maskilim and later scholars, who towed the line of representing the Hasidic movement as a fundamentally traditionalist movement. If R. Nachman is not a traditionalist, the logic goes, he cannot have been a central figure in the movement. But this argument betrays more about the biases of early documenters of Hasidism than about R. Nachman's position in the Hasidic world.[41] To this confusion must be added the difficulty that exists in making sense of R. Nachman's own relations with the Maskilim of his day (a question that will be addressed in chapter 5).[42]

Finally, the very fact that R. Nachman's work was picked up by his contemporaries as well as subsequent polemicists testifies to an identification of him as one against whom to polemicize, and as representative, to some extent, of the Hasidic movement. Why polemicize against an outlier? What sense would it make for opponents of the movement to convince non-Hasidim that R. Nachman and his nontraditionalist ideas are representative of the movement and worth polemicizing against, while at the same time representing him as an outlier? Hasidism was a highly political and politicized movement. Today, it is primarily through literature that this politics is in any way still legible to us.[43] The present study thus offers an intervention into two fields of inquiry that come together in research on R. Nachman's writings: Eastern European Jewish literature and literary historiography, on the one hand, and the literary and intellectual history of Hasidism, on the other.

Some Structural Notes

I have divided the lines of inquiry of this book into three parts: (1) political-aesthetic questions, (2) questions of social and intellectual history, and (3) literary questions. These are of course artificial divisions as these lines constantly interrupt and refer back to each other throughout the book. At the same time, the arc of the argument I present in this book leads from a primarily history-oriented first chapter to a primarily literary-theoretical final chapter. This is in order to build upon the existing research on R. Nachman, which is primarily historical and literary-historical. More importantly, however, this arc is essential for my intervention into the field—presenting the difference between an intellectual-historical reading of R. Nachman's texts and a "properly literary" reading of them by walking the reader through from the former to the latter. While doing so, I demonstrate the necessary but insufficient nature of historicizing R. Nachman's texts in parts 1 and 2, and I then draw literary-theoretical conclusions from this observation in part 3. For the broader argument about R. Nachman's place in the emergence of a "Jewish literary modernity," it is important to move through the more historical aspects of the reading as a lead-up to the literary interpretation of R. Nachman's texts.

In part 1, my discussion moves between context and text, since it is precisely the context of R. Nachman's writing that is so often overlooked in favor of some "deeper" internal meaning. The first chapter, "Positioning R. Nachman," begins by discussing R. Nachman's "position" in spatial and temporal terms, that is, historically and geographically. The chapter focuses on the 1804 "Statute Concerning the Organization of the Jews." As will soon become clear, any effort to "position" R. Nachman must take into account the sociopolitical shifts of his day and the restructuring of the Jewish community that accompanied them. The second chapter, "Representing Difference," details the sociopolitical shifts as they relate to the representation of the Jewish community. It identifies in these shifts a particularly aesthetic problem that is present in this early nineteenth-century reorganization of society. Beginning with Teaching II:28 of the second volume of R. Nachman's collected teachings *Likkutei Moharan*,[44] this second chapter introduces a term that will be central to my argument throughout the rest of the book: *the invisibility of confessional differences*. This key concept refers to the removal of a certain category of markers of difference from the public sphere, as part of the process of creating a modern public sphere. Chapter 2 also introduces us to "The Tale of a King Who Decreed Conversion," which we will read as a commentary on the invisibility of confessional differences. In the third chapter, "The Secret of Our Wisdom," we will continue reading "The Tale of a King Who Decreed Conversion" as well as Teaching I:61 of the first volume of *Likkutei Moharan*. We will see R. Nachman engage the question of communal leadership in light of the social shifts he is witnessing and offer a political-aesthetic strategy for coping with them.

R. Nachman's efforts to make sense of the broad social changes going on around him, and of his own position as a communal leader in such a turbulent moment, involved a reimagining of some of the most traditional cosmogony of the Jewish textual traditions. In part 2 of the book, we turn to questions of social and intellectual history. The chapters in this part explore R. Nachman's *self*-positioning as it ranges from his sense of history and the historicity of his moment, to the challenge of faith that emerged vis-à-vis the rise of Jewish Enlightenment, and to questions of his power to influence these events. This part's two chapters will continue our exploration of the context within which we have resolved to read R. Nachman's work. However, in turning our attention to R. Nachman's *self*-positioning, we will inquire into his agency—discursive, theological, and social—in the processes already described. Chapter 4 reads Teaching 21 of the first volume of *Likkutei Moharan* and discusses R. Nachman's ability and desire to innovate, with a particular focus on the precarious nature of his moment in terms of the traditional Jewish historical narrative. Subsequently, chapter 5 reads Teaching 64 of the first volume of *Likkutei Moharan* and addresses R. Nachman's relation to new possibilities of Jewish existence outside the fold of tradition and communal structures.

In part 3, we turn our attention to the literary reception of R. Nachman's tales. Chapter 6 reframes our discussion in terms of R. Nachman's academic and disciplinary receptions. First, it highlights the scope of extant interpretive frames, and then it discusses more broadly the disciplinary assumptions underlying scholarship on his writing. This chapter is divided between two discussions. The first regards prevalent concerns with R. Nachman's messianic role and its relation to modern Hebrew and Yiddish literature. The second is a discussion of questions regarding the Kabbalistic nature of the tales. Chapter 7 then attempts to move beyond this messianic-Kabbalistic reception by posing explicitly literary-critical questions of R. Nachman's writings. In the first half of chapter 7, we will discuss the various introductions to the 1815 edition of the *Tales*, as well as the first tale, "The Tale of the Lost Princess." In the second half of the chapter, we will read "The Parable of the Wheat" and "The Parable of the Turkey" and relate R. Nachman's tales to the broader political-aesthetic context we have been discussing.

Since historical and sociopolitical contexts play a large role in my reading of R. Nachman, I have made reference to the first (1815) edition of the *Tales* throughout the book. While the Hebrew wording is not different from current editions, I sometimes refer to the Yiddish parallel of the narrative in the 1815 bilingual edition. Highlighting variation and discrepancies between the two versions often demonstrates a point or draws attention to the possibility of a thicker contextual reading. Therefore, I cite the tales in their first edition by indicating the page number followed by the page side with a letter (a or b). While the original 1808 and 1811 volumes of R. Nachman's collected teachings are equally available, the variation with later editions is minor, and there is no running commentary or translation with which to compare the text of the teachings. Therefore, I have not found occasion to make reference to distinct elements of the original editions of the teachings. I reference teachings by volume (I or II), teaching number, and paragraph number so as to make accessible the citation in any edition of the book.

Finally, all translations of primary and secondary sources are my own unless otherwise noted. In my translations of R. Nachman's tales and teachings, I have tried to reflect the idiosyncratic nature of his language as much as possible. Thus, there are instances of inconsistent tenses within sentences and sentences that seem to run on for entire paragraphs. This is in part an effort to convey not only the content but also the form of his teachings and tales—presented orally to his disciples, noted by R. Nathan and then edited for print by the two of them. This is also essential for conveying the content of the texts at hand, since the associative nature of R. Nachman's style relies in part on the strings of filiations he discursively develops. An example of this translation challenge in R. Nachman's teachings is the recurrent word *bechina*. As stated, the associative element is very powerful in these texts, and the marker of free-association is *bechina* (literally "aspect," "facet," "dimension").[45] The semantic meaning is not as important as the formal use of the word as a metastructural indicator of those points in which R. Nachman's exegesis turns into imaginative free association. Therefore, I have chosen to leave the word untranslated so as to highlight its formal function in the narrative flow of R. Nachman's teachings.

Last, by bringing together a diverse set of primary and secondary materials—narrative fictions, teachings, legal history, intellectual history, literary theory, and more—in this book, I aim to enrich the context within which we resolve to read R. Nachman and, indeed, modern literature.

Part I

Political-Aesthetic Questions

Chapter 1

Positioning R. Nachman

Positioning R. Nachman intellectually, theologically, literarily, or even geographically is a multilayered task that involves outlining the various histories within which he operated. We need to identify not only his place in the history of the Hasidic movement, in European Jewish history, and in general European history, but also the complex relations between these histories which form concentric circles within and around his life and work. A fine illustration of this complex background and its indispensability for understanding R. Nachman's thought and writing is already provided by considering the events of 1772, the year he was born.

> The year 1772 is generally regarded as a critical one, or at least an important turning point, in the history of Hasidism. Three decisive events took place in that year which altered both the ideological and the organizational course on which the movement had originally embarked. The spring brought with it the first outbreak of bitter hostilities between the Mitnagdim and the Hasidim in Vilna, whence the dispute quickly spread to other Jewish communities in Lithuania and Galicia. During the summer months Belorussia was annexed to Russia, and Galicia to Austria, in the first partition of the disintegrating kingdom of Poland; as a result, parts of the Jewish (and Hasidic) community in Poland which until then had formed a single cultural and political entity

found themselves arbitrarily separated. At the end of the year, in December, the supreme leader of Hasidism, R. Dov Ber, the Maggid of Mezhirech, died without leaving an "heir" to take charge of the movement in his place.[1]

The year of R. Nachman's birth saw a convergence of major events, the repercussions of which would form crucial contexts of his life. In the history of Hasidism, with the passing of one of its greatest figures at the heart of Hasidic consensus, 1772 marks the beginning of the institutionalization of Hasidism as a decentralized movement.[2] In Jewish history, this year marks a rift within the Eastern European Jewish community, previously united in the Polish-Lithuanian Commonwealth under the governance of the Council of the Four Lands.[3] The conflict between the Hasidim and the Mitnagdim would shape much of Eastern European Jewish history in the following half century, and its traces are present to this day.[4] In European history, 1772 marks the geopolitical expansion of empires (the Russian, Prussian, and Austro-Hungarian) into previously monarchical realms.

The dynamic and complex relations between these historical events are and have been material for other projects. It is not my intention to make any new factual claims about R. Nachman's historical period. Rather, my intention is to offer an interpretation of his writing in light of what we already know of his times. Therefore, I will broadly outline these historical events here only as they relate to R. Nachman. The conflict between Hasidism and the Mitnagdim was the struggle between an innovative popular movement and its conservative traditionalist counterpart, both for religious authority and to fill the broader political vacuum left where the Council of the Four Lands had previously governed. The conflict's containment is due in large part to the subsequent (first) partition of the Polish-Lithuanian Commonwealth, which left the orthodox stronghold of Vilna in the Grand Duchy of Lithuania and the overwhelmingly Hasidic Podolia region in the Kingdom of Poland—at least for the next two decades. The death of the *magid* of Mezhirech, whom Rapoport-Albert calls "the supreme leader of Hasidism,"[5] also coincides with the early institutionalization of disparate and decentralized Hasidic courts. The formation of

Hasidic courts, their emphasis on a single leader known as the *zadik* (righteous man), along with the rising ideology of Zadikism,[6] marks the early consolidation of Hasidism as a "movement." These developments were amplified by the insertion of a tenuous set of imperial borders into the previously united Commonwealth, within which the *baal shem tov* and the *magid* had moved freely. Born into a world just at a moment when it began to change unrecognizably, R. Nachman was to live through the great changes and anxieties of his era.

By the time R. Nachman had reached his twentieth year, further weighty events had occurred. To begin with, the first Hasidic books had been published.[7] This marked a significant ideological turn away from the skeptical and apprehensive attitude toward print technology exhibited by both the *baal shem tov* and the *magid*. For the founders' generation, the medium for reaching the masses of Eastern European Jewry was personal charisma. The generation that followed the *magid*'s death certainly did not neglect this aspect of Hasidism's appeal. On the contrary, the charismatic ideal of the Hasidic leader was solidified into the doctrine of Zadikism. Yet the implementation of print technology as a more effective means of reaching the masses of Jews in Eastern Europe represented an "update" to what it meant for Hasidism to be a popular movement.[8]

In Jewish history more broadly, R. Nachman's first two decades of life saw a series of excommunications issued by the Mitnagdim against the Hasidic movement. These led to aggressive persecution of Hasidic leaders, mostly in the Lithuanian Grand Duchy, resulting in exile, beatings, and complaints to the authorities. To the extent that this ideological divide ran along the new political borders between Poland and Lithuania, it solidified the character of these two communities into the archetypal figures of modern Eastern European Jewish history—the Hasid and the Litvak.[9]

Finally, the French and American Revolutions, though taking place on the other side of the continent and the world, marked a significant breakdown (not to say execution) of existing sociopolitical hierarchies across much of Europe. This broader historical context should inform our understanding of the Hasidic movement as it attempted to consolidate the masses of Eastern European Jews against the old guard of the orthodox rabbinic establishment.

In 1793 and 1795, two further partitions brought about the disappearance of the Lithuanian Grand Duchy and the Polish Kingdom. This marked the final replacement of previously monarchical systems of rule with modern imperial bureaucracy. The majority of the Jews of both Lithuania and Poland now found themselves in the Russian Empire, under the progressive rule of Empress Catherine the Great. Catherine's modernizing efforts and Enlightenment ideology did not affect them for long, however. She died in 1796, and a period of political instability under the rule of her son, Paul I, lasted until his assassination in 1801.

During these last years of the eighteenth century, several further significant events took place. The northern branch of Hasidism consolidated under the leadership of R. Shneur Zalman of Lyadi in the northeastern region of (what had been) Lithuania. In 1796, he published *Tanya*, effectively forming the Chabad school of Hasidism.[10] The following year, the leader of the Mitnagdim, Rabbi Eliyahu, the *gaon* of Vilna, died. Following the *gaon*'s death, and finding themselves under the same external political authority as the Hasidim for the first time since 1772, the Mitnagdim launched another campaign against the Hasidic movement. Their (final) effort was to engage the Russian imperial bureaucracy against the movement.[11] The years following the final partition brought a new kind of anxiety for the Jewish communities of Eastern Europe. With the stabilization of the Russian Empire's borders (for the time being), the question was no longer which political entity they would be ruled by, but in what manner they would be governed and what their legal standing would be under the new imperial bureaucracy.

The five years of Paul I's rule would not provide answers to these questions. His leadership was characterized by conservatism and inconsistent policy, resulting in little expressed concern for the modernizing of the empire, least of all the newly annexed regions to the west. Questions of imperial attitude toward the Jews would only be answered after the assassination of Paul I, whose son, Alexander I, would revive the modernizing efforts of his grandmother Catherine the Great when he assumed power in 1802. One of Alexander I's first orders of business was regulating Jews' legal, economic, and social status, in an effort to modernize this recently absorbed population.

Before this, however, in the summer of 1798, R. Nachman had left the social and political instability of the Russian Empire and set out for the Holy Land with his friend and disciple R. Shim'on. During these travels, R. Nachman encountered a figure who would play a significant role in his later writing: Napoleon Bonaparte.

The encounter took place in early 1799, when R. Nachman found himself besieged in the city fort of Akra. Napoleon's advance up the Mediterranean coast earlier that year had culminated in the siege of Akra. The siege began on March 20 and ended two months later when, unable to take the fort, Napoleon returned to Egypt. R. Nachman had reached Akra only a few days before the siege began.[12] On his arrival, he found the Ottoman forces already busy preparing the city for battle. On Saturday, March 16, R. Nachman witnessed the arrival of British naval forces to reinforce the Ottomans. It was clear they had to leave the city immediately, and R. Shim'on tried to make arrangements for them to board a ship of the—then neutral—Republic of Ragusa (today the southernmost tip of Croatia), but it was already too late to obtain a spot on the manifest. The attempt, however, speaks of a certain familiarity with the political landscape of the embattled Mediterranean that R. Nachman had likely honed over previous months of travel in the region.

On Sunday, March 17, the city was evacuated of all civilians in preparation for battle, and R. Nachman and R. Shim'on were able to obtain a spot on the manifest of an Ottoman trade ship headed for Istanbul. In the turmoil of the general flight from the city, however, they failed to identify the correct vessel and accidentally boarded an Ottoman battle ship. They slept on board that night, and the next morning the mistake was discovered by the Ottoman sailors. But it was too late to disembark. The ship had received its orders, and the captain could not be bothered with the pair of odd stowaways. They were given a rifle and the impression (they did not speak a common language) that they were expected to use it in the coming days. The next morning, the ship set out to sea to the distant thunder of cannons. The battle with Napoleon began two days later.

R. Nachman and R. Shim'on spent several weeks onboard the ship as its sailors battled the French, struggled to navigate difficult weather, and repaired damage to the hull. Eventually, they anchored in Rhodes in mid-April, just before the Passover holiday. The two companions were able to disembark, and, in the market, R. Shim'on found both supplies for the holiday and a contact among the local Jewish community. They spent the holiday of Passover on board the anchored ship, and, a few days later, they were ransomed from the captain by the Jewish community. Now free to continue their journey home, they arrived in Galicia in early June and reached home later that month, just a few months before Napoleon effectively seized power over the French Republic in a coup d'état. Though he never again left the Podolia region, R. Nachman would continue to seek "news of the world" for the rest of his life. Napoleon would continue to loom large over this news and, later in R. Nachman's career, would become a figure of reference in several of his tales.[13]

Around the time Napoleon seized power over the burgeoning French Republic, R. Nachman assembled a small group of followers in Zlatopol. In the summer of 1802, however, and in the wake of a bitter rivalry with another local Hasidic leader—R. Aryeh Leib of Shpola—he moved to Braslav.[14] He would spend the next eight years in Braslav, and it was there that he delivered most of his teachings and tales to his disciples. R. Nachman's move to Braslav coincides with the accession of Alexander I to the emperorship of Russia, and the latter's rule forms the most central backdrop to R. Nachman's intellectual activity. Alexander I's early years would be characterized by an aggressive modernization agenda, and R. Nachman's writings are marked by the processes that Alexander I promoted across the empire.

The Organization of the Jews

Before the annexation of the Polish-Lithuanian Commonwealth to the Russian Empire, Jews had not been permitted to reside within the empire. Following the partitions of the Polish-Lithuanian Commonwealth, the Russian Empire had annexed the Lithuanian Grand Duchy and the Polish kingdom, and, in doing so, it had assumed control over the largest population of Jews in the world at the time. A law from 1744 prohibited the Jews of the former commonwealth from residing in, or even entering, the Russian

Empire without proper authorization.[15] The annexed territories, to which Jewish residence was limited from the time of the first partition, were termed the Pale of Settlement. The modernization of the Pale of Settlement and its Jewish inhabitants was a project to which Alexander I gave particular attention. In fact, one of the first orders of business of the new tsar was to commission a policy committee—the Committee for the Amelioration of the Jews—regarding the Jews of the Pale of Settlement.

> Because of multiple complaints to Us and to the incoming Governing Senate on different abuses and troubles that have harmed agriculture and industry of the population in those Governorates where Jews live, We considered it necessary by the Decree to the Governing Senate given in the 9th day of November 1802, to organize a special Committee to examine this related matter and to determine means to correct the present regulation of Jews.[16]

After decades of internal conflict and external political turmoil, this was the non-Jewish authorities' first concentrated effort to address the issue of modernizing the Jewish population of Eastern Europe.[17] During the roughly two years of the committee's work (from late 1802 to late 1804), R. Nachman repeatedly expressed concerns about the impending *punktin* (clauses or decrees) that the emperor was working on. In fact, the opening paragraph of his biography, *Chayey Moharan* (literally "the life our teacher Rabbi Nachman"), written by R. Nathan Sternhartz, frames R. Nachman's move to Braslav within a genealogy of imperial modernization projects.

> It was the first Rosh Hashana of his [R. Nachman's] dwelling here [in Braslav] . . .
> And at that time it was rumored in the world [about] the decrees [. . .] These decrees started to grow in the days of the Kingdom of Poland, before his Highness the Emperor conquered our country, and then when he first conquered our country the matter was quieted for a while, and after that it was reawakened, [so that now] it is rumored in the world that they want to pass some decrees called "punktin."[18]

R. Nathan then goes on to enumerate various teachings related over the course of the following two years that were told in the context of R. Nachman's concern for these *punktin*. To be sure, R. Nachman was not alone in these concerns. Many leaders, Hasidic and otherwise, were quite engaged, and it is important to mention that the Jewish communities of the various provinces under Alexander I's rule sent delegates to St. Petersburg to meet with the committee.[19] Rapoport-Albert discusses a meeting of Jewish community leaders called by R. Levi Isaac of Berdichev (one of the most significant Hasidic leaders following the death of the *magid* of Mezhirech) in 1802 or 1803, apparently in response to the appointment of the committee.[20] R. Nachman too attended this meeting.[21] Being aware of the communitywide concerns and discussions regarding the committee's work, R. Nathan reports a statement made by R. Nachman sometime during the summer of 1803: "That year he dealt much with the matter of the 'punktin' [. . .] and was cross with those who said that certainly they will not come to pass [. . .] He spoke much of this, that one must be greatly concerned about these decrees, may the merciful God protect and deliver us, and not regard them lightly."[22]

R. Nachman and others were right to take Alexander I's modernizing intentions seriously. The committee's examination led to the "Statute Concerning the Organization of the Jews" of December 1804—instituted in the very same month Napoleon Bonaparte was crowned Napoleon I by Pope Pius VII. This statute had significant effects, which permeate the histories within which R. Nachman is positioned. To be clear, I am not asserting that R. Nachman had read the text of the statute. He most likely did not—at least not in the original Russian and in the format that it was distributed to the local powers across the governorates of the Pale of Settlement.[23] But the topics covered by the committee, and the policies they proposed in the statute as remedy, were known, feared, and fiercely debated among the Jewish leadership of the Pale as the Tsar's intentions to modernize the Jewish population took form. It is therefore worth taking a moment to review the content of the statute that will frame much of R. Nachman's thought concerning the reordering of Jewish society.[24]

The introduction to the statute states that the regulations it sets out "reflected moderation and care about the genuine welfare of Jews, as well as being based on benefits to native residents of the governorates, where those people have permission to live."[25] Dubnow sees this phrase as summarizing the balance that Alexander I hoped to strike between the "welfare of Jews" and the "benefits to native [non-Jewish] residents" among whom the Jews lived in the Pale of Settlement.[26] We should note that the majority of these residents were not Russian but, rather, Poles, Ukrainians, Lithuanians, and others.[27] Nevertheless, little within the statute directly concerns the relationship between Jews and non-Jews. The first section, titled "About Enlightenment," establishes Jews' access to the public education system, from elementary school through university. In secondary and tertiary education, it is stipulated, Jewish children may not wear "Jewish dress," but must wear "Polish or German dress." This, it explains, is "for the purpose of uniformity."[28]

"In the case of Jews who, despite all these motivations, refuse to send their children to common public schools," the statute continues (without specifying the "motivations"), private Jewish schools may be established. However, "among the subjects taught must be one of these languages: Russian, Polish or German."[29] These languages are important since the statute proceeds to define a timeline for the transition of all business records and public documents from Yiddish or Hebrew into one of those languages. "Without this, no document will be accepted," it concludes.[30] By 1808, all elected officials were to be literate in one of these languages, and by 1812 even rabbis would not be appointed without such literacy. Finally, Jewish elected officials, "for general order and uniformity, must wear Russian or Polish dress, if they do not like to wear German dress."[31]

Whether or not Jewish officials liked to wear German dress was not a question of fashion preferences, nor was the aim of the statute to establish a fashion police (though we will soon see the enforcement of dress codes assigned to the police). The repeated mention of order and uniformity as the logic underlying the dress requirements should be understood—as the title of section I, "About Enlightenment," states—as the incorporation of Enlightenment ideas within administrative policy. What is being attempted here is the establishment of a public sphere, separate from the spheres of religion and private life. The removal of private or religious identifiers from public visibility was understood as an important element in the configuration of this sphere and of the possibilities of representing difference within it.

The next section, "About Different Estates and Trades of Jews and [their] Rights," regulates the rights of farmers, manufacturers and artisans, merchants and burghers. The general agenda is clear: making the Jewish population of the Pale of Settlement more productive, through the forced urbanization of nonfarmers, and granting them access to professional guilds and to dedicated government business loans. Importantly, the new regulation of these estates does away with the double taxation scheme to which Jews were previously subject. Jewish businesses and workers are to be taxed equally to their non-Jewish counterparts.

Towards the end of this (the longest) section of the statute, the policing of fashion makes another appearance. "Jews (including their wives and children) temporarily traveling outside of the Pale, have to wear German [style] dress no different than that of others. If they wear traditional dress, they shall be sent back [to the Pale] by the Police."[32] What is interesting in this clause is the relation it suggests between the Pale of Settlement and the "proper" Russian Empire. Within the Pale, Jews may wear "traditional dress" in all private or religious settings. It is only in markedly public settings (public school, public office) that dress codes must be uniform. But outside the Pale, within the territory of the Russian Empire where Jews may not live (nor even enter without appropriate permission and documentation), uniformity is everywhere mandated. In other words, the condition under which Jews may enter Russian territory is that they travel "incognito." Their Judaism, their difference, must not be visible anywhere in the Russian public sphere.

The thought that the difference between Jews and non-Jews would not be evident troubled R. Nachman. What kind of difference is Judaism if it can be made invisible with one stroke of a bureaucrat's pen? Moreover, the thought that Alexander I's legislation could successfully reorganize the social sphere, and in such a way as to produce a public devoid of confessional markers, was baffling to the traditionalist mindset of the Eastern European Jewish community, who had formed under the clear (and clearly visible) difference that the Council of the Four Lands maintained between them and their surrounding society. It is telling that R. Nachman's contemporaries referred to the statue as a *gzerat shmad*, a decree of conversion. In the next chapter, I will discuss the significance of what I call *the invisibility of confessional differences*—to the European Enlightenment projects and policies of social modernization at large, and to R. Nachman's understanding of the changing social and representational structures of his own world in particular. For the moment, however, let's conclude our reading of the 1804 statute.

Section III of the statute, "Obligation of Jews Regarding Above-Mentioned Estates," begins by mandating that "every Jew shall have or accept a known inherited family name."[33] But this was not the really important part of the section, which went on to outline the timeline by which all Jewish-held licenses to produce and sell alcohol of any kind, throughout the whole of the Pale, would be revoked, while any outstanding debt for the purchase of alcohol from a Jew would be voided without compensation. This decree in effect threatened to pull the economic carpet out from under the feet of nearly all non-urban Jewish settlements. Roadside taverns and alehouses and the production and sale of alcohol to non-Jews were the main sources of income and rent payment for most small Jewish settlements. As Dubnow puts it, "with one stroke this clause eliminated from the economic life of the Jews an occupation which, though far from being distinguished, had yet afforded a livelihood to almost one-half of the whole Jewish population of Russia."[34] This legislation would provide the final catalyst for the mass-urbanization of Jewish communities and, as Dubnow continues, "would affect 60,000 Jewish families, or about half a million Jews. Needless to say, within the two or three years of respite which remained before the catastrophe, this huge mass could not possibly gain access to new fields of labor and establish itself in new domiciles."[35] As is evident thus far from the statute, the productivization and modernization of the Jews of the Pale was imagined largely as a top-down process, to be enforced rather aggressively by the imperial administration.

In the context of wider European history, the statute was part of a larger process of modernization undertaken by the Russian Empire. This process included regulating public education and professional (guild) affiliations, overhauling the structure of imperial administration, and incorporating Enlightenment ideas adopted from Western European states.[36] Another element of this broader project was formulated in section IV of the statute, "On the Civil Rights of Jews." Here it was stated quite plainly that Jews "are free and live under the precise patronage of laws given on the level with all other Russian subjects."[37] Equality of all subjects before a unified code of law that applies to all subjects equally was a pillar of emancipation across Europe. This marks a transition away from what we might call "demographic rule," whereby different demographic groups within the same geographic region were subject to different legal systems, and towards a system of "geographic rule," whereby all subjects within a geographically determined area were subject to the same system of laws.[38] The former was the reality for the Council of the Four Lands prior to the disintegration of the Polish-Lithuanian Commonwealth. Jews were there subject to the judicial system established and maintained by the council, and in accordance with Jewish law, while their non-Jewish neighbors were subject to entirely different judicial systems. Only in instances of conflict between a Jew and a non-Jew would the case arrive at a non-Jewish court.[39] The emancipatory legal system, in distinction, covered all subjects within a geographically determined area and purported to grant members of all demographic groups equal access to public legal recourse, regardless of their confessional differences.

Needless to say, Enlightenment ideology and modernization policies proposed the removal of a great deal of power from the hands of traditional leaders of the Jewish community. This is referenced in the very title of the statute, "Concerning the Organization of Jews," which in fact attempted to reorganize the Jewish communities so that in public matters, such as taxation, legal recourse, trade and guilds, as well as general productivity, they would be on par with all other inhabitants of the Pale. At the same time, it allowed for the continued organization of religious life in exclusively nonpublic terms.[40] Thus, section V, "The Position of Rabbis," states that "the rabbinate is just an honorable post."[41] Consequently, the statute makes clear:

> It is forbidden [for rabbis] to inflict any other punishment, except revelation and pronunciations inside the synagogues; Rabbis and other spiritual leaders who dare go against this rule and inflict public punishment,

of whatever kind [such as]: fine by the prohibitions of Paskha [. . .] and kosher meat, and even by condemnation and denunciation will be punished.[42]

Equal access to the law involved denying rabbis their traditional role as adjudicators, as well as their rights to requisitions and compensation from the community.

The process of modernizing the Jews of the Pale would extend well beyond R. Nachman's lifetime, but it formally began in the first years of the reign of Alexander I, during which time R. Nachman was just establishing himself as the leader of his own Hasidic court.[43] R. Nachman's first year in Braslav was marked by the extensive political efforts of the Jewish community (Hasidim and Mitnagdim alike) to assuage the severity of what they suspected would turn out to be a detrimental decree against the Jewish population of the Pale of Settlement. From the perspective of Jewish history, this joint effort initiated a period of cooperation between Hasidim and their orthodox opponents. Indeed, the statute of 1804 included a clause that effectively brought an end to the conflict between these groups: "If in any place there arises a separation of sects and a split occurs in which one group does not want to be in a synagogue with the other group, then it is possible [for] one of them to build its own synagogue and to select its rabbis."[44] From this point on, there could be more than one synagogue per town, and, thus, there was no longer a single position of rabbinic authority to vie for.[45]

This was an important moment in the history of the Hasidic movement, for it allowed the undisturbed establishment of new Hasidic communities across the Pale of Settlement. There subsequently emerged a generation of Hasidic leaders of what would become patrilineal dynastic courts.[46] In the broader context of European Jewish history, the end of hostilities between these two groups set the stage for a new conflict, of which R. Nachman would see only the earliest stages, in which the traditionalist communities of Hasidism and Mitnagdim both found themselves confronted by an emerging generation of Eastern European Jewish Enlightenment thinkers (the Maskilim).[47]

Stepping back further and viewing the statute from the perspective of European history, 1804 marks the heyday of two imperial Enlightenment ideologies, Russian modernization and French emancipation. Commenting on the historiography of the French emancipation during R. Nachman's lifetime, Ronald Schechter complains that, "despite sometimes bitter political differences, the history of the Jews from the Enlightenment through the revolutionary-Napoleonic period has been written with a view to a future that these forces are presumed to have brought into being."[48] The retrospective foreshadowing that Schechter takes issue with sees events such as the Dreyfus Affair and WWII anti-Semitism as natural outcomes of emancipation ideology. By implication, as Schechter puts it, the legislation that resulted from Enlightenment ideology is identified as an "attempt at eradicating the Jews."[49] As Dubnow has documented, many of R. Nachman's contemporaries certainly understood that the tsar's new legislation would cause harm to the Jewish population. Nevertheless, after Napoleon convened the Paris Sanhedrin in 1806, the Jewish community in Eastern Europe was split as to which empire had the better attitude towards Jews—the negotiated emancipation of Napoleon's Republican France or the forced modernization of Russia's "enlightened despot" Alexander I.

The difference of opinion led to some of the worst conflicts within the Hasidic movement at the time, and disagreement between Hasidic courts (and their leaders) on the question of engaging and adapting to the "crisis" of the times was stark.[50] As the Napoleonic wars raged across Europe, the movement was split between those expressing support for Napoleon and those expressing support for Alexander I—on both ideological and pragmatic grounds. This is well demonstrated by a short excerpt from an 1812 letter by R. Shneur Zalman of Lyadi:

> Should Napoleon be victorious, wealth among the Jews will be abundant and the glory of the children of Israel will be exalted. But the hearts of Israel will be separated and distanced from their father in heaven. But if our master Alexander will triumph, though poverty will be abundant and the glory of Israel will be humbled, the heart of Israel will be bound and joined with its father in heaven.[51]

The centrality of this global political conflict within R. Nachman's writings would not emerge until several years later. As Napoleon made his way across Europe, nearing the Pale of Settlement, R. Nachman devoted more and more attention to the emancipatory ideology heralded by Napoleon, distinct as it was in significant ways from Alexander I's. However, the question I want to focus on is not whether forced modernization or negotiated emancipation (or even the denial of emancipation) represented an attempt to eradicate the Jews. To the extent that Schechter is right in pointing out that the common historiographical answer is that both Russian and French policies aimed at this end, we would do well to accept his criticism of implicit historical teleology. Whatever future historical developments might turn out to be, what is common to both Napoleon and Alexander I is an effort to reorganize the social mechanisms that determined inclusion and exclusion. And what is common to the Jews of Europe at the time is their attempt to figure out their place within this reshuffling of the social space. This is a question that R. Nachman engages with fully, through teachings and imaginative fictions, and his engagement is the primary focus of the present study.

In R. Nachman's personal biography, 1804 marks the beginning of his most productive years. Almost all his teachings and publications were produced between 1804 and his death in 1810. The themes we have mentioned—the decentralized structure of the Hasidic movement and the ideology of Zadikism, the conflict with the Mitnagdim, his own conflict with other Hasidic leaders, the 1804 statute, even the arrival of Jewish Enlightenment ideas from Western Europe—all figure in his teachings and tales. His life was a microcosm of these historical forces, and his oeuvre is no different.

R. Nachman's creative years coincide with the reorganization of Eastern European Jewish society. This reorganization was a culmination of the buildup of various political, social, and geographical developments over several decades in the region. His creative period lasts until just before all this volatility disappeared with the post-Napoleonic solidification of Russian borders and reformation policies.[52] Within such a dynamic period, the question of "positioning" R. Nachman historically, socially, or even geographically, is not simple. The standard dichotomy between tradition and modernity does not encompass the multiple traditions and possible modernities that, in his moment, R. Nachman attempted to think through and articulate. What these concentric histories should imply for a study of R. Nachman is that any such "position" will not be static. It is the unabated and unavoidable dynamism of R. Nachman's position that we should keep in mind as we turn to read his work. Indeed, it was through just this dynamism that he himself represented his role as *zadik* to his followers; moving between historical, social, even theological forces, negotiating between faith and heresy, enlightenment and tradition—this was the "position" of the *zadik*.

R. Nachman made great efforts to explore the emergent Pale of Settlement, in all its dynamism. In his books of collected teachings, he intertwines theological insights with political commentary on issues of communal organization. In his teachings, he recasts exegetical discussions of some of the most fantastical narratives of the Jewish textual traditions in terms of deep thoughts on the social structure of Judaism in a modernizing world. R. Nachman also innovated in the spiritual and devotional realms, instituting such practices as regular private conversations between his followers and himself, as well as the practice of seclusion, whereby his followers would spend time alone in nature speaking directly and candidly to God. But the most compelling thing R. Nachman decided to do was to tell stories. The latest count by Zvi Mark has identified 162 stories or instances of storytelling by R. Nachman documented in Braslav literature.[53] Of these, 13 tales told between 1806 and his untimely death in 1810 were collected, edited, and published posthumously. R. Nachman's book of tales narrates a cross-section of the great changes and anxieties of his era.[54]

Chapter 2

Representing Difference

This chapter addresses the particular challenges that emerge in the *aesthetic* construction of this so called "crisis of modernity." The 1804 statute has been flagged as a moment of crisis, a crisis of modernity for Eastern European Jewry on both a sociopolitical and a theological level. This is by no means a new observation. Much work has been done on the many dimensions of this moment.[1] Nevertheless, and as already registered in the introduction, an uncritical use of the word "crisis" prevails in existing observations on this historical moment. The present study, however, is less concerned with historical questions of whether and to what extent the statute marks a "crisis." I am more concerned with the question of how this statute, and more broadly the reorganization of social structures in this historical moment, is *represented* (as a crisis or otherwise). I cannot, therefore, detach the content of reports, depictions, and responses to this moment from their form and the aesthetic stylizations they employ in representing it. And when we insist on keeping both form and content in view, what we find is that representations of this moment are challenged and troubled on an aesthetic level. The nature of the social shifts affects one's ability to describe them, while the description of these social shifts influences one's perception of their nature.

By way of introducing the dimension of aesthetics, I turn to a teaching of R. Nachman that questions the link between the modernization program laid out in the statute and the possibilities of its representation. Specifically, the outlawing of public markers of differences mandated by the statute underscores a political-aesthetic dynamic rooted in the formation of the Pale of Settlement, the literary representation of which greatly concerned R. Nachman. My intention here is to begin underscoring the foundational role he played in the establishment of an aesthetic with which to represent the reality of the Pale. A glimpse of this role can be discerned in Teaching II:28, of the second volume of *Likkutei Moharan*. In this teaching, R. Nachman expresses his anxiety regarding the invisibility of difference in the new kind of public space outlined by the 1804 statute.

> Know that there are differences between Torahs, for there is such a Torah as was not given to be taught, and there is such a Torah as was given to be taught but not written, and there is such that was given to be written, as we find that our sages of blessed memory say (BT Gitin 60b) oral things may not be written etc. And he who knows to distinguish and recognize between Torahs which can be written and cannot be written, he can recognize a man of Israel among the nations and even if the man of Israel is standing among several nations he can recognize him. And this secret is hinted at (Hosea 8:12) "I write for him ever so many things of my Torah, they are regarded as a stranger." That is, when one writes ever so many things of his Torah, that is, many things more than is appropriate, that is, when one writes what cannot be written (as mentioned), then they are regarded as strangers, that is, that he cannot recognize the man of Israel and he is regarded by him as a stranger, that he appears to him as a stranger and non-Jew and likewise he may confuse a non-Jew for a man of Israel (as mentioned). For the main difference between Israel and the nations is *bechina* of what cannot be written *bechina* of oral Torah.[2]

R. Nachman attends to two issues in this teaching, which he will ultimately link with the associative marker "bechina."[3] The first is the relation between the orality of the oral Torah and the fact that it is being written down and published all around him.

There are things that should not—because they cannot—be written down, he insists. His first concern is with the overrepresentation of an essence that cannot be represented. The result of overrepresentation is an eroded ability to identify the object of representation. To put it another way, overuse of the signifier erodes its ties to the signified, all the more so when the signified—the "difference between Israel and the nations"—cannot be represented at all—is "*bechina* of what cannot be written."[4]

In his teaching on this issue, R. Nachman partakes in a debate that reaches back to the first written record of the oral Torah—the Mishnah. And he signals as much in citing BT Gitin. Some major landmarks of this debate are Maimonides's introduction to the *Mishneh Torah*[5] and Moses Mendelssohn's qualms about excessive *printing* of the oral Torah in his book *Jerusalem*.[6] Relating R. Nachman's statements to this ongoing concern with the dissemination of oral Torah is beyond the scope of this book. The focus of this work is on literary representation. This leads to the second issue R. Nachman is concerned with: the inability to tell the man of Israel apart in a crowd, that is, to recognize "the difference between Israel and the nations."

Invisibility of the difference between Jews and non-Jews was certainly a new and growing phenomenon in R. Nachman's time. The Western European Jewish Enlightenment scholars (Maskilim), as well as the burgeoning Eastern European branch of that movement, had already willingly dressed themselves in the European fashion of the day. But invisibility of difference was also being legislated by the emperor himself and enforced by the police. As we have seen, Alexander I's 1804 statute mandated the sartorial conformity of Jewish public officials, students in public schools, and anyone traveling out of the Pale into Russia proper.

> [I. 3.] Jewish children [. . .] attending gymnasiums must wear German or Polish [style] dress *for the purpose of uniformity*.

> [I. 9.] Members of Town Council from among the Jews in the Governorates incorporated from Poland, *for general order and uniformity*, must wear Russian or Polish dress, if they do not like to wear German dress. In the

Russian Governorates where Jews are permitted to live, Jews elected to Town Council must wear German dress.

[II. C & D. 28.] Jews (including their wives and children) temporarily traveling outside of the Pale, have to wear German [style] dress *no different than that of others*. If they wear traditional dress, they shall be sent back [to the Pale] by the Police.[7]

The tsar's interest in his subjects' fashion choices was a marginal aspect of a much wider modernization process that he was driving at the time—whether celebrated or mourned by his subjects. But, if marginal, the appearance of a dress code as a condition for Jewish integration into the burgeoning public sphere was not accidental. It relates to the visual aesthetic dimension of creating a modern public sphere. The *invisibility of confessional differences* was foundational to the emergent public spheres across emancipatory Europe in this time—from Prussian social emancipation, through Napoleonic imperialism, to the enlightened despotism of Alexander I. In fact, the two most frequently mentioned topics in the tsar's new regulations were the revocation of the double taxation to which Jews had previously been subjected in the Russian empire and the normalization of the Jews' outerwear in public and official settings.[8] If we consider these two reforms as reflecting key concerns in the promotion of "general order and uniformity," we see the intertwined nature of uniform law and uniform appearance in a state project that heralded Eastern European Enlightenment. In considering the place of Jews within broader society, R. Nachman reads these two modes of representation—political and visual—as related. And this is the second issue R. Nachman takes up in his teaching: the new challenge facing one's ability to perceive diversity in society: "They are regarded as strangers, that is, that he cannot recognize the man of Israel and he is regarded by him as a stranger, that he appears to him as a stranger and non-Jew and likewise he may confuse a non-Jew for a man of Israel."[9]

European concern with the modern public sphere as a space free from representations of confessional difference continues to this day and has been discussed extensively.[10] What this discussion pays less attention to is the relation between the political-aesthetic dynamic of the modern public sphere and its literary representation. On this matter, R. Nachman offers his most interesting insight, suggesting a link between these two phenomena: a link between the excessive printing of oral Torah, on the one hand, and the invisibility of confessional differences, on the other hand; between the overrepresentation of a Torah that cannot be represented and the under-representation of confessional differences in the public sphere. The overuse of the signifier, which is brought about through the excess printing of the oral Torah, erodes its ability to indicate a signified difference (itself concomitantly losing its public representation), "the difference between Israel and the nations." The signifier and the signified are bound, perceives R. Nachman, "for the main difference between Israel and the nations is *bechina* of what cannot be written *bechina* of oral Torah." [11]

Only one who knows the limits of representation, R. Nachman suggests, will be able to recover the tenuous relationship between signifier and signified. Dealing with changes in the social order requires changes to the order of representation. What would such a representation look like? The effort to represent this political-aesthetic dynamic must represent the invisibility of confessional differences as a sociopolitical problem—that is, it must mark the invisibility of the signified "difference"—and *at the same time* represent it as an aesthetic problem—that is, it must mark the signifier's inability to signify, the erosion of its connection to the signified.

On the sociopolitical level, R. Nachman proceeds one step further with his teaching:

> We find that the main difference *and advantage* of Israel over the nations is the *bechina* of oral Torah that cannot be written. And there is in each and every one of Israel part of the *bechina* of oral Torah. And therefore he who recognizes between the Torahs that can be written and that cannot be written he can recognize between Israel and the nations for that is the main difference between them.[12]

R. Nachman proceeds to affirm that the *main* difference between "the man of Israel" and "the nations" *is* in fact an invisible one. It cannot be seen or written. But he goes a step further. The invisibility of their difference is precisely the *"advantage* of Israel over the nations." Positively valuing the social invisibility of Jewish difference, in the face of imperial policies that would do away with the very same public visibility of Judaism, is also an argument for the compatibility of Jews, as a different social group, with the new configuration of public markers of difference in the Pale of Settlement.[13]

While on the social level, the invisibility of confessional differences relates to one's ability to *discern* such differences in the world, on the literary level, this challenges a text's ability to *represent* those very same differences. On this literary level, then, R. Nachman's teaching outlines a particularly aesthetic challenge. What precisely is the literary challenge produced by the new political-aesthetic dynamic? In this new public sphere, a text that *clearly* represents the "difference between Israel and the nations" does not represent the political-aesthetic order in which Jews must exist in the context of new modernization efforts. But a text that leaves such confessional differences unrepresented does not reflect the sense of crisis that accompanies these efforts. The "crisis" is not merely a sociopolitical one affecting community structures and sentiment; it also simultaneously challenges the very ability to represent this effect. The representation of this crisis encounters a crisis of representation. Producing such narrative fictions that simultaneously mark the invisibility of the signified and the erosion of the signifier is one of R. Nachman's greatest challenges. His success in this regard (which I argue for in this book) would be the constitution of a Jewish literary modernity—a mode of literary representation that contends with this political-aesthetic challenge. To demonstrate R. Nachman's engagement with this challenge, I turn to the fourth tale of his collection, "The Tale of a King Who Decreed Conversion."

A Decree of Conversion

Tsar Alexander I's "Statute Concerning the Organization of Jews" forced Jewish leaders to confront extant notions of the limits of Judaism—geographical, social, and religious. Beyond sartorial conformity, the statute aimed to regulate Jewish communal life in the

Pale of Settlement by mandating, among other things, a "secular" curriculum in Jewish schools and the productivization of the Jewish workforce. The urbanization of Jewish communities was integral to the modernization process, as public schools and professional guilds were centered in urban settings. As we have seen, one way in which Alexander I attempted to force such mass urbanization was by revoking all Jewish-held licenses for the production and sale of alcohol—a major source of income for rural communities and small townships.

While this loss of income was indeed a strong catalyst for the relocation of Jewish communities to urban settings, the implementation of the decree was staggered. The 1804 statute set forth a timeline for the revocation of alcohol licenses, allowing (or hoping) for a process of professionalization and voluntary urbanization. The time frame began with the legislation of the statute in December 1804, marked the first of January 1807 as the date that licenses would be revoked in the large governorates, and designated the first of January 1808 as the date licenses would be revoked in the smaller governorates.[14] For the nearly half a million Jews affected by this particular clause, 1807 would mark a population relocation (from rural Jewish townships to mixed urban settings) on a scale unprecedented in Eastern European Jewish history.

In the eyes of the traditionalist Jewish communities, the imperial imposition of the statute was seen as a *gzerat shmad*, a decree of conversion. In late 1806 or early 1807, around the beginning of the implementation of the clause regarding alcohol licenses, R. Nachman told the fourth tale of his collection, strikingly titled "The Tale of a King Who Decreed Conversion."[15] The title firmly locates the tale within the realm of R. Nachman's contemporary concerns while capitalizing on the many resonances of this dysphemism. Indeed, the exposition throws the narrative back to a previous decree of conversion.

> There once was a king who decreed expulsion or conversion; whoever wanted to stay in the country had to convert, otherwise he would be expelled from the country. Some left everything behind and left in poverty to maintain their faith as Israelites, and some were concerned for their possessions and remained as *anusim*.[16]

> In *tsin'ah* they practiced Jewish religion and in *parrhesia* (in public) they were not allowed. Then the king died and his son became king.[17]

The briskness and lack of detail with which this opening scene is related clearly mark it as the exposition. This first king is not a main character in the story; he simply sets the stage for the tale to begin. The first thing to notice about this exordium is its echo of the Spanish Expulsion, not only in the most basic fact of a king giving Jews the choice to convert or leave, but also in the name it gives the Jews who remain in the kingdom, *anusim*.

For R. Nachman's listeners—familiar with this historical event—the exposition also sets the scene for a break with traditional accounts of the Expulsion, which will take place in the next scene. That is, this exposition could be understood along the lines of a history book, one that will recount the progress made from some originary moment up to the listeners' present. The historical knowledge and narrative expectations R. Nachman is priming in his readers, through the echo of the Expulsion, serve to identify the Spanish Expulsion as the very originary moment of a modern set of concerns in Jewish history—framing the Expulsion as a constitutive break within Jewish historical tradition. This would be nothing new to a listener familiar with the traditional historical narrative.

What narrative (or other) expectations is R. Nachman setting up for his contemporary audience by alluding to the Spanish Expulsion? First, that the Expulsion was a watershed moment for Spanish Jews and European Jewry more broadly.[18] Second, Lurianic Kabbalah develops out of Rabbi Yitzhak Luria's concern with the effects of this moment and in the context of the Safed circle of mystics, several of whom (such as Rabbi Yosef Karo) were expelled from Spain in 1492. Lurianic Kabbalah became the major mythical universe within which Sabbatian and (later) Hasidic storytelling takes place.[19] The Lurianic mystical and literary trend was marked by concern for the expelled communities and the significance of this event for those Jews who, as R. Nachman puts it, "maintain their faith as Israelites."[20] In counterdistinction, interest in those Jews who chose to remain in Spain, as *anusim*, is a marked deviation of the Sabbatian movement from the "normative" redemption plot of Lurianic Kabbalah.[21]

Given the above, it is surprising to find in the next stage of the story, which relates the son's life and rule, that the tale is not concerned with the effects of the expulsion on the lives of the expelled, but will rather investigate the lives of the *anusim* who remain in the country. Leaving the listeners' expectations hanging at the end of the exordium is an effective way to set up the world of the tale as a departure from traditional narratives of the Expulsion. Since at first glance the exposition seems to give no indication of the tale's concerns, it prepares the way for the dissociation of the Spanish Expulsion from the narrative of Jewish history that R. Nachman's listeners would have been familiar with.[22] Thus, the narrative sets up the Expulsion as a break, and as constitutive of a tradition from which R. Nachman's present narrative will then depart.

In addition to this subsequent departure, the exordium also introduces the theme of Jewish encounters with, and existence within, a homogenizing broader culture. This is entirely in line with the theme we saw R. Nachman develop in Teaching II:28 regarding the existence of the "man of Israel among the nations." In historical terms, this theme is evoked by the tsarist reforms taking effect around the time R. Nachman told his tale. In literary terms, R. Nachman evokes this theme by framing the narrative of his tale within a reference to the Spanish Expulsion. Moreover, in focusing his narrative on those Jews who chose to become *anusim*, the dynamics of the political-aesthetic through which the representation of the "difference between Israel and the nations" is troubled in his own historical time can be more finely discerned.

The second scene introduces us to the main character of the tale, a Marrano minister in the court of the king. This second scene will trace the question of "the man of Israel among the nations" back to the character of Mordechai from the Book of Esther. The tale relates that there was a plot in which some ministers conspired to kill the king. The minister whose Judaism is unknown to the king and court warns the king. Having survived the assassination attempt and captured the conspirators, the king rewards the minister publicly for his loyalty. Later in the tale, we discover that all the kings have kept a Sefer Zichronot (a book of memories, as did King Achashverosh), and the last king of the tale will desire to read from it on a sleepless night.

When the minister first considers what his response should be upon learning of the conspiracy, his internal dialogue is related: "Well, why am I a Marrano? Because I wished to spare my fortune and possessions. Now that the country will be without a king it will be that man will swallow his neighbor alive, for there cannot be a country with no king."[23] We should focus for a moment on the minister's logic. In particular, the questions here are: What exactly does the minister fear would happen to a country that has irrecoverably (the possibility of the king's son assuming the throne does not seem to occur to him) lost its king? What makes the king such an indispensable figure? These questions are in regard to both the minister's reasoning and the internal logic of the tale itself.

The first answer is that, as a depiction of this minister's reasoning and motivation, the perceived indispensability of the king is an important detail since the tale is ultimately also the story of how the minister learns he was wrong to think this and of how he comes to grasp the possibility of a kingless country. As the main character of the tale, the conflict the minister will overcome is his fear of this kingless reality and the anarchy such a prospect suggests to him. This fear has already prompted him to remain in the country and subsequently to expose the plot against the king. It is the logic by which he operates. This logic is further emphasized by the fact that R. Nachman alludes here to a verse from Pirkei Avot: "Rabbi Hanina, deputy to the Priests, would say: Pray for the wellbeing of the rulership [literally "kingship"], for were it not for the fear of it, a man would swallow his neighbor alive."[24] This allusion serves to mark both the dilemma the minister will have to overcome and the overcoming of outdated modes of thought about the relation between Jews and sovereignty.

A second answer is that, as an echo of R. Nachman's own postmonarchic world, which has indeed affirmed the possibility of a kingless country, the minister's lesson is also his own. What is involved in coming to terms with this affirmation is the reconciling of new forms of imperialism with traditional thought on sovereignty (such as the gloss on Pirkei Avot)[25] and with existing structures of engagement (such as the recent memory of the Council of the Four Lands), through which Jews encountered shifting conceptions of homogeneity and equality in their broader culture. In that sense, for the minister to be proven wrong is for the tale to affirm the possibility of such reconciliation. While kings die and are replaced, the minister never dies. He continues to engage with the subsequent generations of this lineage and advances toward affirming the possibility of reconciliation between a persistent "difference between Israel and the nations" and the invisibility of such confessional difference in the public sphere inaugurated by the first king of the dynasty.

Having introduced the narrative world of the tale through an allusion to the Spanish Expulsion, the various episodes of the minister's interaction with the following three kings further allude to two biblical accounts of relationships between Jewish ministers and non-Jewish kings in whose courts they serve, namely, the Book of Esther and the Book of Daniel. The structure of the tale mirrors that of the Book of Daniel. Both provide an account of a minister who serves subsequently in the courts of four kings. Like the Book of Daniel, in this tale, the reign of each of the four kings demarcates the successive chapters in the narrative. R. Nachman weaves together episodes from historical and textual traditions that relate a Jewish minister finding his place in the court of a non-Jewish king. In these traditions, he identifies (or imagines) a former engagement with the questions that preoccupy his own context—the place of the Jews among the nations and the representation of their difference. Thus, the tale weaves a narrative thread that extends from Babylon to Persia to Spain and all the way to the Pale of Settlement under Alexander I. In weaving together these discrete moments, R. Nachman also limns the rich tradition of breaks, on which his stylization of the emergent public sphere *as* just such a break will draw. Let us return to the beginning of the tale and track the question of a public sphere in the four scenes that are demarcated by the four kings' lives.

[Scene 1]

The first of the four scenes concerns the decree of conversion, which I discussed previously. We are given no motivation for the king's decree because the tale explores effects, not causes. The primary (and intentional) outcome of the king's decree is the creation of a homogeneous social sphere, one in which the "expulsion" of confessional difference leads to its lack of representation in the public realm. The secondary (and unintentional) outcome is that, having been "expelled," these differences don't disappear. The king intended to create a single homogeneous public sphere but ended up creating a second sphere where these differences continue to exist, even without representation. This second sphere is characterized by the narrator in the final line of the exposition when he presents the tension inherent to the lives of the *anusim*: "In *tsin'ah* they practiced Jewish religion and in *parrhesia* (in public) they were not allowed." *Tsin'ah* and *parrhesia*, then, are the poles of the political-aesthetic tension in which the *anusim* exist.

Parrhesia is a Greek word (παρρησία) with a long history in Jewish textual traditions, and its use in the sense of a public sphere is understandable.[26] But the secondary sphere—*tsin'ah*, the underbelly of the lack of representation—is undefined and unfamiliar. In the Yiddish version of the tale, the narrator interjects parenthetical clarifications of both these terms for the lay reader, rendering *parrhesia* as "for [the] people [to see]," and *tsin'ah* as "for concealment," which further underscores the issue of public visibility or invisibility at hand.[27] In *tsin'ah*, invisible differences continue to exist. What kinds of differences are these? And how might we characterize their lack of representation? In his initial vagueness, the narrator presents one of the central questions this tale will deal with—investigating the contours and characteristics of this secondary sphere. This investigation is what sets the plot in motion. From the possibilities faced by the narrator, we may extrapolate what R. Nachman seeks to explicate. The constitution of the Pale will define and determine the political-aesthetic dynamics of its modern public sphere. However, there is tension between this "modern public sphere" and the realm in which, with no public representation, "the difference between the man of Israel and the nations" will invisibly continue to exist. This tension is what R. Nachman's narrative seeks to explicate further.

There are two possibilities for translating *tsin'ah* into R. Nachman's contemporary terms. Where do invisible differences continue to exist? Is it in a secret realm, such as anti-imperial secret societies like the Freemasons occupied at the time? Conspiratorial accusations on just these lines had already been leveled against the Hasidic movement by their orthodox opponents in the tumultuous period of conflict between them. Or would invisible differences continue to exist in a private sphere, such as that which resulted from the separation of church and state in the German emancipation? The 1804 statute had taken a small step in this direction by outlawing rabbinic sanction of any kind—what the statute calls "public punishment" for ritual violations. Coercive power was reserved for the state, while "exhortation and persuasion" alone were for the rabbis.

The secret and the private—each maintains a different tension with the modern public sphere. Working through the difference between them, the main character of the tale, the Marrano minister who serves in the king's court, explores the political-aesthetic dynamic introduced by the king who decreed conversion. We meet this character in the second episode, in the reign of the first king's son. The tale follows the minister as he serves in the courts of each of the subsequent three generations of this royal dynasty. In each, the minister's contact with the king will engender an attempt to work out the relationship between the kingdom's public sphere and the minister's *tsin'ah* Judaism.

[Scene 2]

The second king is a stern ruler. As mentioned, a plot forms against him in the court. The minister hears of it and decides to inform the king of the conspirators' plot "without their knowledge,"[28] and the plot is foiled. The secret plot was reported in secret to the king, but is this secret of the same order as the minister's Judaism? The second king has just learned a lesson in secrecy for the plot against him was indeed secret, yet it was by no means a private affair.

"What honor can I give you for saving me?" the king asks. "Say what privilege you would like and I will provide it."[29] The king is about to learn a further lesson, this time in privacy. In return for publicizing the secret, the minister now wishes to publicize the private. "The principle of my privilege" replies the minister, "is that I may be allowed to be a Jew in public."[30] The king is displeased with the minister's wish yet is obligated to grant it. The next day, the minister goes out in public wearing his *tallit* and *tefillin* (prayer shawl and phylacteries), the symbols of his Jewish faith. Then the king dies.

Death has a formal function in the tale. It marks the structural breaks between scenes, demarcating the shifting relations between public, private, and secret. If for the first king "private" and "secret" are indistinguishable, and both opposed to "public," for the second king, they become mutually exclusive. On the one hand, the plot to kill the king was secret but not private. On the other hand, while the minister's religion is no longer a secret, it is not public in the sense that it is not part of the homogenizing efforts of the king. The second king's rule, then, sets up the tension between these elements, not as they relate to the public, but as they relate to each other. With the death of the second king, the third scene once again reconfigures this relation.

[Scene 3]

The third king was very wise, tells R. Nachman. Fearing the kind of plots his father had survived, he summons the astrologers and bids them predict what he must guard himself against so that his royal line will not be extinguished. The astrologers tell him "his seed will not be felled, just that he should be guarded from ox and lamb."[31] The king has this chronicled in the royal archives (R. Nachman uses the precise term from the Book of Esther, *Sefer HaZichronot*) and then dies. This third scene is the shortest and least detailed of the four. Its function in the narrative flow is to insert the riddle of ox and lamb. These remain, as Ora Wiskind-Elper points out, "symbols whose meaning is left hermetically sealed."[32]

The king's challenge before his death is to interpret this runic warning, and the astrologers' prediction poses a twofold riddle. First, he must determine whether "be guarded from" means that he must distance himself from "ox and lamb" or whether the "ox and lamb" will protect him in some way, a slight yet significant difference. This signifier "be guarded from" is unable, as it were, to signify, implying one thing and the opposite at the same time. Second, the king must determine what is signified by the ox and lamb. This riddle is one of the relation between signifier and signified. The ability of the signifier ("be guarded") to signify its meaning is eroded, and at the same time, the signified of ox and lamb has no perceptible representation in the king's environment.

The king walks on a razor's edge, for the future of his dynasty depends on the solution to this riddle. Will its successful resolution ensure the king's survival or bring about his line's ultimate extinction? But, having documented this runic prediction in his *Sefer Zichronot*, this third king dies, and his son becomes king. The fourth and final scene, the account of the fourth king's life and rule, is by far the longest and can be divided into two sections.

[Scene 4, Part 1]

The fourth king is a great and wise warrior who conquers many lands. Believing he has understood the riddle, he decrees that there be no oxen or lambs anywhere in his realm. "He therefore has no fear of anything,"[33] relates R. Nachman. This will prove to be an ironic statement since, in the second part of the scene, the king's erroneous resolution of the riddle will bring his dynasty, and the tale, to an end. Before we get to this, however, the first part of the scene proceeds to investigate the relation of "the public" to the idea of social homogeneity.

In the account of the fourth king's reign, we find an even more explicit reference to the Book of Daniel. The king constructs an idol in the image of "a man, his head of gold, his body of silver and likewise the rest of his organs from other types of metal," just as in Nebuchadnezzar's dream: "As for that image, its head was of fine gold, its breast and its arms of silver, its belly and its thighs of brass."[34] R. Nachman then tells of the fourth king: "And he became a great wise man and encountered an art by which to conquer the entire world without war."[35] Could there be a greater expansion of "the public," a larger totality than "the entire world?" How then is such a feat achieved? "For there are seven parts to the world, and seven planets, each of which shines in one part of the seven parts of the world, and there are seven types of metals, for each of the seven planets shines with a different type of metal."[36]

R. Nachman's knowledge of astrology is (for the moment) beside the point. What is pertinent is the fourth king's recognition of the cosmogonic heterogeneity of the universe. And the art (or technology) by which the world is conquered without war is entirely dependent on this recognition. As mentioned, the image of the idol, whose organs are comprised of the seven metals that represent the seven planets, alludes to Nebuchadnezzar's dream in the Book of Daniel. Yet, in Daniel's interpretation of the dream, this image represents the fleeting rulership of Nebuchadnezzar's

Babylon, one of four kingdoms that rise but then fall before "the God of heaven [shall] set up a kingdom, which shall never be destroyed; nor shall the kingdom be left to another people; it shall break in pieces and consume all [other] kingdoms, but it shall stand forever" (Daniel 2:42). A kingdom that breaks apart and yet consumes all other kingdoms and stands forever is the very opposite of that made by our fourth king, whose attempt to solidify the world into a single kingdom will not prevent his ultimate demise.

How does this idol function as a technology for peaceful world domination? The various metals offer advice by glowing or not glowing in reaction to the king's questions.[37] Each metal can only offer advice regarding the part of the world it corresponds to. If the construction of the idol is an attempt to represent cosmogonic heterogeneity in the totality of a single man's image, its functioning entails the attempt to solidify the variety of human knowledge in a single consciousness. Unlike the first king's attempt to dominate through imposing public homogeneity, with this new technology, the fourth king will attempt to dominate the world through recognition of its heterogeneity. The first king's perceived overlap of totality and homogeneity is undone by the fourth king. Which of these, then, is the "public" to be associated with? Is it the infeasible homogeneity of a single country's population or the equally impossible totalizing of the entire heterogeneous world?

Through the fourth king's innovation, perceptions regarding the limits of inclusion shift from those associated with the Spanish Expulsion to those characteristic of R. Nachman's contemporary political realities in the Pale of Settlement. Ferdinand and Isabella did not intend to create a second realm of invisible differences, and, in the aftermath of the Expulsion, the inquisition dedicated great resources to combatting the seemingly unexpected realm of invisible differences.[38] Around the turn of the eighteenth century, it becomes clear that models of social emancipation had broken sharply with former inquisitorial attitudes. Emancipation policies embraced the invisibility of confessional difference as a strategy for containing and managing difference under the expanding imperial bureaucratic mechanisms of the day. R. Nachman's tale fictionalizes and narrates this shift in the political attitude toward "the difference between Israel and the nations."

To return to the fourth king, R. Nachman further complicates the plot by explaining the mechanism of the idol's functioning. "And that idol of a man was not capable of all this except on condition that the king would humble the lofty and exalt the lowly."[39] It may be a stretch to call the idol a "technology" and its functional mechanism "social revolution." However, the demand to reshuffle social hierarchies and classes as a condition of possibility for the impossible totalizing of the world's heterogeneity will finally present itself to the fourth king. It will take the form of a demand to resolve the locus of tension between the mutually exclusive "private" and "secret," on the one hand, and, the "public" he is so concerned with expanding, on the other.

To maintain the idol's functional mechanism, the king begins to strip his ministers and generals of their titles and privileges. "What is your privilege?"[40] he asks the minister, who replies: "That I may be allowed to be a Jew in public."[41] In order to satisfy the idol's functional mechanism, the king must reverse the minister's privilege. But what is the reverse of the minister's public privilege? What must the king take away in order to humble the minister so that the mechanism of his own totalizing efforts will continue to function? Which is the opposite of the public that the king must exalt in order to consolidate the heterogeneous world into a totality: privacy or secrecy?

We may imagine two possibilities. First, in an attempt to reverse the minister's public privilege to be a Jew, the king abolishes the secrecy of Judaism, whereupon the minister is swallowed up in the heterogeneity of the public—a heterogeneity that includes "public Jews" among many other groups. Or, second, attempting to reverse the minister's public privilege to be a Jew, the king reduces him to the secrecy of his previous life as a Marrano. If under the second king the minister's secret was released from its private realm, the fourth king would reduce his privacy to a secret. In an echo of the initial exordium against "public Judasim," the king chooses the latter, and the minister "once again became a Marrano."[42] This will prove to be a mistake. The former, in fact, would have saved the king's lineage from doom. The fourth king chooses to oppose "public" to "private." Ironically, reinforcing the opposition between public and private ends up disrupting the king's ability to define the limits of inclusion and exclusion, visibility and invisibility. The tense complementarity of these two poles no longer suffices to define the social limits of the kingdom. The fourth king's decree establishes "the secret" as that which temporarily brings to a halt the totalizing project.

[Scene 4, Part 2]

The second part of this final scene begins by returning to the riddle of the ox and lamb.

> Once the king went to sleep, and saw in a dream that the skies were clear, and he saw all twelve signs of the zodiac, and he saw that the ox and lamb that are among the signs of the zodiac, that they were laughing at him, and he woke in great anger and very fearful, and he commanded to bring the book of chronicles (*Sefer HaZichronot*) and found written that by ox and lamb would his seed be felled, and a great fear overcame him.[43]

The fourth scene began with the king's decree that there be no ox or lamb anywhere in his country, which left him with no fear of anything. The dream marks the beginning of the second part of this scene, in which the king is entirely motivated by his fear. And this fear is once again brought on by the runic ox and lamb.

Let us pause for a moment to recall that in his interpretation of the ambiguous meaning of the astrologers' warning, the fourth king has decided to guard himself against the secret of the ox and lamb rather than to believe that the secret would guard him. His fear of the secret is compounded by his recognition of the complementarity of public and private at the exclusion of the secret, which is how we interpreted the manner in which he stripped the minister of his privileges.

The king summons all his dream interpreters, but none can interpret his dream. Now his fear transforms the king into a paranoid conspiracy theorist: There is a great secret, he believes, to which he has no access. All he has is the knowledge of its existence and the terror of its fateful significance. The content of the secret is beyond his ken. Then the wise man enters the scene.

The wise man finds a dramatically altered king. He is no longer the fearless ruler, bent on a totalizing project. He no longer looks out over his kingdom and sees the vast public his great grandfather had begun constructing and which he, in his great wisdom, has perfected without war. He is now a fearful and obsessive ruler, one who can no longer see far enough to recognize "the public" that has been his dynastic project. Though he does not recognize the connection between "the secret" and the secret Jews of his kingdom (nor does the reader at this point), this connection has nonetheless begun to strain his grasp of reality—inserting everywhere, in place of the narrative plot, the possibility of a complot, a conspiracy, the very possibility the riddle is meant to guard against.

The wise man will boast an impressive knowledge of what R. Nachman calls "our wisdom"[44]—astrology. He tells the king that "there are 365 courses of the sun, and there is a place which all 365 courses shine upon, and there grows an iron rod, and he who has fear, when he comes to that rod he is saved from fear."[45] The wise man explains of his knowledge of astrology, "it is a tradition from my father."[46] The king is invited to the place where the iron rod grows.

As it turns out, our fourth king is not the only one who seeks the iron rod, or (we might surmise) wishes to be saved from his fear. The road to the rod leads through a great fire, and many kings are walking this path, accompanied by the Jews of their kingdoms wearing their *tallit* and *tefillin*. These kings are all walking through the fire unharmed on their way to the rod because, the tale explains, "since those kings had Jews living in their countries, therefore they were able to walk through the fire."[47] The wise man seems unaware of this explanation or at least unwilling to disclose it. He refuses to walk through the fire, explaining that this too is part of the tradition received from his father.

The fourth scene ends rather abruptly. The king and the wise man have a disagreement. The wise man doesn't want to walk through the fire but the fourth king, seeing other kings walking though it unharmed, wants to proceed toward the iron rod. The king is too controlled by fear, and too intent on overcoming it, to listen to the wise man's warning. The wise man ends the disagreement by saying: "I do not want to go, if you want to go, go [whereupon] the king and his seed went, and the fire came over them, and he was burned with his seed, and they were all felled."[48] The astrologers' warning comes true. Clearly, he was not guarded correctly from ox and lamb. But what happened?

[*Afterword*]

The king's death marks the end of the narrative, yet the riddle is still unsolved. In a short afterword narrated by the minister, the secret of the riddle is revealed. Surprisingly (or not), the unrepresented signified "ox and lamb" turns out to be the Jews of the country, whose public representation of their difference had been preempted by the first king. The Marrano minister puts the final proverbial nail in the king's coffin, explaining, "[B]y me was he felled, for the astrologers saw and did not know what they saw, for an ox is used to make *tefillin* and a lamb is used to make *tzitzit* for a *tallit*, and by them was he felled."[49] The identification of the minister with the ox and lamb and the explanation that they were the cause of the king's demise strengthen the representational relation between them—that is, as *lacking* representation in the king's homogeneous world.

The minister's explanation—"by me was he felled"—also marks his recognition of his own error in thinking there could be no such thing as a kingless country. Not only does he now live in such a country, but he himself was the instrument of its formation. The question is in what way was he such an instrument? The kings that were saved from the fire had Jews living in their countries, the minister explains. But this late king had Jews living in his country too. It is just that they were not allowed to practice (that is, wear *tallit* and *tefillin*) in public. The relegation of difference to a realm of secrecy is at the heart of the dynasty's undoing.

The ending of this tale would seem to suggest a positive valuation of the public representation of confessional differences. After all, that is what saves *other* kings in the tale from death, and leads *this* dynasty to its end. Yet, recalling the conclusion of Teaching II:28 points to a less determined resolution: "[T]he main difference and advantage of Israel over the nations is the *bechina* of oral Torah that cannot be written."[50] The thought that a loosening or unstable relation between signifier and signified is the main difference and in some way an *advantage* that Jews have over their surrounding societies stands in tension with the ending of the tale, which suggests that a clear representation of that difference is advantageous for the rulers of those societies.

R. Nachman will not resolve the question of whether invisibility of confessional differences is advantageous and, if so, for whom. Indeed, it was in his day only just emerging as a large-scale social and aesthetic question. Yet neither will he naively imagine that he can simply avoid the question, the political-aesthetic dynamics of which are already quite tangible to him, as we have seen. What he will do—and quite innovatively—is take on this question as a literary challenge and go on telling stories that capture the complex and even paradoxical existence of "the man of Israel" in the new order. As we shall see, a further aspect of R. Nachman's thought on these matters relates to the role of the Hasidic leader (or *zadik*) in such a moment.

Chapter 3

The Secret of Our Wisdom

In late 1807, a couple of months before the alcohol licenses were revoked in the smaller governorates, R. Nachman dedicated his Rosh Hashana sermon to the impact of the 1804 statute. Published as Teaching I:61 in the first volume of his collected teachings, his sermon harshly criticized the loosening of Jewish communal leadership structures and raised questions regarding rabbinic responsibility in light of the decrees.[1] While this teaching fits within a wider constellation of issues R. Nachman is concerned with, I bring it into focus here for two reasons. First, it is historically and topically close to those concerns we have explored in "The Tale of a King Who Decreed Conversion," which themselves are bound up with the 1804 statute. These concerns are particularly evident in Teaching I:61 in R. Nachman's explicit dismay at the relocation of Jewish communities. What is less evident, however, and what I will attempt to flesh out in the following pages, is the way R. Nachman's comments on the function of good communal leadership in this teaching relate back to "The Tale of a King Who Decreed Conversion," which he had told earlier that same year. Teaching I:61 helps us highlight the broader field of social actors implicated in the "crisis" of this moment by turning our attention to a hitherto unmentioned actor—communal leadership.

In the previous chapter, we attended to two characters in "The Tale of a King Who Decreed Conversion." The first was the king. R. Nachman represents his concerns with the tsar's 1804 statue by fictionalizing and narrating the outcome of the king's decree in the tale. The second is the Marrano minister. In this second character, we find a fictional representation of the set of concerns we have seen R. Nachman express in Teaching II:28. The fictional tale allows the narrator to explore the various possibilities of representing and responding to an emerging challenge to "the man of Israel among the nations," namely, the invisibility of confessional difference. But now we may recall that, beyond "the man of Israel," there is another figure in Teaching II:28, referred to as "he who knows to distinguish and recognize between Torahs which can be written and cannot be written, he [who] can recognize a man of Israel among the nations."[2] This "he who can recognize" is not the man of Israel but an external observer whose esoteric knowledge of the limits of representation allows him to overcome the erosion of the bind between signifier and signified in two senses. First, his knowledge of Torahs that were and were not given to be written allows him to make public just enough and not too much of the invisible difference. Second, he can discern in the invisibility of confessional differences a social variety otherwise imperceptible.

This brings us to the third character of "The Tale of a King Who Decreed Conversion." He has hitherto escaped our close attention due to the fast-paced and hectic unfolding of the narrative, yet we have seen him play a crucial role in leading the king to the fires of his ultimate end. He is the wise man. Let us recall what we have read of the fourth scene. The first half of the scene is marked by the fearlessness and conquering prowess of the fourth king. It includes the construction of the idol from the Book of Daniel and ends with the decision to revoke the Marrano minister's privilege by relegating his Judaism to the realm of secrecy. The second half of the scene begins with the king's dream of ox and lamb and his waking in a dramatically altered state as a fearful king no longer in charge of his own destiny. The wise man is entirely contained within the second half of this scene. In fact, he is the most active character in this section of the tale. However, once the king is dead, the wise man "returns to his home" and we hear nothing more of him.[3]

In order to appreciate the role of the wise man in the tale, we must first observe the extensive parallelism between the two halves of the fourth scene. In particular, the parallel is between the king in the first half and the wise man in the second. Recall that the fourth scene immediately follows the documenting of the astrologers' warning in the third scene. The riddle of ox and lamb has just been introduced, when the fourth scene begins with the fourth king deciding on an interpretation. "And he ordered that there be no ox and lamb found in his kingdom, so that he and his seed should not be felled. He therefore has no fear of anything."[4] As with the fourth king in the tale, the wise man is first presented to us in the context of an attempt to interpret the riddle of ox and lamb, which has returned to the story by way of the king's dream. However, he does not offer a straightforward interpretation, resolving neither in favor of nor against the ox and lamb. In fact, he offers an interpretation of the dream that seems at first to have nothing to do with the ox and lamb. A further point of parallel lies in the source of their knowledge. The riddle has been passed down from the third king to his son, the fourth king, as a transmission from father to son. Likewise, the wise man prefaces his interpretation of the dream by stating that "he has received wisdom from his father."[5]

Following the fourth king's interpretation of the riddle, the narrator in the first half of the scene elaborates on the astronomical wisdom the king has encountered, explaining that each of the seven planets illuminates one of the seven parts of the world and corresponds to one of the seven types of metal. As we have read, the king's knowledge of astronomy allows him to develop a mechanism "to conquer the entire world without war." Whenever the king needed to make a decision, he would face the part of the idol made of the metal corresponding to the part of the world relevant to his decision. "And when he should act—it would shine and illuminate that limb [made of the corresponding metal], and when he should not [act]—the limb would go dark."[6] While the king's idol represents the totality of "the entire world," it does so artificially. The metals are not naturally found in combination and, in fact, represent seven distinct planets. They have been artificially combined by the king, and discrete parts of the idol light up at different times, regarding different decisions in discrete regions of the world.

The next parallelism now emerges into view because the wise man also possesses an impressive knowledge of astronomy. Immediately following the mention of his received wisdom, the narrator relates this knowledge: "For there are three hundred and sixty-five courses of the sun, and there is a place where all three hundred and sixty-five courses illuminate there."[7] It is to this place that they must journey to save the king. The word "illuminate" appears only twice in this tale.[8] It appears once in the description of the response the king receives from the idol, where, as we have just seen, the relevant limb "illuminates" to answer the king's question, and it appears once in the wise man's account of the place they must journey to, which all three hundred and sixty-five courses of the sun "illuminate" simultaneously. These two usages point to a parallelism deeper than a mere possession of astrological knowledge, relating to the content of that knowledge as well. In comparing the astrological content, we find a telling divergence between the two characters. The king knows of a way to artificially combine multiple astrological elements, and yet the "illumination" of these elements betrays their discrete nature. The wise man knows of a place where the "illumination" of multiple astrological elements naturally combines. The king's astrological illumination reflects the imperceptibly fragmented totality that is his "entire world." The wise man's astrological illumination, on the other hand, marks the underlying unity of a perceptibly fragmented phenomenon.

This divergence in the content of knowledge relates to a further divergence in the way the king and the wise man relate to their received knowledge. The king's interpretation of the riddle leads him to an overdetermined action—to decree that there be no oxen or lambs in his kingdom. The wise man, even when pressed by the king, refuses to disclose more than the relevant knowledge he possesses and simply repeats three more times the same formula by which he introduced his knowledge: "I have received wisdom from my father."[9] In contrast to the king, the wise man acts upon his wisdom in an entirely underdetermined manner. He reveals just enough but not too much, emphasizing repeatedly the existence of his received wisdom while refusing to elaborate more of its content than is necessary for determining his actions.

A comparison may also be made between the kinds of determinations each man seeks for the riddle. The wise man is more concerned with addressing the king's fear than the nature of the ox and the lamb. The reason he is recounting his received wisdom is because, in the place where the three hundred and sixty-five courses of the sun illuminate there is an iron rod, and "he who has fear, when he comes to the aforementioned rod—is saved from the fear."[10] The wise man is not proposing to resolve the riddle of ox and lamb but to help the king deal with his fear of it being unresolvable.

In the first half of the scene, by contrast the king determined that the object of his fear was the physical oxen and lambs in his kingdom. His fear left him after his decree that no such animals could be in his kingdom. Yet if there are no such animals, a dream about them should not inspire fear. What frightens the king in the second half of the scene is the suggestion that the riddle is less straightforward than he had thought. He comes to fear not the ambiguous signifier (be guarded from), nor the absent signified (the ox and lamb, which he has expelled), but rather the loosening of the bind between signifier and signified. The king fears the indeterminacy generated by the riddle—an indeterminacy that mirrors the one produced for the minister by the first king's decree. This indeterminacy is what R. Nachman has referred to in Teaching II:28 as "the main difference *and advantage* of Israel over the nations."[11]

The wise man offers to help the king overcome his fear of this indeterminacy. He may not have any concrete solution to the riddle. In fact, there may be no way of reestablishing the kind of bind between signifier and signified that existed before difference became invisible. But it is possible to come to terms with it and stop fearing it. This is the wise man's proposal, and the king agrees to go along with it. Having set out to reach the iron rod, we discover that the king is so motivated to overcome his fear that he is resolved to arrive at any cost. As the party nears the rod, the wise man spies a great fire ahead of them. Other kings are seen to pass through the fire, accompanied by Jews wearing their *tallit* and *tefillin*. The king, seeing others successfully passing through the fire, wants to continue. The wise man refuses, simply repeating, "I have received wisdom from my father," while refusing to elaborate upon that wisdom.[12] The king is not satisfied, and, despite the warnings of the wise man, he insists on proceeding into the fire, whereupon, the narrator reports, both he and his seed perish.

The difference between our king and those who pass through the fire unharmed is the visible presence of Jews in the countries of the latter. The other kings are not walking the same path toward the rod by coincidence. They have all set out to overcome their fear. And yet they allow Jews to represent their difference. Our king has expelled what did not accord with his understanding, the ox and lamb of the astrologers' prediction and the Jews of his great grandfather's decree. He actively upheld the decree by revoking the Marrano minister's privilege of being the only Jew allowed to wear his *tallit* and *tefillin* in public. His persistent investment in an overdetermined invisibility as a response to indeterminacy ultimately prevents him from reaching the rod and alleviating his fears of the same indeterminacy.

As the wise man returns home, the narrator introduces the tale's afterword, in which, as we have seen, the wise man correctly interprets the dream of the fourth king. In doing so, he solves the riddle of the connection between signifier and signified—not for the king, but for the Marrano minister. We have already explored the relation between this tale and R. Nachman's concerns with the 1804 statute and have analyzed the representations, in the kings and in the Marrano minister respectively, of concerns with a totalizing "public sphere" and the invisibility of confessional differences. To understand the manner in which the character of the wise man is implicated in R. Nachman's narrative exploration of these themes, I turn now to Teaching I:61 and R. Nachman's discussion of the role of communal leadership.

Canceling the Script of Our Hand

R. Nachman has much to say in criticism of his fellow communal leaders, and the road Teaching I:61 takes before leading us to a discussion of the wise man is somewhat circuitous. However, the intellectual scatology of this route is unavoidable, both in relating R. Nachman's affect on the issue and in setting up the positively valued counterexample of sage leadership. By having faith in sages and following their teachings, R. Nachman begins, one finds the middle ground from which one should veer neither right nor left.

> For all the studies that a person studies, he must receive and extract from them true sentences [. . .] sentences of comportment, that one know how to comport oneself, as

much towards himself as towards others [. . .] but when one's faith in sages is faulty, one is sentenced to weariness of the flesh, that is to constraints, as our rabbis of blessed memory wrote (BT Eruvin 21b) whoever mocks the words of the sages will be sentenced to boiling excrement, as it is written "and much [mockery] is weariness of the flesh"[13] [. . .] and when the body is clean, then the brain is clear, and one can extract true sentences, proper comportment, but when one is sentenced to constraints, due to faulty faith in sages as mentioned above, then fetid fumes rise to the brain, and confound and confuse one's mind, and thus he is not able to extract true sentences, *bechina* of (Habakkuk 1:4): "For the wicked besets the righteous, therefore judgment emerges deformed," that is, by the fetid fumes that encircle and surround ones brain and confuse him, by this does his judgment emerge deformed, *bechina* of "sentences they have not known." (Proverbs 149:20)[14]

R. Nachman here offers what is perhaps the most eruditely circuitous way of calling someone "full of it" that exists in Jewish textual traditions. The importance of these opening lines of the teaching is not just in setting up the scatological double-entendres that will run throughout this teaching, regarding the constraints that unfit leadership may be causing, the extraction of sentences, and the like. It also sets the affective tone for the criticism that follows. It is a tone of disgust with unfit leadership and a sense of great damage that they are doing, as well as a humorous tone, mocking the ineptitude of certain communal leaders. In the following section, R. Nachman directly identifies the adverse results of the 1804 statute with the staffing of leadership positions by unfit rabbis.

And there are leaders who receive the title rabbi, whose learning is from such constraints. And not only are they unable to comport themselves as mentioned, and certainly they are not able to lead others, and [yet] they assume for themselves greatness to lead the world [. . .] for they have a great evil inclination to lead the world [. . .] and by ordaining rabbis that are unfit, the script of our hand is weakened, and it has no validity, and the script of

> their [the Russian Empire's] hand is given power, and by this do they decree that our scripts should have no validity, but only their scripts, and Israel will be obliged to study their script, and by this do they also decree to expel sons of Israel from [their] place of habitation [. . .] to places where there have never been Israel, for the ordination that one ordains the rabbi and [ordains] the script, they are [of] one *bechina*.[15]

This terrible decree was the result of people putting their trust in rabbis who are not fit to lead, rabbis who "have a great evil inclination to lead the world" and who themselves have no faith in the sages.[16] So R. Nachman begins his explicit comments on the 1804 statute. In his criticism, he focuses on the linguistic education mandated by the statute. When we trust in unfit rabbis, he observes, "the script of our hand is weakened, and we give force to their writing, and all sentences must be by [the empire's] writing, as 'sentences they have not known.'"[17] "Sentences" here can mean both grammatical sentences and judicial decrees. This pun exists in the previous section of the teaching as well, where R. Nachman plays with the meaning of the Hebrew word *mishpat*, which also means sentence both in a grammatical and a judicial sense. The clash of sentences, he suggests, is both judicial and linguistic. It is crucial to insist upon our own sentences, as writings and as ordinances because the Russian Empire's sentences, he continues, lead to the deportation and relocation of Jews from their homes.

The object of R. Nachman's critical comments moves from mandated linguistic education, through regulations on the official legal languages for business and taxation purposes, and concludes with the relocation of Jews. While, from our own perspective, the topics R. Nachman strings together may appear to be nonsequiturs, he is clearly taking his cues both from the timeline of the 1804 statute and from the topics that the overarching modernization plan has bound together along this timeline. Here is the language of the statute:

> [I.6] Among the subjects taught [in Jewish schools] must be one of these languages: Russian, Polish or German.

[I.7] After six years have expired since the publication of this regulation, all bookkeeping and other merchant's documentation and correspondence between Jews must be written in one of these languages: Russian, Polish or German, or contain a translation on one side [of the page].

[I.8] All Jews who reside in the Russian Empire have the right to use their language in all matters related to their faith and in everyday life. They must, beginning January 1, 1807, use Russian, Polish or German languages in all public documents, deeds, bills of exchange, bonds, obligations, etc. Without this, no documents will be accepted.[18]

As is evident in these ordinances, the issue of linguistic regulation links education and financial topics in the span of three consecutive clauses. The linguistic regulation on business and taxation documents had just taken effect in January of that same year—on the very same date as the first revocation of alcohol licenses, leading to the first wave of relocation.

An unfit rabbi is one whose faith in the sages is faulty, and by this fault can extract only crooked sentences. By thus detracting from "our" sentences, he detracts from the force (both linguistic and judicial) of the script of our hand more generally. We must believe there is a force to our sentences, even if it is not perceptible, even if we find it difficult to represent, R. Nachman tells his students. Not having such faith is the sign of unfit communal leaders. In the following section, R. Nachman links his criticism of unfit leadership to a question we have already seen him take up in Teaching II:28, namely, esotericism and the limits of representation.

And by this is taken from us the wisdom of the course of heavenly orbs [. . .] and is given to them. For in the beginning this wisdom was given only to us, as it is written (Deuteronomy 4:6): "For this is your wisdom and understanding in the sight of the nations"; and our rabbis of blessed memory commented (BT Shabbat 75a): "What wisdom and understanding is [appreciated] in the eyes of the nations? This is the calculation of astronomical seasons and constellations." For there is sense in that, that the secret remains with us, even though we inform them of the wisdom [we possess]. For certainly we must inform them of the wisdom [we possess], so that they know [. . .] that we possess this wisdom [. . .] And if so, since we inform them, it is no longer a secret, for [now] they also know. But there is sense in this, that we might inform them of the wisdom, and nonetheless the secret remains with us. And this is the *bechina* of: "For this is your wisdom and understanding in the sight of the nations"—specifically in the *sight* of the nations [. . .] only that they [should] know that we have the secret. For we do not inform them [the content of] this wisdom [. . .] only that we possess the secret.[19]

The result of bad leadership is not merely these decrees, R. Nachman explains. More fundamentally, bad leadership takes "our" wisdom and delivers it to "them." This occurs because unfit leaders do not know how to maintain the balance between the public, private, and secret aspects of communal existence. "It makes sense that the secret [of our wisdom] remain with us," he declares.[20] But we must reveal to "them" our wisdom. That also makes sense. "For this is your wisdom and understanding in the sight of the nations" (Deuteronomy 4:6), quotes R. Nachman. The wise course is to reveal to them the existence of the secret and yet not to give away the content of the secret "[o]nly so that they will know that we have the secret."[21]

The current teaching may be seen as offering a qualification of Teaching II:28, in which R. Nachman was concerned with the overrepresentation of an essence that cannot be represented. What he now establishes is that the right leadership will know to clearly exhibit the existence of "our secret" without giving away its content. Thus, the impossibility of representing this particular essence does not imply that one should entirely relinquish the question of representation. Indeed, the rabbinic interpretation of the verse from Deuteronomy suggests "there is sense" in representing the *existence* of a secret, a difference, the content of which cannot itself be represented.

This is precisely the mode through which the wise man engages the fourth king in "The Tale of a King Who Decreed Conversion."

He repeatedly insists he has "received wisdom from his father," yet he refuses to share the content of this knowledge.[22] He never offers the king any further reason for his refusal to approach the fire, even as he sees the other kings passing through: "By and by [the wise man] saw the fire, and he saw that through the fire were passing kings and Jews wrapped in *tallit* and *tefillin*."[23] The narrator then interjects the information the wise man is unwilling to share: "And this [that they passed through the fire unharmed] was because there were by those kings Jews dwelling in their kingdom, therefore they were able to pass through the fire."[24] To emphasize the wise man's aloofness, his own voice then returns to the narrative: "[S]ince I have received wisdom [. . .] therefore I do not desire to walk any further."[25]

The idea of publicly exhibiting the existence of something that should not be publicly represented echoes the concern R. Nachman voiced in Teaching II:28 with the excessive publication of the oral Torah. However, while the latter offers a broad comment on the effects of this undesirable dissemination, it does not relate any social agent responsible for the writing of that which "was not given to be written."[26] The present teaching directly implicates the contemporary communal leadership in this process, which results in the "cancelation of our script" and "our sentences." The undesirable dissemination referred to in Teaching II:28 is here presented as an insistence upon revealing the *content* of "the difference between Israel and the nations." Overstepping the boundaries of what should be represented and, indeed, of what *can* be represented, unbalances the community as they negotiate the invisibility of their own confessional difference.

When attempting to walk this fine line between revealing and concealing, the unfit communal leadership does so without faith in the sages. Therefore, they either overpublicize "our" difference or omit it altogether. Both responses, says R. Nachman, are tantamount to canceling the script of our hand. What can be done about this lack of faith in the sages? R. Nachman turns to a possible remedy in the next section of his teaching.

> But he who has already sunk into such constraints, there is water that purifies from this filth, *bechina* of (Ezekiel 36:25): "I will sprinkle clean water upon you, and you shall be clean: I will cleanse you from all your uncleanness

> and from all your fetishes"[27] [. . .] and this water is *bechina* of disagreement, *bechina* of (Numbers 20:13) "the waters of *meribah* [quarrel]."[28] And that is why disagreement is called *plugta*, *bechina* of (Psalms 65:10): "the channel of God full of water";[29] for from every disagreement there is made a book, *bechina* of question-and-answer [. . .] in the beginning when he had no faith in sages, he would mock them, as it is written (Ecclesiastes 12:12): "making of many books without end and much [mockery] etc." That is, he mocks the increase of [the sages'] books.[30]

Faith in the sages means accepting not merely the validity but also the necessity of their disagreements. We will see the foundational role of disagreement in R. Nachman's thought when I discuss Teaching I:64 in chapter 5. For now, the point to emphasize is that an intellectual leadership that does not air its disagreements and so validate the dialectical process of engaging and adapting to the changing sociopolitical environment does a disservice to its constituents. Moreover, a communal leadership that does not have faith in the intellectual leadership, but would rather mock the increase of books and deliberations in the face of political and aesthetic shifts, disrupts the rebalancing of public, private, and secret by which these shifts need to be addressed.

Finally, R. Nachman relates the esotericism he develops in this teaching to questions regarding the dissemination of Torahs and the difference between those that are and are not given to be written.

> And by this are all [the judgments] sweetened [. . .] by the correction [and reestablishment] of faith in the sages, by which the books of the holy Torah are increased [. . .] And the wholeness of the Torah is by the oral Torah, for the written Torah has no wholeness except by the oral Torah [. . .] by the increase of books produced by disagreement (as mentioned above) then does the Torah attain wholeness.[31]

That which is given to be written and that which is not given to be written must both exist in complementary fashion in order for the Torah to be complete. The oral Torah cannot be written down lest differences will become undiscernible (as R. Nachman has stated in Teaching II:28), and the written cannot be neglected due to the juridical weakening of "our" script, or the result will be its cancelation. Both Torahs must continue to be actively maintained, each in its proper mode. By reestablishing faith in our sages "are all the judgments sweetened," states R. Nachman, alluding to judgments both divine and imperial.[32]

How is this to be achieved? R. Nachman turns the peculiar esotericism of this teaching into a rule of thumb for the fitting conduct of sage leadership. In his response to "their ordinances" as decreed in the statute, R. Nachman develops a *politics of secrecy*. The teaching ends by quoting Proverbs 11:13: "He that goeth about as a talebearer revealeth secrets, but he that is of a faithful spirit concealeth a matter." One who is not trustworthy will reveal secrets, which is tantamount to canceling the script of our hand. But the wise man, the right leader, will *obviously* conceal a matter. A leader who promises to reveal secrets, or to explicitly account for "the difference between Israel and the nations," is not to be trusted, for he will surely deliver "our" sentence into "their" hands. Nor is one who claims there is no secret to be trusted because wisdom must always be maintained "in the sight of the nations." There must be a concealment, and it must be obvious. There is a delicate balance between revealing and concealing, through which the right leadership should engage the representation of difference in the age of its invisibility—publicizing the existence of a secret that cannot be publicized. Discursively maintaining an awareness of difference—even as its form is imperceptible and its content is not representable—is a way of adapting to the new political-aesthetic order. It is a way of admitting that the visibility of difference is not necessary, and perhaps not fully possible, and yet doing so without dissolving the distinctions underlying the concept of social difference.

We have thus far discussed the figure of the wise man as a character in the tales and as a community leader in the teachings. However, the similarity implied between this figure and the author himself is unmistakable. The question I will turn to in the next part regards the position R. Nachman ascribes himself—as a *zadik*, as a community leader, as a sage—in the processes of imperial bureaucratic expansion and modernization. This is a further question of positioning R. Nachman—along an historical narrative, in a tenuous social position—while asking what precisely promises to enable or threatens to inhibit his communal leadership efforts.

Part II

Questions of Social and Intellectual History

Chapter 4

Was R. Nachman an Innovation Such as the World Had Never Seen?

Where do the previous chapters leave us in our attempt to "position" R. Nachman? Is he a reactionary "conservative" thinker or a forward-looking "progressive" thinker? It may seem at this point that much of his writing is reactionary. While he is responding to a changing environment—the 1804 statute, emancipation policy, and Enlightenment ideology—his response is entirely delimited by the possibilities and perils of an incoming tide over which he has little control and against which he must be guarded. On the other hand, we have seen R. Nachman suggest his own political aesthetics, such as the "politics of secrecy" discussed in the previous chapter. We have also seen him offer a forward-looking argument for the compatibility of Jewish difference with the emerging invisibility of confessional differences. Thus, he may seem to be a progressive thinker in the sense that his contemporary reflections translate into forward-oriented actions.

I would like to address the question of the reactionary and progressive components in R. Nachman's thought by refracting it into two complementary questions. The first asks about R. Nachman's ability to innovate, intellectually and aesthetically, upon his sociohistorical "position." This question has circulated in scholarship, and answers have been rather emphatic. As Arnold Band comments on *Sippurei Maasiyot*, R. Nathan Sternhartz's editorial introduction "is evangelic since it heralds the first publication of this new, sacred text [. . .] It is obvious from the first section of the Introduction that Nathan was fully conscious of the novelty and daring of this publication."[1] David Roskies too suggests that R. Nachman "did not want to create a seamless narrative out of disparate traditions—he ripped out all the seams and started over."[2]

As opposed to scholars of "literature" like Band and Roskies, who may be inclined to an inflated sense of R. Nachman's progressiveness (or even revolutionism), some intellectual historians and students of "Jewish thought," such as Yehuda Liebes, have taken the opposite view, namely, that R. Nachman was a deeply conservative thinker: "It is only natural that such a radical innovation, and self-consciousness of such innovation, would not emerge among traditionalist Judaism without awakening resistance [and yet,] what novelty is there in one who tried so hard to preserve the old and fight against any innovation?"[3] Liebes in fact perceives a paradox between R. Nachman's express desire for innovation and what he reads as his deep traditionalism. The solution he proposes is that, in the face of a modern rationalist imperative to innovate, R. Nachman insisted upon (and even amplified) "the old" traditionalist confines of the Hasidic movement.[4] Joseph Dan, in an introduction to the tales of R. Nachman, expresses a similar tension, arguing that "it is quite natural for an innovative, revolutionary movement to emphasize its adherence to tradition rather than to emphasize its new departure."[5] What Dan adds is an understanding that this question ought to be posed to the Hasidic movement in general, not merely of its individual figures. But by pointing to the difficulty of even *posing* this question—of clearly distinguishing between reactionary and progressive positions—I would like to address the complications and impossibilities we must consider when addressing R. Nachman's work within our existing disciplinary structures. As we explore these difficulties, however, we will also strive for a fuller appreciation of his position and self-positioning within the concentric historical circles outlined in the opening chapter.

This leads to the second question, which concerns the extent to which R. Nachman's "position" is the result of a conscious *self*-positioning on his part. Discussions of R. Nachman's conformity and innovation must take note of his very self-conscious self-fashioning, which is in turn echoed by R. Nathan. Expressions of self-worth and self-evaluations abound in R. Nachman's teachings and biography. A particularly persistent example of a discursively self-produced tension between conformity and innovation can be found in R. Nachman's (and, in his editorial capacity, R. Nathan's) contradictory pronouncements on his innovativeness and conformity. Our attempt to appreciate R. Nachman's position, if it is not to fall into a simplistic reading of his writings as either merely reactionary or radically generative, must take into account the great efforts at *self*-positioning that he consistently exerted throughout his career and across his intellectual project.

Is Innovation Possible?

In discussing the possibility of identifying R. Nachman's innovation, or lack thereof, I must begin by acknowledging my own puzzlement at the relation between disciplinary divides and his writing. At times, it has been unclear to me whether the literature on R. Nachman exhibits some confusion (or even error) regarding his disciplinary positioning, or whether he is (as one may be tempted to project anachronistically) truly an interdisciplinary figure in the world of letters, one whose innovations span multiple and diverse fields of study. Neither is simply the case. The very possibility of this anachronism—of imagining we might somehow divide and discipline his project in an effort to define an innovation—is contingent upon an ideological encounter in which R. Nachman himself partook; an ideological encounter that itself pivots on conceptions of innovation. Before we can even make sense of the question "was R. Nachman an innovation?" we must first agree upon what innovation is and the scope of its possibility. Such agreement was markedly absent in R. Nachman's own context.

Let us begin with two present-day working definitions of innovation in the study of Jewish texts and then work our way back to the early nineteenth-century moment in which these definitions emerge as possible and yet separate conceptions. The first is prevalent within the discipline of Jewish thought, the second, within the discipline of literature—the two disciplines within which R. Nachman is most productively studied today.[6] The first definition is as follows: *Innovation is manifest as the idiosyncratic selection and configuration of traditional (old) sources, particular to a given writer or group.* If we wanted to dispute this definition, we might point out that it merely retrojects the question of innovation to a past time at which the "old text" itself was (or was not) actually new. But disputation is not my intention here. On the contrary, noting the problem of such retrojection in fact highlights the shared set of assumptions between this definition and the concept of "the decline of the generations." As historical time passes, we find ourselves declining, moving farther and farther away from an origin-moment—be it in terms of innovative genius or divine revelation—and thus farther from an ability to comprehend the meaning (historical or theological) of such a moment.[7]

In contradistinction, the second definition would be as follows: *Innovation is manifest as a text's lack of dependence upon previous textual sources and norms in producing its meaning.* In this conception, it is the rupture that separates the literary text from the traditional source that is a condition of possibility for *modern* Jewish literature.[8] In this context, it is imperative to note that the possibility of, and indeed desirability of, a rupture from tradition is the underlying ideology of modern notions of "progress." As historical time passes, we draw nearer and nearer to a future moment inflected with redemptive overtones. We progress toward a fuller comprehension of the meaning of history, which will be revealed in a kind of epistemological end-moment that is yet to come. The modern notion of progress would be the inverse proposition to that of "the decline of the generations," both in terms of its valuation of the passage of historical time and in terms of the human attainment of knowledge. It is not my intention to critique either of these definitions nor their underlying ideology. Rather, I propose to examine these definitions as themselves an innovation in so far as they structure the disciplinary divide between the study of Jewish thought and modern Jewish literature. Moreover, the appearance of a conceptual and ideological clash, which pivots on these seemingly mutually exclusive attitudes, is in itself an intellectual-historical moment that must be appreciated. Recognizing the appearance of a clash is integral to our attempt to make sense of the temporal aspects of the question of R. Nachman's innovation, as well as of the temporality underlying contemporary disciplinary boundaries. We cannot ask about R. Nachman's "innovation" without implicating in that very articulation a historical-intellectual process, which is as much enabling of our own perception of innovation as it is of

R. Nachman's ability or inability to innovate. Moreover, R. Nachman himself reflected upon this same process and in those same writings in which we are attempting to identify an innovation.

The conceptual separation of "thought" from "literature," or the philosophical from the aesthetic, was a transformation that took place in the late eighteenth and early nineteenth centuries. This was part of a far broader shift in European intellectual attitudes. As Pierre Macherey puts it:

> Literature and philosophy are inextricably entwined. Or at least they were until history established a sort of official division between the two. That occurred at the end of the eighteenth century, when the term "literature" began to be used in its modern sense [. . .] The encounter which constitutes Literature and Philosophy as autonomous essences confined to the respective fields that both define them and establish their limits, is a product of history.[9]

This same process did not elide the Jewish textual context, where the word *sifrut*, formerly designating the work of the scribe, took on the modern significance of literature.[10] The broader implication of separating out these textual realms was that this enabled, and even defined, new conceptions of innovation. It is in this late eighteenth-century moment that the working definitions of innovation I have proposed at the outset of this chapter seem to take form.

In R. Nachman's Hasidic context, these separate conceptions of innovation have their roots in the (theological, ideological, cultural) negotiation that took place between the Hasidic movement's powerful drive to innovate and the traditionalist society within which it emerged and operated. This can be illuminated by reading the position R. Nachman takes within his own contemporary debate about innovation. More generally, within the Hasidic movement, R. Nachman is a productive case study through which to track these debates and ideological formations of innovation, both because he explicitly discusses innovation and newness with his students on many occasions and because his presumed innovation doesn't fall neatly into our own disciplinary divides.[11]

Moreover, the separate conceptions of innovation I have cursorily defined, and the disciplinary divisions they support, distract us from identifying an important component of R. Nachman's writing, namely, the lack of any discernible distinction between what contemporary disciplines might designate as Jewish thought and literature. While it is clear from the conversations R. Nachman had with his students that he was quite aware of contemporary efforts to distinguish between different concepts of innovation, his own writings do not seem to support any such division. This does not merely prefigure our own difficulty in firmly positioning his writing within a discipline but (read contextually) is itself a comment on the conceptions of innovation he was (and we are) familiar with.

The fact that R. Nachman is difficult to position within disciplinary distributions is evident in the secondary literature that we have already noted. As we have seen, scholars of literature see him as an innovator, the "Forerunner of Modern Hebrew Literature."[12] This link between innovation and literature is no coincidence. Meanwhile scholars of Jewish thought, such as Ada Rapoport-Albert, Yehoshua Mondshein and Yehuda Liebes, see him as firmly rooted in traditional texts and practices—which makes it more difficult to pinpoint his innovations.[13] I have already cited Liebes's article "The Novelty of R. Nahman of Braslav," which suggests that R. Nachman's innovation lies in the fact that, in the face of a rapidly changing reality, and despite a powerful drive to innovate, he innovates nothing.[14] Resisting innovation is his innovation. But if we turn to the discipline of literature, we find a different understanding of R. Nachman's texts. Ora Wiskind-Elper, Arnold Band and David Roskies all mention the Brothers Grimm in their work on R. Nachman's tales. Yet despite the fact that romanticism is a body of thought as well as a body of literature, none identify his teaching as part of the body of romantic literary thought (the key word here being *thought*).[15] In other words, R. Nachman's writings are conventionally divided quite neatly: His teachings are discussed as Jewish thought, his tales as literature.

To an extent, R. Nachman is a particular case of the broader difficulties we encounter in general discussions of the Hasidic movement. Arthur Green exhibits this general problematic when he asks: "What, if anything, is new in Hasidism?"[16] But he proceeds to set the bar for what counts as "new" rather low: "Hasidism represents a *new* selection and interpretation of earlier Jewish sources [these selections] interplayed with one another creating the *particular* [. . .] texture of Hasidism."[17] Here the new is a particular selection and configuration of *other* (older) sources. This says nothing about the Hasidic text itself. At the very least, this approach highlights the difficulty in identifying Hasidic writing as a new mode of textual production. And this is the very crossroads within which Hasidism itself is located: The development of the idea that a particular selection and configuration could in itself already count as new. To begin outlining these crossroads—and this is where we can begin to track the roots of some "new" definitions of innovation—we may point out that this is not what the early Hasidic writers said about themselves.

Early Hasidism makes the strong claim that the *baal shem tov* had come to lay down a new path. This path had never been seen before, and "amounted to a new revelation of God's truth."[18] Opposition from the Mitnagdim soon followed. Not surprisingly, observes Jacobs, "repeatedly one finds in the mitnaggedic polemics the taunt that the Hasidim make claims for their *zaddikim* quite impossible for those in 'our orphaned generations.'"[19] Ultimately, however, while applying a "decline of the generations" logic to Hasidic miracle tales, the more pertinent claim of contemporary orthodoxy was that innovation on tradition is not desirable and should be tightly regulated.[20] From the first outbreak of hostilities between Hasidism and Mitnagdim in 1772 to the pragmatic end of these hostilities in the aftermath of the 1804 statute, Hasidic writers were challenged to explain how one may be such an innovator and yet remain within the confines of traditional Eastern European Jewry.

It is in this context that we should read various paradoxical statements of R. Nachman. For example: "I will take you by a new way—a way that has never before existed. It is indeed an ancient way. And yet it is completely new."[21] Again: "I am traveling a new path which no man has ever travelled before. It is a very old path, in fact, and yet it is completely new."[22] Such statements, voiced by a third generation Hasidic leader, and uttered a few years after the conflict with the Mitnagdim had subsided following the 1804 statute, should be read as a step back from the claim of radical innovation voiced by the *baal shem tov*'s circle half a century earlier. R. Nachman here voices a shift in the concept of innovation that was being negotiated at the turn of the eighteenth century.

The subsequent Hasidic generation will express a conception of innovation that is already similar to that of the discipline of Jewish thought today. R. Nathan's words demonstrate this in the following excerpt from *Chayey Moharan*:

> Once he [R. Nachman] was sitting with the holy rabbi the *magid* of Terhovitza—apparently it was on Shabbat during the third meal and he [R. Nachman] tugged the *magid's* beard affectionately and said: "An innovation such as me there has never yet been in all the world." Editor's note: There is no need to wonder about the Patriarchs, Moses, etc., for who can understand the sacred meaning of his [R. Nachman's] remark? Simply his meaning would seem to be that *such* an awesome innovation, in just *such* a manner, with *such* revelation and *such* concealment, and with all that includes, there has certainly never yet been.[23]

We hear in the editor's note the assumption that the particularity of R. Nachman's selection and configuration of sources *is* his innovation.[24] Yet R. Nachman's own paradoxical statements about innovation mark an in-between moment. He is "positioned" in between the earlier claim that radical innovation upon tradition *is possible* but not desirable (this is the clash between the early generations of Hasidim and the Mitnagdim) and the later claim that such innovation *is not possible* and that the only possible innovation lies in selecting and configuring the (old) traditional texts in a new (that is, particular) way. This latter aspect of R. Nachman's writing is what is attended to by the discipline of Jewish thought. So much for disciplining R. Nachman's activity within the realm of traditional writing.

Yet another "new" concept of innovation was emerging around the same time. This was expressed in the realm of storytelling and literature. In the Jewish world, it begins with Naftali Hertz Wiesel (whom R. Nachman followed closely) and the Jewish Enlightenment. Literary scholars such as David Siff suggest that, for R. Nachman, the emerging concept of the "author," coupled with the effects of print technology, offered a way to radically innovate upon traditional ideas.[25] Storytelling was a way for R. Nachman to express ideas that could not be otherwise publicized—that in other mediums would be considered undesirable radical innovation—and reach a far greater public in so doing. However, by no means was this limited to Jewish writing.

Here we arrive back at the link already identified between Hasidism and romanticism. Several researchers follow (or circle) the disciplinary boundaries of literature to the point of imposing them on R. Nachman's work. Band states that "Hasidism, certainly by 1780, had effected a radical change in the attitude toward the tale."[26] Juxtaposing the Hasidic tales with the Brothers Grimm's publications of the same year, Band argues that it is precisely this change that places collections such as *Shivchei HaBesht* and the tales of R. Nachman squarely within modern Jewish literature. David Roskies further suggests that it is the very act of storytelling that is the greatest innovation of R. Nachman, who "was the first Jewish religious figure to place storytelling at the center of his creative life."[27] As "a kind of romantic philologist, like the Brothers Grimm [R. Nachman] did not want to create a seamless narrative out of disparate traditions—he ripped out all the seams and started over."[28] R. Nachman's literary genius "is measured," writes Wiskind-Elper, "not by his conformity with established forms but by his break with them."[29]

The constitutive break between the literary text and traditional writing authorized the contradistinctive innovation, in which selecting and configuring old texts would at best be no more than a form of writing in quotations and, at worst, plagiarism. (R. Nachman was accused of both by his opponents.) The conception of textual innovation as departure from traditional sources also underlies the tendency exhibited by researchers such as Zvi Mark and Joseph Dan to read R. Nachman's tales as devices of concealment for his most radical innovative ideas in the realm of messianism and (even) politics.[30] Whether storytelling (and literature, in that it is constituted by this departure) was the proper vessel for R. Nachman's innovative thoughts or whether literary innovation became the proper category for his storytelling is left indeterminate.

We might do better to focus our discussion on the difficulty that pertains to positioning R. Nachman's writing as a whole. Our considerations above suggest that the question to ask should *not* be whether R. Nachman is merely selecting, interpreting, and configuring old texts or whether he is authoring new ones. I suggest that, to move forward, we should problematize the framework into which this question falls, namely, the division between old traditional-textual commentary and new imaginative storytelling. This is for several reasons. First, eventually we would end up claiming he did both in any event. But in order to claim this, we would have to rely on disciplinary divides that force us to ignore large parts of his corpus (no matter which side of the divide one stands on). Second, as I have argued, such a division already relies on conclusions drawn in part from a negotiation that was still ongoing in R. Nachman's own time, a negotiation between various conceptions of innovation. Insisting upon this disciplinary divide, and inserting it into R. Nachman's writing, would be a retrojection of categories that were themselves formed only as an ideological compromise-formation against an effort to reject Hasidism altogether (and I suspect this may be true for several other Hasidic writers was well).[31] Last, at least for a reading of R. Nachman, the division between commentary and storytelling is simply untenable. Rather than falling into this framework, we should ask: In what way does R. Nachman's writing itself engage emerging divisions between literature and philosophy?

In order to begin outlining a way to read past disciplinary divides, we might begin by noting the absence of such divides in R. Nachman's writing. R. Nachman (and the Hasidic movement in general) certainly emphasizes and centers storytelling in a way that was both unfamiliar to his opponents and seemingly detached from traditional textual practices. While in terms of "literary studies" this is surely innovative, R. Nachman's own words of introduction to the first edition of his collected tales suggest that he sees storytelling as equally innovative in terms of "Jewish thought":

> Before he told the first tale of this book, he said: "in the tales the world tells there are many hidden and very lofty things, but the tales have been ruined for much is missing from them, and also they have been confused and are not told in [the correct] order, for what belongs in the beginning is told at the end and vice versa, and such [confusions], but in truth there are in the tales the world tells hidden and very lofty things.[32]

Was R. Nachman an Innovation?   85

The editor, R. Nathan, is sensitive to the possible misunderstandings of these lines. After all, as literature is defined more and more by its independence from tradition, a story that is merely the selection and reconfiguration of other (older) tales is either a quotation or plagiarism. He is quick to explain:

> Know that the tales our Rabbi told are mostly entirely new tales that had never been heard before [. . . , and] also sometimes he would tell a tale of those that the world tells, but he would add a lot, and change and correct the order, until the tale was entirely different from what the world tells.[33]

We hear here an editorial voice very different than R. Nachman's, claiming he was an innovation the likes of which the world had never seen before.

Moving to R. Nachman's teachings, we find a similar overlap between contemporary disciplinary divides. R. Nachman derives his teachings, commentary, and exegesis from stories. The teachings in *Likkutei Moharan* are usually based on a story or narrative. The first eighteen are based on readings of the known Talmudic fabulations of Rabba bar bar Hanna. In fact, R. Nachman told his students that it was Rabba bar bar Hanna himself who told him in a dream to look more deeply into his fabulous tales of sea voyages and desert caravans.[34] R. Nachman's imaginative teachings are both literary readings of these stories and exegeses of traditional Talmudic passages.

Furthermore, the teachings in *Likkutei Moharan* are themselves structured as narratives. That is, R. Nachman's reliance on speculative metaphysics (and Kabbalah) often serves the purpose of structuring his commentary around a narrative. Explicating the relation between the story he is discussing and the mystical narrative that determines the structural progression of the teaching is often the driving force of the teaching. A common rhetorical structure of his teachings is to begin by presenting a verse or saying and then proceed to expound a seemingly unrelated teaching. Then, at some point, he will introduce a narrative (such as a fabulous tale by Rabba bar bar Hanna), and through the rhetorical link of the teaching to the narrative he will end up explaining the initial verse.

The narrative thus functions as the pivotal point of the teaching as well as the eventual link between the opening verse and the didactic end of the teaching.

R. Nachman narrativizes his teachings so that they stand independent of the traditional text they seem to originate in, and he selects and reconfigures narratives in order to rhetorically structure his teachings. It would seem that both his teaching and his storytelling fit within both our definitions of innovation. Both modes of writing select and reconfigure traditional (older) sources as well as exhibit a lack of dependence on previous sources and norms. And on top of all this, R. Nachman's writings have become canonical sources for the study of Hasidism and, increasingly, for the understanding of contemporary Judaism. All this would imply that in R. Nachman's writings the two conceptions of innovation offered at the outset are not mutually exclusive nor even divided. On the contrary, any attempt to appreciate the richness of his writing forces us to approach their complementarity.

The Temporality of the Question

As stated above, both of our present definitions of innovation imply an underlying notion of history as either leading farther away from a moment of understanding or increasingly closer to such a moment. I have named these opposing ideologies "the decline of the generations" and "the modern idea of progress" respectively. We have concluded that R. Nachman's writings do not easily submit to either notion of innovation, and certainly not to one at the exclusion of the other. We must now inquire into the underlying temporality of a position that is able to maintain a view of both "decline" and "progress" in a way that does not exclude either. This also relates to R. Nachman's *self*-positioning. He explicitly reflects on his own moment in an effort to take his bearings from both temporalities, as he discusses *when* along these axes of decline and progress he is himself positioned. One particularly instructive text on this issue is Teaching I:21.

In Teaching I:21, R. Nachman returns to an idea that appears again and again in his writings, namely, that there is knowledge outside of human comprehension that orbits human comprehension. When one understands, knowledge enters one's mind and no longer orbits one's comprehension. However, it is characteristic of our historical moment that certain knowledge remains forever in orbit. The comprehension of this knowledge would mark both a radical epistemological transformation and the transgression of a temporal limit. "As we see there is some deep wisdom, that there is no ability in the human mind to comprehend completely [. . .] such as [the questions of] understanding and free will."[35] The examples R. Nachman offers for questions that humans do not have the ability to comprehend are the philosophical questions of epistemology ("comprehension," "understanding") and free will. However, he proceeds to explain that the fact that we cannot comprehend free will is precisely the reason we have free will.

> And know that this is the main force of free will: so long as the mind is not large enough to understand comprehension and free will, then free will is in place, for one has the power to choose life or its opposite. But when this orbiting [knowledge] would enter one's mind [. . .] and it would reveal to humans the [understanding of] comprehension and free will—then free will will be cancelled. For by increasing his mind, one would leave the realm of human and enter the realm of angelic, and free will would be cancelled.[36]

R. Nachman begins with the assumption that if one had ultimate knowledge of true and false, right and wrong, if one *knew* the "correct" choice, then it would no longer be a choice—it would simply be the "true" or "right" thing to do. Being truly free to choose between good and bad, right and wrong, means never having this self-evident certainty. It means never ultimately possessing the knowledge that would be required in order to make the "right" choice. This is the human predicament, as opposed to the angels, who, in Jewish legendary and mystical tradition, have no free will. Our limited human comprehension is the prerequisite for free will because it both allows and necessitates that we make choices between apparently equally viable options.

For R. Nachman, nowhere does this notion of free will apply more forcefully than in faith in God. Joseph Weiss writes of R. Nachman's observation that the great power of reason and science is that they turn faith into a leap. Faith becomes a leap over the division inserted between rational thought and religion, a leap into the abyss of doubt. Only by freely choosing to believe in God, that is, by believing despite the absence of proof or certainty in God's existence, only thus is true faith accomplished. Doubt is thus the primary prerequisite for faith. R. Nachman develops this paradoxical notion of religious faith based on his notion of free will. Furthermore, it is the rationalist project of the Enlightenment that enables one to confront most clearly his doubt in the existence of God. Since by seeking the knowable truth, science and reason have consequently also further delimited the realm beyond what is humanly knowable.

We live now in the most auspicious time for faith, R. Nachman tells his students. This is because neither the history of the world nor the coming days of the Messiah will be as felicitous a time for true faith. Before the Enlightenment and the age of reason, we were incapable of true faith. Since our knowledge was riddled with prejudice, it was not possible to discern reality from imagination nor truth from preconception. It was impossible to maintain a faith free of prejudice and thus a faith that was not a result of one's erroneous sense of epistemological certainty in the existence of God. For God cannot be "known" by humans, only believed in.

> And this is what our sages of blessed memory said (BT Brachot 17), that in the days to come the righteous will sit with their crowns in [upon] their heads [. . .] for sitting indicates the lack of free will [. . .] for it indicates the lack of change, for movement indicates change from one will to another will, and sitting indicates the lack of change, that is the lack of free will. And this will be because "their crowns"—that is, what orbits their minds [will be] "*in* their heads"—and not encircling their heads, that is the [knowledge that] orbits their mind will enter their mind [i.e., be comprehended by them], and they will know and attain all that [knowledge], and they will transcend the human and rise to the level of angel, and free will will be cancelled.[37]

In the coming days of the Messiah, on the other hand, there will equally be no possibility for true faith, since God's existence will be self-evident to all: "For the earth shall be full of the knowledge of the Lord, as the waters cover the sea," R. Nachman quotes Isaiah 11:9. In the days of the Messiah it will be *knowledge of* God, he explains, not *faith in* God, that will dominate human minds.[38] But now, when science and reason can prove conclusively that God is neither an empirical reality nor a necessary presupposition of existence, now that the abyss of doubt gapes more widely than ever, adherence to God is truly a leap, truly an act of faith. Only in the age of reason are we truly free to believe.[39]

It is worth pausing on the temporality implied in these remarks. Movement along the axis of decline has distanced humans from the possibility of faith by diluting it with prejudice masquerading as knowledge. The farther along this axis history progresses, the less true faith becomes. On the other hand, movement along the axis of progress brings us ever closer to a time in which faith will be impossible since it will be supplanted by knowledge. Individually, decline and progress lead away from the possibility of true faith. However, in his own historical moment, as R. Nachman sees it, the axis of decline and the axis of progress intersect to form a temporality from which any movement would be regressive. And yet it is from this temporally determined (and delimited) in-between moment that a new horizon of faith is opened, and true faith is finally (if temporarily) possible.

The edge and what lies in between are persistent preoccupations of R. Nachman, and we will expand on them in the next chapter. But by way of concluding the present discussion, I would like to highlight the great discursive effort at *self*-positioning that R. Nachman makes in attempting to outline his own temporality as an in-between moment. As we turn to the next chapter, and the next teaching, we should keep in mind that his "position" is both spatial and temporal. More importantly, discerning between these two modes of "positioning" is not a division that can be maintained. In turning our discussion to R. Nachman's spatial position, we will encounter his discursive construction of "the edge" as a designation that maintains both the spatial and temporal aspects of the position he is attempting to forge.

Chapter 5

Was R. Nachman a "Jewish Intellectual"?

R. Nachman moved to Uman in the final year of his life. There, much to the chagrin of his disciples, he lived in the home of a Jewish Enlightenment scholar. In this residence, Joseph Weiss writes, he felt

> the sensation of living at the limit—a very characteristic sensation to R. Nachman all his life. R. Nathan [his disciple and scribe] tells that while living in the home of Nachman-Nathan [Rapoport]:[1] "He said: here we are now at the limit and edge of Israel where the limit of Israel ends, for everything has a limit and an end."[2]

The "limit of Israel" is as characteristic a phrase in the depictions of Hasidic leaders as it is in the characterizations of Jewish Enlightenment figures, that is, Maskilim or intellectuals. Speaking of R. Nachman as an exemplary Hasidic leader, Weiss states that "they are figures at the very limit, at the limit of Judaism, whom the fascination of the limit and what lies beyond it has overtaken."[3] Paul Mendes-Flohr, in his book *Divided Passions*, similarly characterizes the Jewish intellectual as "one who lives at or between boundaries cognitive, cultural, and social. Straddling these boundaries, the Jewish intellectuals find themselves divided between the respective claims of the provinces of thought, norms and values in which they simultaneously reside."[4]

The shared articulation of R. Nachman and the Maskilim in terms of such a "limit of Judaism" raises the question: Was R. Nachman a Jewish intellectual? However, as R. Nachman's words quoted above illustrate, this "limit" is a position that, well before the academic study of Hasidism or the Jewish Enlightenment, R. Nachman already attributed both to himself and to the Maskilim he engaged. For this reason, I will not inquire into this limit as a descriptive or definitive statement regarding the social position of Hasidic and Jewish Enlightenment figures. Rather, I will begin by reading this "limit" as a discursive *self*-positioning of one individual member of these groups—R. Nachman himself—and ask about the perceived overlap of these groups in his eyes, in terms of their liminal position and transgressive operations.

Proposing to understand this language of limits as a discursive self-positioning, we must (ironically) first define the limits of this discourse of limits. That is, we must ask: The limits of what, exactly, are being invoked here? As we have already seen Mendes-Flohr enumerate, these are "boundaries cognitive, cultural, and social." But, importantly, there is a theological question here too: What is the limit of faith beyond which lies heresy? How far into the realm of rationalism (the hallmark of Jewish Enlightenment, as far as Hasidism was concerned) could one venture before ending up in the realm of heresy?[5]

Braslav ideology, explains Weiss, "sees a special role in the zadik entering among the investigators and the books of investigation (that is, books of heresy) [. . .] The most explicit expression [of this] is found in Teaching I:64."[6] The question of whether these "investigators" straddled the limit or simply exited Judaism altogether is a question R. Nachman struggles with in Teaching I:64. As we have seen, this is also a defining question in Mendes-Flohr's account of Jewish intellectuals. Thus, we need to give more consideration to the social implications of an ideology that ascribes to the *zadik* the role of fraternizing with the Maskilim. We cannot stop at the Braslav critique of rationalism as a form of heresy, as does Weiss, when this critique is part of an ideology that calls for engaging with the very same heresy.[7]

In the present chapter, I will outline the definition of "Jewish intellectuals" as it relates to the social, epistemological, and geographical limits of R. Nachman's contemporary Jewish society. I will then move on to read R. Nachman's Teaching I:64, "Come thee unto Pharaoh,"[8] in these terms, and propose that this teaching is a central text in understanding R. Nachman's reception (which is by no means the same as acceptance) of his contemporary Maskilim. My reading of Teaching I:64 will begin with an outline of the shared topography of the limit, within which R. Nachman sees himself and the Maskilim operating. R. Nachman's presentation of this topography is, in theological and mystical terms, primarily borrowed from Lurianic Kabbalah. However, in paying attention to the central role of the "investigators" (the Maskilim) in R. Nachman's articulation of this topography, I will highlight the geopolitical, social, and epistemological aspects of their shared "limit of Israel."

Last, I will discuss the differences between the operations of the *zadik* and the Maskil in relation to this limit. The question of how to position himself and his own transgressive aspirations vis-à-vis the "investigators" and the gravitational pull of the limit was, for R. Nachman, part and parcel of a larger question about positioning himself within the early nineteenth-century restructuring of traditional Jewish and, more broadly, European society. In Teaching I:64 he considers the various kinds of "limits" that encircle Jewish society—theological, social, and epistemological—along with the possibilities and implications of their respective transgression. R. Nachman's introduction of a "vacant space" between the limit and its infinite beyond is what makes Teaching I:64 so significant—as an early theorization of "the Jewish intellectual" and in its positioning of the zadik as the marker of an alternative horizon.

What Is an Intellectual?

"The men of letters of the eighteenth century [. . .] being out of touch with practical politics indulged in abstract political theories and vague generalizations," writes George Huszar in the first pages of *The Intellectuals*.[9] He is speaking of the role that French intellectuals played in the Revolution, but extends his observation to European men of letters in the late eighteenth century more generally. The politicization of letters (and men of letters) in this period is not a novel observation. Contemporaries of R. Nachman, such as Madame de Staël in her *Politics, Literature, and National Character*,[10] had already articulated this process. From Alexis de Tocqueville to Raymond Williams the increased involvement of men of letters in politics, and the effects of this trend, have been well documented.[11] For reasons that fall beyond our present scope, questions and possibilities of the relation between politics and intellectual activity received new articulation in late eighteenth-century Europe. A variety of writers, poets and philosophers took up politics and government, whether as topics of writing or as occupations. These men came to comprise their own social group and were known as "intellectuals."[12] Though they had little practical political experience, they did have, as Huszar notes, "great confidence in [their ideas] and thought that under the rule of reason a sudden and radical transformation of a complex society was possible."[13] Such intellectuals took on key roles in the revolutions and reformations of the period, and the revolutions and reformations of Jewish society were no different.

But, one might object, how could a Hasidic *zadik* be considered an intellectual? Our first reaction would, for two reasons, probably be to see this as a contradiction in terms. First, we tend to think of the intellectual as an enlightened, rational, perhaps even secular figure. Thus, the Berlin rabbi Moses Mendelssohn might be considered an early Jewish intellectual, while his contemporary, the Polish R. Yisra'el Baal Shem Tov, would not. However, this "secular hypothesis" is certainly not true of the non-Jewish intellectuals in R. Nachman's lifetime. Nor is it unproblematically true of Mendelssohn or of Eastern European Jewish Enlightenment figures for that matter—regardless of R. Nachman's choice to refer to them as "heretics."[14] Furthermore, the earliest non-Hasidic documentation of Hasidism was performed by Maskilim. Through harsh criticism and biting satire, these early accounts set up an opposition between the *zadik* as a corrupt populist leader exploiting the prejudices of the Jewish masses and the Maskil as a modern rational intellectual operating above the masses. This opposition—in which the secular hypothesis is ingrained—has been passed down through historical work on both groups over the past two centuries.[15]

The second reason we might not think of the *zadik* as an intellectual is that research on intellectuals as a social group has tended to focus on the intellectuals' liminal position vis-à-vis the society in which they operate—hence the invocation of "exile," "inter-space," and "in-between-ness" in many representations of "the intellectual."[16] Of course, these sorts of invocations assume certain social structures of inclusion and exclusion that allow someone to occupy such in-between positions. Such structures had just begun to form in R. Nachman's day, as political emancipation and tsarist reforms rearranged societies across Europe. The reorganization of society in terms of emancipation ideology and modernization policy was an important precondition for the emergence of the kind of in-between social space that has been central to the conceptualization of "the intellectual" (and, to an important extent, of "the Jew" as well).[17]

The Possibility of a Jewish Intellectual

The point I want to emphasize relates to the contingent nature of any social position associated with the above categories. The possibility of an in-between space—a space not entirely excluded and yet not quite within society, from which an intellectual can be both a "public" figure and an "outsider"—is first and foremost a possibility that relates to social organization, prior to any personal or intellectual disposition one may have. The early implementation of Enlightenment ideology at the turn of the eighteenth century is where R. Nachman and the figure of the intellectual meet, both ideologically and historically. The contingency of this social position relates to the possibility of Jews leaving their tradition and having somewhere to go (even an in-between space—Mendes-Flohr calls this "straddling"), somewhere not fully absorbing and thus also not fully "other" or "gentile."

This in-between social position, so central to understandings of the intellectual, was just being carved out and negotiated during R. Nachman's lifetime. Certainly, medieval and early-modern social conditions in Europe contained no such widely accessible space. As a group, Jews were, for the most part, either fully identifiable and socially contained (as in the ghettos of Italy), or they were absent (as in England). If there was a difference between Jews and the non-Jewish surrounding society, it was visible. If such difference was not desirable, it was expelled.[18] In the late eighteenth and early nineteenth centuries, with the spread of Enlightenment ideology that promoted the separation of church and state along with political programs of emancipation, this social reality began to change. In R. Nachman's immediate context, this was expressed by the effort to include Jews of the Pale of Settlement under a unified legal code. Alexander I's 1804 statute worked to outline new borders for this space—in terms ranging from geography to attire—and was an early articulation of the changing structures of inclusion, within which Jews and intellectuals alike would come to be defined and represented by later thinkers. In his social imagination, R. Nachman represents the emergence of these spaces in the processes of reordering society.

Paul Mendes-Flohr argues that we should not think of Jewish intellectuals as individuals who "achieve intellectual distinction by virtue of their self-transcendence as Jews in order to serve the larger cause of humanity."[19] Mendes-Flohr's remark certainly applies to the way we think of R. Nachman, who was firmly rooted in the Hasidic movement and exhibited no such effort to transcend his own Jewishness. His attempts to make sense (and, later, his stories) of the changing world around him did not lead him to transcend the traditional tenets upon which Jewish society in Eastern Europe was predicated, at least, no more so than the broader Hasidic movement. However, following Mendes-Flohr, if we define the Jewish intellectual as an in-between figure, straddling boundaries with divided and simultaneous residence, we might note that R. Nachman was hardly such a figure either. Nor could he be. The requisite social space for such "straddling" was just taking shape—geographically in the Pale of Settlement, politically in Alexander I's 1804 statute and socially with the appearance of the first Eastern European Maskilim.

The Maskilim certainly meet the definitions offered thus far of Jewish intellectuals. They were both scholars of Judaism and seekers of "heretical" knowledge. They were men of letters who took up politics as both topic and occupation. They lived at the limits of the Jewish community, identified as both Jews and intellectuals (an identification that includes and excludes them simultaneously). This double relation between the Maskilim and the Jewish community is enabled by a new answer to the question about where one ends up when leaving the traditional Jewish world. The Maskilim were not the first to pose this question to the Eastern European Jewish community. Hasidism had done so half a century earlier. Was it possible to step out of traditional Jewish settings and end up in between, where one might still be a subject of Judaism but as a nontraditional member? Or would one, such as the Mitnagdim had argued decades earlier, end up outside the fold entirely, ex-community? For its orthodox opponents (the Mitnagdim), in the final decades of the eighteenth century, Hasidism fell entirely outside the fold of the traditional community. There was no in between, no straddling of borders. But, in the early nineteenth century, at the time of the emergence of the first Eastern European Maskilim, the "topographical" question of ideological borders was reopened.

One character who for R. Nachman represents an exemplary position at the limits of Judaism is the Talmudic rabbi Elisha ben Abuya—the famous rabbi-turned-heretic, referred to simply as "Other" by the rabbis of the Talmud. R. Nachman sees Elisha ben Abuya as caught, like himself, in the gravitational pull of the limit, between rabbinic knowledge and gentile culture. Most importantly, R. Nachman represents Elisha ben Abuya as posing questions similar to his own, questions that concern the nature of the limit and its transgression. R. Nachman recalls the Talmudic question and its answer: "What was it about 'Other' [i.e., Elisha ben Abuya]? Greek song never quit his mouth, and when he would rise from his study, several heretical books would fall before him."[20] What draws R. Nachman's attention is this image of a rabbi in study, constantly humming non-Jewish tunes, who rises from his study of Jewish texts only to reveal he is also engaged in the study of heretical texts. With his similarity to the "investigators" of R. Nachman's day, Elisha ben Abuya will appear toward the end of Teaching I:64. R. Nachman sees Elisha ben Abuya as straddling the boundary between faith and heresy, and he values Elisha ben Abuya's contribution toward making sense of his own changing topography.

One important aspect of R. Nachman's writing is his understanding of such liminal positions as a *self*-positioning. This is true of his understanding of Elisha ben Abuya as it is of his own social position, which he will elaborate in Teaching I:64. Though this insight is never explicitly extended to understanding the Maskilim, it nonetheless recalls Antonio Gramsci's intervention regarding the perceived social autonomy of intellectuals. In his consideration of the social phenomenon of intellectuals, Gramsci cautions not to conflate the historical continuity of the institution of intellectuals with "that social utopia by which the intellectuals think of themselves as 'independent,' autonomous" social actors.[21] The "traditional intellectuals" are institutional actors, he explains, their "self-assessment" notwithstanding.

In his book *How Strange the Change*, Marc Caplan makes an instructive use of Gramsci's discussion in "The Intellectuals" to highlight the social aspect of relations between orthodox, Hasidic, and Enlightenment actors.[22] Gramsci's insight regards the relationship between the types of intellectuals he theorizes, in the process of social change. In Gramsci's words:

> One of the most important characteristics of any group that is developing towards dominance is its struggle to assimilate and to conquer "ideologically" the traditional intellectuals, but this assimilation and conquest is made quicker and more efficacious the more the group in question succeeds in simultaneously elaborating its own organic intellectuals.[23]

Gramsci defines the "organic intellectual" as an alternative type of intellectual, whose authority does not derive from an institutional attachment but rather an attachment to new classes of emergent social structures. Following this typology, Caplan proposes that "in Reb Nakhman's era, the eighteenth-century conflict between traditional rabbinical scholars (*misnagdim*) and the charismatic Hasidic movement can thus be understood in part as an instance of the dialectic between traditional, institutional intellectuals and organic ones."[24]

This paradigm is also useful for understanding the relationship between Hasidism and Haskalah, continues Caplan. "To a certain extent, the nineteenth-century conflict between Maskilim and Hasidim also recapitulates the conflict of institutional and organic intellectuals."[25] Both the old guard of orthodox intelligentsia and the emerging Eastern European Jewish Enlightenment circles were attached to, and indeed authorized by, institutions. The former derived their authority from prepartition social structures associated with the Council of the Four Lands. Within a generation, the latter associated themselves with imperial bureaucracy, staffing education committees and working as Hebrew book censors.[26] It is clear from R. Nachman's writing that he is concerned with an emergent intellectual stratum that he does not see as deriving authority from any "organic" connection to Eastern European Jewry. In that sense, the Maskilim R. Nachman is engaging with can be understood as "traditional intellectuals." However, what typifies the Maskilim, from R. Nachman's point of view, is their ability to stretch to the limit the bonds of affiliation with their Jewish environment. A consideration of the Hasidic *zadik* as an "organic intellectual" is a fascinating prospect for another study. Presently, my focus in reading Teaching I:64 will be R. Nachman's evaluation of the Maskil in counterdistinction to the *zadik*, in terms of the overlap he identifies between their shared social position at "the limit of Israel."

This shared position excludes the orthodox "traditional intellectual" over and against whom (in part) the limit was defined by Hasidism and Haskalah alike. Therefore, my focus will not be on the perceived clash between "institutional" and "organic" intellectuals. R. Nachman is sketching a subtler and more socially nuanced position vis-à-vis these categories. Gramsci cautions that "the most widespread error of method seems to me that of having looked for this criterion of distinction in the intrinsic nature of intellectual activities, rather than in the ensemble of the system of relations in which these activities [. . .] have their place within the general complex of social relations."[27] In reading R. Nachman's engagement with the Maskilim we would do well to keep this in mind. The point I would like to stress before moving on to Teaching I:64 is that even if the "autonomy" of one's social position is imagined or discursively self-produced, it nonetheless requires a context of social relations that allow one to imagine such an in-between space. And that act of imagination is itself an intellectual feat.

The Topography of the Question: Teaching I:64

Teaching I:64 of *Likkutei Moharan* is widely recognized as setting out a basic tenet of R. Nachman's worldview. In this teaching,

R. Nachman lays out the topography of the limit and the possibilities he sees of crossing it. In particular, he develops his concept of the "Vacant Space" as an in-between space that only a select few may successfully navigate. The most comprehensive interpretation of Teaching I:64 has been given by Joseph Weiss and provides an essential background to my own reading.[28] However, Weiss's efforts are limited to the philosophical understanding of the concept of Vacant Space and deal exclusively with the epistemological thesis R. Nachman develops. My task here will be to consider the social implications of the Vacant Space, and to understand its significance to R. Nachman's identification of an emerging possibility of in-betweenness in relation to which both he and the Maskilim operate.

An important focus of my reading will be the character of "the investigator," who constantly maintains a tension with "the *zadik*" in this teaching through comparing and contrasting social positions and roles. Moreover, while many have recognized the importance of this teaching to R. Nachman's worldview, no one has discussed the contrast set up within it between the *zadik* and the Maskil. Nor has any attention been given to what we might call the rescue operation, which R. Nachman imagines himself leading in relation to the "investigators." The thrust of Teaching I:64 is not a private idiosyncratic moment in the mystical or existentialist mind of R. Nachman. It is social, and it is relational. It relates constantly to the position of the investigators, to an unrecognizable "man of Israel" who has already made a significant step towards immersion "among the nations." The persistence of the investigators as a reference point signals the deep social concerns that motivate the theological speculations R. Nachman undertakes here.[29]

Teaching I:64 begins with a summary of a classic idea in Lurianic Kabbalah, namely, that of the Withdrawal.[30]

> God desired to create the physical world for His mercy, for He wanted to reveal His mercy, and if there were no world, upon whom would He have exhibited His mercy? [. . .] When God wanted to create the world, there was no space to create it, for everywhere was the infinite divinity, He therefore withdrew the light [of His own

infinite divinity] to the sides, and by this Withdrawal³¹ a Vacant Space³² was created, and within this Vacant Space, there came to be all the days and measurements, that are the creation of the world (as it is written in *Etz HaChaim* in the beginning).³³

Note that R. Nachman concludes the first paragraph of this teaching with a bibliographic reference to *Etz HaChaim*, the major work of Lurianic Kabbalah.³⁴

R. Nachman then turns to one of the basic philosophical-theological paradoxes that arise from the Lurianic idea of God's withdrawal. If it was necessary for God to withdraw Himself in order to allow the creation of anything separate from His infinity, then the Vacant Space, and with it the entire physical world that was created therein, would be entirely devoid of divinity. Insisting on the withdrawal of divinity from the physical world is the only way to ensure the world does not get swallowed up by the infinite divinity and thus lose its very existence, predicated as it is upon it being separate from God. Yet, if we accept this premise, we are forced to admit that the physical world we inhabit is a Godless world. Thus, Lurianic Kabbalah seems to force us into a radically transcendental view of divinity.³⁵ For the Hasidic movement, whose founder's motto was "the whole earth is full of His glory,"³⁶ this was not an easy conclusion to accept.

Weiss has suggested that the basic theological tension at the heart of the Hasidic movement is that of reconciling divine immanence with divine transcendence. He sees this tension as resulting from the attempt to reconcile the opposing ideas of Zoharic and Lurianic Kabbalah in Hasidism's popularization of mysticism.³⁷ For R. Nachman, suggests Weiss, this attempted reconciliation produces his deepest critique of rationalism, the rejection of the "law of non-contradiction."³⁸ R. Nachman subsequently claims that, within the Vacant Space, God both exists and does not exist, and—most significantly—that this is not merely some inconsistent epistemological position but is rather the empirical recognition of the ontological contradiction that is the foundation of the Vacant Space. In other words, this ontological contradiction *is* the space within which the physical world came to be. As R. Nachman puts it: "For we must say that two opposites are within [the Vacant Space]: existence and non-existence [of God]."[39]

Weiss identifies the law of noncontradiction as paradigmatic of rationalist thought in R. Nachman's day. In his teaching, R. Nachman develops his most elaborate and comprehensive rejection of the Enlightenment's rationalist ideal. In other teachings, R. Nachman focuses his criticism on the futility he sees in the rationalists' endless production of questions, converting every answer into a new question to be answered.[40] Here, he raises the stakes, so to speak, by attempting a more comprehensive engagement with rationalism. Thus, R. Nachman begins the next section of the teaching: "And know, that there are two kinds of heresy: there is heresy that comes from external wisdom, and about which it is written (Ethics Ch.2): and know what to answer a heretic; for this heresy has an answer."[41]

Weiss explains that this first kind of heresy is produced by "the questions that form out of the encounter between religion and the sciences,"[42] that is, between religious beliefs and rational investigations. These questions can be resolved rationally. R. Nachman's implicit reference in "know what to answer a heretic"[43] relates to the verb "know," which is to say that the contradictions of religion and reason are epistemological and thus resolvable through reason. Moreover, states Weiss, "in this realm of [epistemological] contradiction rational thought is king, and discursive thinking is not only one's permission but one's obligation."[44]

"But there is another kind of heresy," R. Nachman continues. The contradictions of this other heresy may appear to emerge out of rational investigation, but they do not. "There are several questions and contradictions among the investigators, that in truth are not related to knowledge, and the questions are null and void, but since they cannot be resolved through human reason, they therefore appear to be [epistemological] contradictions."[45]

In this typology of contradictions, Weiss explains, R. Nachman "turns the ontological terms of Lurianic Kabbalah into logical terms,"[46] concluding that the creation of the world through the Withdrawal also brought about the existence of epistemological contradictions, that is, the apparent contradiction between scientific observation and religious faith.[47] It also brought into existence the rational faculty required for their resolution.

R. Nachman then circles back to the ontological realm, in which the withdrawal of divinity implies its existence and nonexistence within the created world itself (rather than within human perception of it). The ontological contradiction produces the second kind of heresy, the heresy that derives from the Vacant Space, that is, from the space in which divinity does not exist. It leads to heresy when it is confused with a resolvable, epistemological contradiction. The shift R. Nachman offers here, explains Weiss, moves away from seeing the Withdrawal, and the resulting existence and nonexistence of God, as a logical contradiction. That is, R. Nachman does not want to see this contradiction as resulting from epistemological fallacies we experience as humans, as a result, that is, of fallibilities in our ability to know or perceive anything about the physical existence of our world. Instead, R. Nachman proposes a view of the contradiction between faith and reason as precisely the *successful* perception of the manifestation of the ontological contradiction formed by the Withdrawal, which is the condition of possibility of our created existence.

For Weiss, the first sections of Teaching I:64 serve as a point of departure to elaborate upon R. Nachman's concept of "the question" (that is, religious doubt) as the ultimate recognition of the ontological contradiction and, thus, paradoxically, the ultimate experience of faith. From this point on, Weiss focuses his discussion on the realm of epistemological questions, specifically on the human experience of doubt, which R. Nachman seeks to transform into faith.[48] As I proceed through this teaching, by contrast, I will consider the many levels on which the Vacant Space is a limit within the ontological, epistemological, and social topography of the world. From this perspective, R. Nachman's challenge is to find a mode of crossing the limit, a "leap of faith" from one type of (resolvable) contradiction to the space of the second (unresolvable) type, without (like the Maskilim) falling into and becoming mired in heresy.

In his next paragraph, R. Nachman elaborates upon the Vacant Space as a limit: "God fills all creation and encircles all creation [. . .] so there must be a space between the filling and the encircling, for if not so, then all would be one."[49] Having concluded that God both does and does not exist within creation, R. Nachman draws our attention to a new problem. What precisely were the ontological effects of God's withdrawal? If divinity exists (even contradictorily) within the world as well as all around the area from which it withdrew, then existence is still within the continuous infinity of divine presence. But such infinity was precisely what had to be limited and contained in order for the individuation of existence to be possible. Here R. Nachman offers his most radical understanding of the Vacant Space as the space that interrupts the continuity of the infinite divinity that surrounds existence from the ontologically contradictory form of divinity that fills all existence. "It is the Vacant Space [and not God] that surrounds all of creation, and God, who surrounds everything, surrounds the Vacant Space [but between God's filling and God's encircling of everything] in-between divides the Vacant Space."[50]

It is worth emphasizing again the radical nature of this proposal. R. Nachman states that there is a space in which God, in a noncontradictory yet fully ontological sense, does not exist. And, he continues, this space, which he calls the Vacant Space, lies in between the created world we inhabit and the infinity that is beyond. The radical nature of R. Nachman's understanding of the Vacant Space becomes even clearer when we consider the various provinces this in-between space divides. First, it is an ontological space that divides both the created world from the infinite divinity and the paradoxical existence of God within the world from His infinite existence outside of the world. Second, it is an epistemological space that marks the limit of rational thought's ability to comprehend reality and so buffers between the province of reason and the unattainable knowledge of God that exists in the infinite beyond. The Vacant Space is the realm in which, as Weiss articulates it, "the law of non-contradiction does not hold true for itself."[51] Lastly, and what is most important to emphasize in the present reading, it is also a social space. As such, it separates the faithful from the "investigators," and it is the space within which heretical books circulate. The Vacant Space is thus a social buffer zone, which falls between traditional Judaism and the non-Jewish world, and within which the Maskilim and their heretical ideas exist outside of the Jewish faith but not yet absorbed into the non-Jewish world that surrounds them.

What are we to do with such a Vacant Space, vacant of God, of the basic tenets of reason, of religious faith, and full of heresy and irresolvable contradiction? Or, to ask this otherwise: Where does R. Nachman position himself within this topography? "And know, if there is a *zadik*, who is *bechina* of Moses, he must deliberately look into the ideas of this [second] heresy," he tells us. This overlap of social and (for lack of a better term) speculative-philosophical realms is a key to understanding R. Nachman's teachings in general and the topography of the Vacant Space in particular.

One way to understand this overlap, as Magid states, is to recognize that "theological speculation is always contextual, emerging via imaginative interpretation rather than via pure philosophical argumentation."[52] Could we then not say the same for social speculation? Certainly, it is a speculative project R. Nachman is undertaking. He arrives at the in-betweenness of the Vacant Space by contemplating the question of the limit—theological and rational, ontological and social—of his changing world. As the *zadik* whose role is to explore the Vacant Space, the multifaceted nature of any possible maneuver R. Nachman might consider attempting within it must form a central observation of our reading.

In many ways, the topography of the Vacant Space is comparable to the in-between space of Mendes-Flohr's Jewish intellectual. It is where one ends up when stepping out of the limits of Jewish tradition and from where one can no longer budge. For R. Nachman, to be lodged between tradition and its inaccessible surroundings is to fall into heresy. For the Maskilim, he imagines, the transition is one-directional. That is, they lose the ability to return to the fold of tradition. But this is not true for the *zadik*. In that sense, R. Nachman's Vacant Space is at once open and restricted. It is restricted in the sense that it is not propitiously accessed by just anyone. After all, the Maskilim access it at the price of irreparable heresy, which to R. Nachman is hardly a propitious result. But it is open in the sense that those who are able to act propitiously within it (the *zadikim*, that is) are also able to return from it to the fold of Jewish tradition.

This ability to return has an important social function. It mediates between the community and its outliers. The *zadik*, in R. Nachman's social imagination, is able not only to return from the Vacant Space but also to bring back with him those Maskilim who have fallen into heresy. The *zadik* saves these Maskilim from being trapped in the Vacant Space. In epistemological terms, this means recognizing the difference between resolvable rational contradictions and irresolvable ontological contradictions mistaken for the former. In social terms, this means maintaining relations with the Maskilim and attempting to draw them back into the fold by entertaining their heretical ideas. No more than a handful of such Maskilim lived in R. Nachman's surroundings, mostly in Uman, and he was in touch with them all.[53] In fact, and as mentioned, he spent the final months of his life living in the home of a Maskil.

On a local level, it appears that R. Nachman's efforts were mildly successful. R. Nathan and later Braslav biographers recount regular meetings between R. Nachman and the Maskilim of Uman and report several Maskilim attending the mourning rituals over R. Nachman's passing and even returning the following Rosh Hashana to pray with R. Nachman's followers at his grave.[54] Hayim Liberman tells us that "the maskilim enjoyed coming to visit R. Nachman and even played chess with him. R. Nachman is known to have visited Hirsch Ber Hurwitz."[55]

An open space as opposed to a limit, as the separation between the traditional and the "external," is R. Nachman's innovation, not only in metaphysical but also in social terms. It conceptualizes a space within which Maskilim may exist—and get stuck, perhaps—without totally detaching from Judaism. In his conceptualization of the Vacant Space as a place from which the *zadik* "retrieves" the heretics, it is certainly not a desirable position to be in. But in R. Nachman's own terms it is a position that nonetheless allows for a shift in one's relation to Jewish tradition, from the continuity along which religious leaders of the time positioned themselves, to the kind of contiguity that the Vacant Space maintains with the created world.[56] To the extent that R. Nachman represents the existence of an in-between space—theological, epistemological, and social—his writing and thought document the processes by which an opening is formed between Jews and their non-Jewish surroundings. However, documentation is still far from being approbation. R. Nachman remained critical of Maskilic ideas all his life. This is mirrored in the many layers on which Teaching I:64 operates and the general antiphilosophical position R. Nachman proceeds to articulate in response to Maskilic transgressions of the Vacant Space.

Antiphilosophy

How does the epistemological significance of maneuvering in the Vacant Space relate to the social significance of its exploration? To answer this, let us return to the investigation of the limits of rationalism. My guide will be Bruno Bosteels's discussion of "antiphilosophy."[57] The speculative metaphysics of R. Nachman's Vacant Space is comparable in several ways with what Bosteels describes as an antiphilosophical system. First, as is evident from the critique of rationalism contained in Teaching I:64, R. Nachman's position opposes a strict rationalistic understanding of the world as much as it opposes a naïve antirationalism. That is, R. Nachman differentiates between contradictions that cannot be resolved by reason (the contradictions of the Vacant Space) and those that can be resolved by reason and with regards to which, as Weiss states, "discursive thinking is [. . .] one's obligation."[58] In developing his position, R. Nachman's "rejection of systematic thinking is in itself astonishingly systematic."[59] Furthermore, this systematic rejection of systematic thought follows the contours of what Bosteels identifies as the exemplary antiphilosophical position, namely, one that is "[o]pposed to the universality claims [sic] of truth but [. . .] also forever in search of a radical gesture that would be able, if not fully to replace, then at least continuously to compete with the prestige of truth in philosophy."[60] For R. Nachman, this gesture is found in the paradoxical nature of faith we discussed in the previous chapter.

Let's read Bosteels's characterization of antiphilosophy and then return to our present teaching.

> We can distinguish a few general clues that serve to detect an antiphilosophical approach to thinking: first, the assumption that the limits of language coincide with the limits of the world; second, the reduction of truth to being nothing more than a linguistic or rhetorical effect, the outcome of historically and culturally specific language games; third, an appeal to what lies just beyond language, or at the upper limit of the sayable, as a domain of meaning irreducible to truth; and, finally,

in order to gain access to this domain, the search for a radical act, such as the religious leap of faith or the revolutionary break, the intense thrill of which would disqualify in advance any systematic theoretical or conceptual elaboration.[61]

As we read through the rest of Teaching I:64, we will encounter the first, third, and fourth of these "clues."[62] Let's return to R. Nachman's words.

> And know, if there is a zadik, who is *bechina* of Moses, he must deliberately look into the ideas of this [second] heresy, and even though they cannot be resolved [. . .] For these contradictions and questions of this [second] heresy that come from the Vacant Space, they are *bechina* of silence, for there is no resolution for them. For the creation [of the world] was through speech, as it is written (Psalms 33[:6]): "By the word of the Lord were the heavens made, and all the host of them by the breath of His mouth." And in speech there is wisdom [. . .] And speech is the limit of all things, for He delimited His knowledge within the letters [with which the world was created].[63] But in the Vacant Space [. . .] there is no speech, nor knowledge without letters, and therefore the contradictions that come from there, they are *bechina* of silence [. . .] That is why one may not enter [the Vacant Space] and look into these words of heresy and contradiction except for a zadik who is *bechina* of Moses who is *bechina* of silence, for Moses is *bechina* of silence, in the *bechina* that he is called "'slow of speech." (Exodus 4[:11])[64]

Since letters and words are the building blocks of the created world, as the idea of God creating the world through speech suggests, the limits of language are the limits of the created world. Language can articulate contradictions that emerge from creation because it is made of the same substance as creation—words and letters. Furthermore, God "delimited His knowledge within the letters,"[65] making language the vessel of knowledge. In the Vacant Space, there is no creation, so language cannot articulate it, and knowledge of it is not possible. The very articulation of the question "Does God exist?" is a putting into words of God's paradoxical existence and nonexistence and causes the ontological precondition of existence to appear as an epistemological contradiction. This is what happens when one attempts to put into language a knowledge of what lies beyond it, that is, beyond what words can create. In antiphilosophical thinking, Bosteels continues, "so much weight is given to the effects of language and the change it can produce that the principle of non-contradiction, cornerstone of classical logic if there ever was one, no longer applies [. . .] When taken to an extreme, this privileging of rhetoric over logic can easily lend the argument a mystical overtone."[66]

R. Nachman concludes that it is not possible to say anything about the function of language in the Vacant Space since it has none. At this point, R. Nachman's teaching shifts the discussion to the function of language in the created world. This will lead quite explicitly to a discussion of the social realm.

> And know, that disagreement is *bechina* of the creation of the world. [God] withdrew His light to the sides, and there was Vacant Space, and within it He created all of creation [. . .] by means of the words [that He inserted into the Vacant Space]. And so is the *bechina* of disagreement, for if all scholars[67] were one, there would be no space for the creation of the world, if not for the disagreement between them, whereby they divide from each other, and each pulls himself in a different direction, by this is there formed between them *bechina* of Vacant Space, which is *bechina* of withdrawal, in which is the creation of the world [accomplished] by means of speech.
>
> For all the words that each of them speaks, all are only for the creation of the world, which is done by them in the Vacant Space between them. For scholars create everything by means of their words [. . .] But caution is needed not to speak too much, only as is needed for the creation of the world, no more.[68]

R. Nachman elaborates several points about the social aspect of this teaching. First, he connects the cosmology of the previous sections to the topography of social discourse. Every scholar is a microcosm of the grand Lurianic cosmological drama. Scholars have the dual role of withdrawing from the Vacant Space between them and of filling it with words of creation. "This decisive role of the speaking subject, finally, constitutes a fifth and final feature that is typical of antiphilosophy,"[69] Bosteels concludes. For Bosteels, there is a mystical overtone to antiphilosophy. The centrality of the speaking subject is clear in this passage from Teaching I:64. However, mysticism and esotericism are integral parts of R. Nachman's system. Recall the constructive role of disagreement in Teaching I:61, as well as the prescribed limitations on the speech of the sages, who are to reveal the secret just enough and not too much.

Having mapped the ontological onto the epistemological and social realms, we can now more clearly articulate the critique R. Nachman produces by framing epistemological questions in Lurianic terms. The epistemological unity presumed by rationalism is what scholars must withdraw from in order for a social world of discourse to be created. R. Nachman's scholar is empowered with the ability to create this world. But he is also stranded within the Lurianic drama: Every time the scholar disagrees, he creates Vacant Space, which he can fill with words. And yet every instance of filling Vacant Space with creation, as R. Nachman has radically argued, is also the simultaneous creation of a buffer between the withdrawn and the created therein. The scholar, in this sense, is always isolated from the world he creates by the Vacant Space necessary for his intellectual individuation and existence. The scholar here resembles the infinite divinity, whose every attempt at creation is also a distancing of Himself therefrom. The ontological terms in which God created the world are mapped onto the epistemological terms in which scholars create knowledge within that world.

In the next section of the teaching, both the ontological and the epistemological terms of "world creation" are mapped onto the social terms of community inclusion and exclusion. Unlike language, the *zadik* is able to operate in the created world as well as the Vacant Space. In social terms, the *zadik* straddles both sides of the divide, at once within the paradoxical created world, drawn by the gravitational pull of the limit, and at the same time outside of the world, engaging with heresies and heretics in all three realms. This is first and foremost R. Nachman's self-positioning.

His self-assigned role is the exploration of the possibility of an in-between space. In the next section, we come to R. Nachman's chosen precursor of such exploration, Elisha ben Abuya.

> And know, that by means of the melody of the zadik that is *bechina* of Moses, he raises the souls from this heresy of the Vacant Space into which they have fallen. For know, that each and every discipline of study in the world has a particular tune and melody, which is particular to that discipline of study. And from that melody is derived that discipline of study. And this is *bechina* of (Psalms 47[:8]): "sing ye praises with understanding";[70] that every understanding has a particular song and tune. And even the discipline of heresy, it has a tune and melody particular to the heretical discipline of study. This is what our sages of blessed memory said (Tractate Hagiga 15:): "What was it about 'Other' [Elisha ben Abuya]? Greek song never quit his mouth, and when he would rise from his study, several heretical books would fall before him." For one depends upon the other, for by means of the song that never quit his mouth, by that [song] the heretical books would fall from him. For that song was particular to that heresy and the blasphemy within it.[71]

R. Nachman incorporates Elisha ben Abuya's famous heresy into his own topography of heresies. The Greek song is not an outcome of heresy, but its source. Elisha ben Abuya has access not only to the words of Greek heresy contained in books, but also to its source in the Vacant Space, where there are no words, only melodies.[72] In this move from the cosmological nature of melodies to their place in Elisha ben Abuya's mouth during study, R. Nachman here continues to indicate the overlapping nature of the cosmological with the social topography of the Jewish community. That is, Elisha ben Abuya's liminal place within the social topography turns out to be a cosmological position within the Vacant Space as well. And this identification of the overlap between cosmological and social reveals the true extent of Elisha ben Abuya's heresy and shows it to be akin to that of R. Nachman's contemporary Maskilim.

Transgression of the limit of the Vacant Space is also the position R. Nachman ascribes to himself. His relations with the Maskilim are not evidence of a heretical inclination but of a desire to contest heresy. His exploration of heretical ideas is presented in terms of maneuvering in the new social space, in between the limits of Jewish tradition and its beyond. This effort contains redemptive power. He continues: "And faith too has a melody and tune particular to that faith, and as we see that even beliefs of non-Jews in their erroneous aspects, every faith of non-Jews has a particular melody, which they sing and with which they pray in their houses of worship."[73]

The idea R. Nachman develops next is that there is also a melody of ultimate faith, with which it is possible to cross over the contradictions and heresy of the Vacant Space and end up in the infinite light of divinity that lies beyond. "For this is the melody that pertains to faith in the infinite light itself,"[74] he explains. This melody of ultimate faith, and hence the possibility of crossing the Vacant Space entirely and passing into infinite divinity—which would, in social terms, mean crossing into the broader non-Jewish culture without losing one's Jewish faith—will only be revealed in the days of the Messiah.

> And *bechina* of this melody of ultimate faith, no one can merit except the zadik of the generation who is *bechina* of Moses, who is at that level of faith, who is *bechina* of silence.
>
> And therefore by means of the melody of the zadik, who is *bechina* of Moses, by this are raised up and exit all the souls that have fallen into this heresy of the Vacant Space [. . .] for by this melody and faith is all heresy annulled, and all melodies are included and [thus] annulled within this melody, that is above everything.[75]

Once in a generation, there is the phenomenon of a *zadik* able to venture into the Vacant Space unhindered and unharmed. This "zadik of the generation" is able to raise up those who have fallen into heresy, into the Vacant Space, into the social in-between that they are now lodged in.[76] The messianic moment in this teaching lies in the fact that this unique *zadik* does not raise the souls out of the

Vacant Space back into the fold of tradition, but rather raises them into the infinite beyond, on the other side of the Vacant Space. The initial possibility of successfully crossing over into the Vacant Space is reserved for a select few *zadikim*, but R. Nachman's messianic horizon raises the image of all Jews departing from "the created world." Rather than getting stuck in the Vacant Space, however, they manage to cross over to the infinite divinity. What it would mean in social terms for Jews to cross into "the great beyond" of European society is not discussed in the teaching. Imagining all Jews crossing the limit is a messianic image for R. Nachman, and he ends Teaching I:64 with it.

In conclusion, let us return to definitions of the Jewish intellectual—"a tangible historical and social configuration in Western society,"[77] Mendes-Flohr claims, notwithstanding its elusiveness and methodological problematic. If we accept this definition of "the intellectual," then R. Nachman was certainly not a Jewish intellectual. Nor did he see himself as one. However, R. Nachman was invested in developing a language—at once theological and social—with which to make sense of the position his contemporary Maskilim were occupying. R. Nachman articulates the position of his contemporary Maskilim *as* that of "intellectuals" in a sense already operative in his day (and in line with our more contemporary representations of "the intellectual"). In doing so, R. Nachman opens a window onto a moment from which this "configuration" can be seen as taking shape but is, however, not yet as "tangible" as when Mendes-Flohr sees it. R. Nachman also anticipates a question that is largely absent from definitions of "the intellectual" yet which is of utmost concern to his own reality as a religious leader: What lies beyond this in-between space, and is it really possible to get there? The Maskilim, he suggests, will not arrive on the distant shore. For the infinite beyond is not accessible through reason or language. It requires a leap of faith.

We might append, however, that this inaccessibility through language also implies a problem of representation. An immersion of Jews into their non-Jewish surrounding—without losing their particularity or faith as Jews, yet rendering invisible their confessional difference from the broader society—is a messianic horizon particularly in tune with the anxieties of R. Nachman's contemporary world. The difficulties of representing such a horizon have been outlined extensively in our reading of Teaching II:28. And yet, while recognizing the impossibly messianic horizon of new and emergent social structures, R. Nachman nonetheless attempts to withdraw from the Vacant Space of extant social discourse, like a scholar—discursively, epistemologically, and socially—and to create this moment as a crisis of representation.

The unrepresentable must be marked as such in order for the difference it subsumes to persist. This would require reimagining the nature of the relationship between political and aesthetic representation in explicitly literary terms (a reimagining that, as we have seen in the 1804 statute, was already taking place in social terms). To put it in literary terms, the invisibility itself must be aestheticized, dissociated from the political realm where it is subsumed by the public sphere and inserted into the aesthetic realm of literary representation. To put this invisibility into literary terms is R. Nachman's challenge in the context of constituting a Jewish literary modernity. To bring about this dissociation is what we will see him attempt when we turn our focus more explicitly to his literary efforts.

Part III

Literary Questions

Chapter 6

Was R. Nachman the Messiah?

Turning our attention now to more overtly literary concerns in R. Nachman's tales, we encounter two questions that stand out as those most commonly posed in the study of his writings. The first question is: Did R. Nachman think he was the Messiah? (A question which may, depending on the audience, amount to asking, "*was* R. Nachman the Messiah?") The answer (regardless of the audience) has been a resounding "yes." I have thus far ignored this question entirely, for reasons that will become clear in the present chapter. The second question, which I have touched on briefly, is: Should we include R. Nachman's writing in the category of Modern Hebrew or Yiddish Literature? While this may seem an odd question to ask about the (perhaps, self-perceived) Messiah, this too has mostly been answered in the affirmative.[1]

These questions are at best irrelevant, and at worst distracting for a literary reading of R. Nachman's work. The first question is tangential to any attempt to focus on the intricacies of his social thought and imaginative writing, and even more so once we consider R. Nachman's own understanding of what the messianic moment would look like in social terms.[2] As for the second question, the initial "yes" never cashes out into a clear affirmation of R. Nachman's writing as modern literature. Eager statements of inclusion such as Arnold Band's are not hard to find: "While these collections of hasidic tales have not generally been included in histories of *Modern Hebrew Literature*, the arguments Dov Sadan and others have proposed for their inclusion are quite convincing."[3] The obvious problems with fitting R. Nachman into the categories of "Hebrew" and "literature" are that he published teachings as well as tales, and that it is unclear whether they were in fact delivered in Hebrew or Yiddish. Eventually, statements such as Band's are qualified, and R. Nachman becomes a "forerunner" of modern Hebrew or Yiddish literature, or simply contemporaneous with it.[4] "If we use the term [modern] generically, referring to a period of time—the last two centuries, for instance—[then the tales of R. Nachman] are of the 'modern' period. If 'modernity,' however, is measured by the secular, inquisitive, and historic spirit,"[5] continues Band, then the tales of R. Nachman are not modern. I hope it is clear by now, however, that R. Nachman had an immensely inquisitive and historical spirit, and that the socio-political turmoil that foreshadowed (what Band terms) "modernity" was of great interest and concern to him. Why then has the scholarship on R. Nachman been unable to produce a clear articulation of his relation to "modern literature?" For the most part, because it has been asking tangential or distracting questions.

The duality of R. Nachman's perceived relation to the category of "modernity"—yes and no, a contemporary and a forerunner—is instructive. It certainly illustrates the difficulty that exists in placing his thought and writing within readily available categories, be they modern or messianic. But this duality also signals what is broadly overlooked in the reception of R. Nachman, namely our own contemporary attachment to a dichotomy, the structure of which was only just taking shape in R. Nachman's lifetime. That R. Nachman might have had some other notion of modernity, some idiosyncratic appreciation of the risks and opportunities that lay in the social upheavals of his time—as the previous chapters have demonstrated that he did—has not been a thought present in his literary or academic reception. The very question "did R. Nachman think he was the Messiah?" already presumes the stability of a dichotomy between traditional and modern, messianic and literary—a stability entirely uncharacteristic of R. Nachman's literary and intellectual context. This dichotomy is precisely what we should be questioning as a tenable port of arrival, not presuming as our point of departure. In that sense, beginning one's reading of R. Nachman's tales with the question of his messianic role or beginning one's reading with the question of his place in modern literature are in fact the very same dichotomous, anachronistic point of departure.

This point of departure is shared regardless of disciplinary boundaries and generic foci in the study of his tales. Several scholars of Hasidism have read them as moral parables,[6] popular theosophy,[7] or psycho-biographical documents.[8] These scholars have tended to privilege the tales' informative aspects while for the most part ignoring their literary qualities. Others have recognized the literary qualities of the tales, reading them in conjunction with myths and folktales,[9] interpreting them through literary-structural analysis,[10] and discussing their narrative elements within the broader context of a tradition of Jewish narratives.[11] Yet for all the variety of approaches and concerns, there is one question nearly all these literary scholars ask: Did R. Nachman think he was the Messiah?

In this chapter, I will analyze the literary assumptions that underlie such messianic readings by designating two frameworks of interpretation—the allegorical and the symbolic. I will outline—in theory and practice—these frameworks, within which many literary readers seem to operate. My contention will be that, while recognizing the literary qualities of the tales, in their over-commitment to allegorical and symbolic frameworks of interpretation these readers have nonetheless fallen short of an interpretative approach that fully appreciates the rich complexity of these tales' aesthetic. In particular, the conjunction of allegorical and symbolic frameworks creates an un-explicated link between the Kabbalistic narrative of redemption and R. Nachman's own biography and experience. As a result, the conjunction of these frameworks compulsively leads to the question of R. Nachman's messianic destiny.

Following the discussion of interpretive frameworks, our entry point into a literary discussion of the tales will be through a consideration of the most common question dealt with in such literary readings—the question of the missing ending.[12] Naturally, there are many other literary devices to be discussed in these tales, and I will touch on some of them. Yet, more than any other, the missing ending has been most widely recognized—even in nonliterary readings and even though its particular literary quality and significance have not been sufficiently explored. In the present chapter, I will examine the manner in which the allegorical and symbolic frameworks produce their interpretations and how this relates to their understanding of (and even production of) missing endings in R. Nachman's tales. The next chapter will begin with a reading of the first tale of the collection, "The Tale of the Lost Princess," which has famously been read as missing its ending. My own reading of this tale will complicate the conventional relation between messianism and redemption. I argue that R. Nachman's thought on redemption should be placed within the broader European horizon he is a part of. Offering a reading of R. Nachman's tales that is attentive to their aesthetic qualities and conventions does precisely that. It implicates the tales in a broader sociopolitical setting than allegorical and symbolic trends of interpretation currently allow.

Allegory and Symbol as Interpretative Frameworks

The concepts of allegory and symbol (and their interpretive applicability) have a long history of oscillating between complementarity and competition, at least since Greek aesthetic theory.[13] Modern landmarks in this intellectual history of literary theory are Italian Renaissance thought and German romanticism. In recent literary theory, Walter Benjamin and Paul de Man stand out as theorists of these terms.[14] In particular, Gershom Scholem's intellectual engagement with his friend Walter Benjamin has colored the interpretive framework of subsequent readers of R. Nachman's tales as well (I will touch on this later in the present chapter).[15] It is not surprising, therefore, that a literary reception of the tales should fall between these troubled yet productive antipodes.

The first conceptual framework through which the tales have been read is the allegorical. This interpretative approach tends to locate the meaning and significance of the tales in the removed realm of the allegorical referent. Whether the tales express a messianic vision or a moral lesson, they do not state it explicitly. The meaning of the tales is thus removed from their content, and the reader must access this meaning by way of revealing the allegorical correspondence of a tale's narrative to the transcendent realm of its significance. This realm has been largely recognized as that of Kabbalistic redemption narratives.[16]

It is worth noting that the allegorical reading not only binds the tale's content to a removed correspondent as a means of identifying its (allegorical) significance, but that this binding is exclusive. Allegorical correspondence is based on a one-to-one reference of the tale's "materials" to the tale's "significance," to use Yoav Elstein's terms.[17] The king in the tale cannot stand for God as well as for a human ruler. The king's assistant cannot represent the Messiah as well as R. Nachman himself, unless of course we accept that in the transcendent realm they are one and the same.[18]

Paul de Man posits allegory as a text's insistent reference, both to its own possible multiplicity of meanings and to the impossibility of linking it exclusively (through the act of reading) to any single, closed meaning.[19] What I refer to here as the allegorical framework in the reading of R. Nachman's tales is nearly the opposite of this sense because it serves to narrow the multiple possible referents of the narrative, producing a closed, exclusive reading. What it does have in common with de Man's understanding of allegory is its insistence on a realm of significance outside the text itself, to which it constantly refers. Further similarity lies in the shared observation that our inability to encounter a stable meaning in the text turns every reading into a "misreading" since it constantly refers to an external realm beyond what is being read. This realm, for de Man, is that in which the impossibility of closing the meaning of the text exists in the form of its own deconstruction. For R. Nachman's allegorical readers, this realm is that of a closed Kabbalistic narrative.

Allegorical reading, as an interpretative framework employed by readers of R. Nachman, relies on what Walter Benjamin calls "the antinomies of allegory" whereby "any person, any thing, any relationship, can mean absolutely anything else."[20] However, in Benjamin's notion, allegory "is both of these—convention and expression—and they are inherently in conflict with each other."[21] Allegorical readings of R. Nachman have tended to underplay this "dialectic of convention and expression"[22] by reading the tales (merely) as an expression of convention. This expression is asserted by the recognition of the exclusive reference of any and every person, thing, and relationship, to its correlative in the Kabbalistic realm. This all-encompassing recognition constitutes the narrative of the tale as an allegorical expression of a conventional Kabbalistic redemption narrative.

As opposed to the outward-oriented gaze of the allegorical reader, the symbolic reader locates the meaning of the tale within the overabundance of its narrative. For example, following this framework, Joseph Weiss has proposed that R. Nachman is always the hero of his tales, and the tales express his complex personal-religious experience as a mystic.[23] Arthur Green deepens this reading within the symbolic framework, asserting that R. Nachman is not only the hero of his tales, but every character in them.[24] The meaning of the tales is thus located within the narrative unity, expressed not by reference to a metaphysical order but by the very present dilemmas and conflicts of the characters. What presents itself to the reader is the immanent complexity of reality, an immanence that these tales are a part of and an expression of.

If in the allegorical framework the separation of narrative material from transcendent significance is what needs to be bridged by the reader, in the symbolic framework, there is no such separation. As Benjamin puts it, here "the unity of the material and the transcendental object, which constitutes the paradox of the theological symbol, is distorted into a relationship between appearance and essence."[25] That is, the appearance of the tales, "suffering terribly from over-complexity,"[26] is both the essence of their meaning and the unity through which it is expressed. This immediacy of complexity does away with the notion of reference-as-bridge and, in contrast to the allegorical reading, is able to support an internally coherent proliferation of significance. Thus, R. Nachman may share the experiences of both the prince *and* the pauper, the wise man *and* the simple man. No one of these characters maintains a singular referential tie to any part of the tales' meaning. The tales express the rich sum of human experiences that constitute both self and reality.

Benjamin proposes this notion of the symbol as part of his reading of the turn romanticism took from baroque. "The idea of the unlimited immanence of the moral world in the world of beauty is derived from the theosophical aesthetics of the romantics,"[27] he suggests. It comes as no surprise to find that R. Nachman's periodization within the German romantic tradition often accompanies discussion of the applicability of the symbolic framework to the tales. "Reb Nachman was a kind of Romantic philologist, like the Brothers Grimm," writes Roskies, adding only the qualification that his "restorative program was more cosmic and dialectical."[28] As we have already discussed in chapter 4, such romantic periodization is tenuous at best. At any rate, within the logic of such a periodization, and following Benjamin's argument, the symbolic and allegorical frameworks may indeed be understood as maintaining dialectical tension with one another.

The Messianic Synthesis

No necessary notion of exclusivity—which requires these two frameworks to be opposed to one another or discount each other in some way—is being proposed here.[29] Rather, I would like to emphasize the fact that the most prominent of R. Nachman's readers have tended to identify the challenge they are faced with as that of finding a balance between these two interpretative frameworks. The theoretical background to this focus on the dialectics of allegory and symbol, as well as the methodological tendencies of the various readers, has its origins in Gershom Scholem's pioneering work on the Kabbalah, particularly in his understanding of its modes of expression.[30] Scholem himself was influenced in this conceptualization, and the methodology it implied, by the work of his friend Walter Benjamin cited above.[31] While Scholem himself never gave much attention to R. Nachman (a single mention in his monumental *Major Trends in Jewish Mysticism*), his understanding of Jewish mysticism's modes of expression has left its mark on the study of R. Nachman's tales.[32] Indeed, it is not surprising to discover that among the readers most committed to these frameworks, to their perceived dialectical tension as to their attempted synthesis, are two of Scholem's most prominent students, Joseph Weiss and Joseph Dan.

Weiss proposes both R. Nachman's identification with all the heroes in his tales and their allegorical meaning. As a mystic, he explains, R. Nachman must express himself carefully, keeping any potentially heretical ideas away from the public. At the same time, he must find a way to fully express his rich internal experiences. Weiss thus sees allegorical expression in the tales as the epitome of R. Nachman's self-censorship, as part of the mystic's esoteric project.[33] The allegorical reading serves, in his opinion, to reveal the rich mystical experience reflected in the tales.[34]

Dan proposes a different balancing of these frameworks by suggesting that the tales contain multiple layers. The most basic layer of the tales' "materials" is made up of folk motifs. Above this is the "symbolic" layer, comprised of Kabbalistic symbols, which the "materials" refer to allegorically. Finally, there is the layer of meaning that emerges from the unique manner in which R. Nachman reorders both the folk "materials" and the Kabbalistic "symbols." To reach the meaning of the tales, however, Dan argues, it is not sufficient to identify the "materials" and their allegorical relation to the "symbols."[35] Only by recognizing the complex dynamic within which these allegorical referents (themselves Kabbalistic symbols) structure the tale's narrative does the reader come to recognize the expression of R. Nachman's unique personality.[36]

A more recent example of the effects of synthesizing these two frames can be found in Marc Caplan's reading of R. Nachman's seventh tale.[37] Caplan, the most theoretically informed reader of the tales to date, exemplifies the preoccupation with R. Nachman's messianic role, while simultaneously theorizing its limitations:

> Stated directly, the secret [. . .] is the evident heresy that Reb Nakhman is, or at least might be, the Messiah [. . .] Understanding the story as a mere corollary to Reb Nakhman's eschatological aspirations makes the task of interpretation hermetic: the wandering, melancholic king is Reb Nakhman; the messianic destiny ostensibly reserved for this character signifies the actual spiritual status of his creator.[38]

Caplan goes on to challenge the interpretive coherence of the allegorical framework, stating that "although conventional exegesis [has] typically read Reb Nakhman's stories as allegories, they function as such only in the particular, peculiar sense that Benjamin suggests."[39]

Here is my first intervention into the literary concerns with R. Nachman's tales. The tales may indeed refer allegorically to Kabbalistic narratives and symbolically to R. Nachman's life experience. But neither of these frameworks provides *in itself* a properly literary reading. For a start, they do not account for the aesthetic elements in the tales. In fact, and as we will discuss shortly, they tend to pull the reader away from such considerations. What is more, they severely limit the interpretive activity to various forms of identifying correlations, thereby removing from sight a range of other possible interpretations.

Each of the two frameworks has one primary operation. The allegorical framework works to correlate the tales with Kabbalistic narratives, primarily those of messianic redemption. The symbolic framework correlates the tales with R. Nachman's biography and life experience. Now, with the discovery that the tales correlate with *both* Kabbalistic narratives of messianic redemption *and* R. Nachman's own life and experience, readers find themselves compelled to raise the question of a correlation between messianic redemption and R. Nachman's biography. And it is precisely the attempt to create an interpretive link between these two frameworks within a single reading that compulsively leads to the question: Did R. Nachman think he was the Messiah?

Each of the interpretive frameworks I have outlined involves asking different kinds of questions about R. Nachman's tales. Thus, each reader notices and highlights different literary devices in the tales (at the expense of others). Let us move to discussing the relation between reading strategies and interpretative frameworks and work our way back to the literary devices they identify. The attempt to synthesize these two interpretative frameworks is also echoed in the form of reading strategies. And while each of the interpretive frameworks may privilege a certain literary element in the tale, thereby narrowing the range of interpretations, the "messianic synthesis" is what ends up drawing attention most sharply away from aesthetic questions.

Reading Practices of the Allegorical and Symbolic Frameworks

Allegorical reading locates the referent of the text outside of itself. The meaning of the text emerges only once an identification of the external content is made. This external content is the locus of the tale's meaning—not what it says but what it means. The practice of allegorical reading is thus the search for the corresponding extra-textual. It is an activity of revealing "the hidden," the inexpressible esoteric secret, as Weiss puts it.[40] Thus, it has the effect of sealing the meaning of the text within Kabbalistic convention. By its commitment to a single reading, it binds what is revealed in the text to what is concealed beyond it, thus constituting the monological expression of meaning revealed through one-to-one reference.

Such allegorical reading, focused as it is on the extratextual, tends toward an identification of what is *not* part of the narrative with the main meaning of the tale. Thus, literary devices of concealment are understood as omission and read precisely as loci of significance. The anticipation of an unarticulated meaning both preconditions this understanding and creates an increased sensitivity to concealment. What has been recognized as the missing ending of several of the tales, and the way these have been read, is the clearest example of such sensitivities. For the allegorical reader, the location of the ending outside of the text amounts to its location in the heart of the tale's meaning. In this way, many have asserted that knowing the ending of the tale would amount to understanding it. In the sense that whatever remains unarticulated in the end is precisely what the tale wishes to convey. The monological expression of meaning—a single possible reading dependent on the identification of a single possible referent—leads to a closed reading. That is, it leads to a reading that "unlocks" the secret of the text and identifies its "real" meaning by articulating the singular synthesis of (the presumed dichotomy between) text and meaning.

To articulate our critique more explicitly, we may follow de Man in questioning the epistemology of the metaphorical key that unlocks the concealed meaning of R. Nachman's tales: "One may well begin to wonder whether the lock indeed shapes the key or whether it is not the other way round, that a lock (and a secret room behind it) had to be invented in order to give a function to the key."[41] This is to ask whether R. Nachman's mode of expression is, in fact, as Caplan sees it, "the natural habitat for allegory."[42] Or perhaps it was in the interest of a literary reception of sorts, along the lines of Scholem's conceptualization of Kabbalistic modes of expression, that R. Nachman's readers postulated a concealed meaning for his tales, one that would fit the key of an interpretative framework they already possessed. The meaning would have to be postulated in accordance with the key's double function.

Allegorical reading both enables R. Nachman's tales to be read as more than esoteric texts and, at the same time, maintains their strict referential link with Kabbalistic tradition.[43]

In dialectical opposition to the allegorical reading, the symbolic reading does not recognize a gap to be bridged by a monological relation of reference. Instead, it recognizes the simultaneity with which the tales express R. Nachman's biographical experiences. The significance of the tale as a complex unity (rather than its individual "materials" or "symbols") is constituted by the dialogical relation of reflection it maintains between its narrative and that of R. Nachman's life. Thus, the meaning of R. Nachman's life is expressed by the tale, and the meaning of the tale is expressed by R. Nachman's life.

The symbolic reading presumes this reflection, a *mise-en-abyme* of R. Nachman's tales and biography. In this dialogical relation, the correspondence of one with the other reveals the unity of both. This symbolic correspondence is distinct from the allegorical reference in several important ways. First, it presumes that meaning emerges from a consideration of the entirety of the tale, not its individual elements or "materials."[44] Second, it is two-directional (dialogical rather than monological) in the sense that R. Nachman is a representation of his characters as much as the characters are a representation of R. Nachman. Third, presuming the correspondence of biographical experience and textual narrative, the symbolic reading is not concerned with anything literary outside of the text.[45] There is no presumption of an external, transcendent realm of reference wherein lies the meaning of the tales. The meaning is immanent in the narrative and encompasses the tales as well as the life and experience of R. Nachman.

This last difference is also my next point of criticism. The overdetermined symbolic unity largely ignores those areas where there is no overlap between R. Nachman's life and his tales. Experiences that did not exist in R. Nachman's life (such as the experience of being the redeeming Messiah) cannot be reflected in the tale. Similarly, any element of this symbolic correspondence concealed by the narrative is, by definition, not an element of correspondence, for it is unable to reflect either the significance of his life or (by dialogical extension) of the tale. Both loci of concealment are beyond the scope of the text to be considered. Such a reading, then, is concerned with that which is revealed in (or by) the text. As opposed to the allegorical reading's increased sensitivity to concealment within the text, the symbolic reading is overly sensitive to revelations (both narrative and narratorial) in the tales. Reading the tales as a whole, it presumes their explicit (revealed and overlapping) unity with R. Nachman's life and experience.

Beyond the text of the tales, there are several elements that a symbolic reading must account for within the scope of its interpretation. These are elements that reveal the correlation between the tales and R. Nachman's life. As Green suggests, such correlation may be revealed by R. Nachman in his own teachings and statements, whether generally concerned with storytelling or referring to a specific tale. Though "there is nothing directly autobiographical about any of Nahman's writings [. . .] the constant involvement with self [. . .] make[s] it clear that Nahman's own writings, teachings as well as tales, are absolutely vital as sources for [. . .] the inner life of their author."[46] Such correlation can also be found in the writings of his scribe and biographer R. Nathan Sternhartz, which offer interpretations of both R. Nachman's thought and his biographical accounts.[47]

Narratives that end with explicit statements that the end of the tale is missing may serve as good illustrations of the argument thus far. The way such tales have been read reveals the conjunction of the two reading practices, and the manner in which the double correlation this conjunction allows (Kabbalistic and biographical) leads to the question of R. Nachman's messianic role. Such endings further illustrate how this question leads away from a concern with the literary-aesthetic character of the tales. This will be our topic in the next chapter. Before turning to a reading of such tales, however, I'd like to take a short detour and discuss in more detail another prominent scholarly assumption already alluded to about R. Nachman's tales, which equally preempts properly literary readings—the assumption that these tales are in some sense "Kabbalistic stories."

Kabbalistic Stories

There is no doubt that widespread allusions to works of Kabbalah abound in R. Nachman's writings. The task of properly identifying them and relating their appearance to their "source" has occupied many researchers, who have studied both the tales and the teachings.[48] R. Nachman himself signals both his familiarity with and interest in engaging with such works. In his collected teachings, for instance, there are series of teachings grouped by their reference to parts of the *Zohar*. In his tales, too, many studies have highlighted these allusions.

Such identification, as detailed above, is the most prominent method for interpreting R. Nachman's tales. However, this widespread method has produced a rather narrow interpretive frame within which his tales are read. The persistence of this methodology has limited the interpretive approach to the tales and, in so doing, has constituted the tales *as* "Kabbalistic stories."[49] The method of identifying such allusions (and its resultant allegorical readings) is overdetermined in interpretations of R. Nachman's tales. As a result, the focus shifts from literary analysis to a correlation between the tales and a set of (primarily) Kabbalistic tropes. The circular logic—moving from an assumption about Kabbalistic stories to a methodology of identifying references, which in turn produces (or reinforces) the interpretive assumptions about the tales' allegorical reference—is exemplified in the opening pages of Marianne Schleicher's *Intertextuality in the Tales of Rabbi Nahman of Bratslav*.[50]

> *Sippurey Ma'asiyot* consists of thirteen tales that have many traits in common with fairy tales [. . .] Nevertheless, these tales refuse to reveal a coherent meaning by themselves, as fairy tales ought to do [. . .] The content of these tales only becomes accessible [. . .] through the interaction with external sign systems.[51]

The basic interpretive assumption here is that the tales cannot be understood without identifying their reference to "external sign systems." The methodological conclusion is that such identification—"intertextuality," as Schleicher refers to it—would "reveal a coherent meaning," or make "the content of these tales [. . .] accessible." This approach is an instance of what I have called the allegorical interpretive framework. What leads from the allegorical to the "Kabbalistic" is the identification of the "external sign systems" as "imagery from biblical and rabbinical literature, from various mystical trends, and *particularly* from the kabbalistic text corpus *Sefer haZohar*."[52]

For the student of literature, such an approach has many theoretical, practical, and methodological limitations. The best illustration of this can be found in the way readers of R. Nachman have addressed the question of endings in his tales. As mentioned, Dan has identified the Lurianic redemption myth as the overarching narrative to which R. Nachman's tales maintain an allegorical reference.[53] In terms of an overdetermined Kabbalistic reading, the end of R. Nachman's tales would thus refer to the "end of time," the "messianic redemption" that is the telos of the Lurianic myth.[54] With such interpretive presumptions, it is no surprise to find that most readers have concluded that the endings of many tales are "yet to come."

In fact, it was not until the early 1970s that the adjective "Kabbalistic" was appended so broadly to various aspects of the writings of R. Nachman.[55] Yet what precisely is intended by this adjective remains to this day only loosely defined.[56] Among the readers of R. Nachman, Green recognizes the intended function of the tales as preparation for the advent of the Messiah,[57] while Dan calls R. Nachman's collection of tales "one of the most intriguing Jewish literary and mystical texts [. . .] a fusion of literature and mysticism, using profound concepts drawn from Kabbalah and Hasidism."[58] Arnold Band, on the other hand, insists:

> [R. Nachman's] stories are based only on his own personal experience. Still, we do find major kabbalistic elements [. . .] serving as major *motifs* within the tales. But there is a basic difference between "using" kabbalistic ideas and "expressing" them in the tales: those elements which are present in the tales ceased to be building blocks of a mystical theology and became chapters in the mystical biography of Rabbi Nachman's soul.[59]

The question of whether the use of "Kabbalistic motifs" makes a text Kabbalistic is one I will address presently. But the point to note first is that the adjective "Kabbalistic" is never—in any of the research quoted above—defined or explained in any significant way. The majority of studies attributing this appellation to the stories of R. Nachman are conducted within the discipline of literary studies. For the most part, the term is taken to signal the prevalence of allusions to "the Kabbalah" in R. Nachman's tales. The definition of "the Kabbalah," in turn, is almost exclusively derived from Gershom Scholem.[60] The result is that many studies end up inadvertently—even unknowingly—taking sides in the ongoing debate about Kabbalah as an object of academic study. Indeed, in the context of the more specialized debate on Jewish mysticism, the adjective "Kabbalistic" seems quite out of place here.

At present, the debate regarding the study of the Kabbalah can be summed up in a disagreement (which I will here imaginatively construct) between Elliot Wolfson and Boaz Huss.[61] Wolfson subscribes "to the view that mystical experience, like experience more generally, is contextual."[62] Nevertheless, he proposes that there are "deep structures that may be illuminated through a comparative study of various mystical traditions."[63] Huss, on the other hand, insists that "the various cultural phenomena presently included in the field of study of Jewish mysticism [should be studied as] cultural productions that formed out of political needs in specific historical, economic and social frameworks."[64] For the student of Jewish mysticism, this difference—between Wolfson's Chomskian "deep structure" approach to mystical experience, on the one hand, and, on the other, Huss's resistance to both "deep structures" and the category of "experience" itself in the study of Kabbalah—is certainly a central issue. But, for the student of literature, this debate simply does not contribute to our attempt to make sense of the term "Kabbalistic stories."[65]

Viewed as a contextual expression of a deep structure of mystical experiences attained by the writer, the adjective "Kabbalistic" would be misleading with regard to R. Nachman's tales. This is so because no claim has been made (by R. Nachman, his disciples, or academic scholarship) that his tales express such experiences.[66] Viewed as texts that should be regarded and interpreted as "cultural productions that formed out of political needs in specific historical, economic and social frameworks,"[67] calling R. Nachman's tales "Kabbalistic stories" is already redundant.

Nevertheless, denying the proliferation of allusions to major texts of Kabbalah in the writings of R. Nachman is equally misleading. He refers repeatedly not only to terms and symbols, but even to specific books of Kabbalah.[68] These allusions will lead us to a central question: How are we to read these references without, on the one hand, introducing theological assumptions about the nature and reality of religious experience—assumptions we have already argued are tangential from a literary-aesthetic perspective—while, on the other hand, giving these references the attention they merit as persistent components of R. Nachman's stories?

I would like to suggest a different implication for the academic use of the adjective "Kabbalistic" in studying the tales of R. Nachman. Let us consider "Kabbalah" as a discursively constructed object that is defined through its relation to two other such objects; on the one hand "religion," and on the other hand "Jewish nationalism." Viewed from this perspective, the adjectivization of this object with regard to a collection of stories takes on a different significance. Huss historicizes Jewish mysticism as an object of academic study that emerged in the midnineteenth century in Germany and France.[69] Understood as the particularly Jewish expression of a universal mystical experience, it was framed within the broader academic interest in mysticism at this time.

Richard King criticizes the broader interest in a universal mystical experience as presuming a problematic interpretation of its object "mysticism." Mysticism was a category hitherto operative only in the context of Christian religion, and Christian religious *experience* in particular. The basic assumption of this new discipline, King explains, was that "mysticism" could be fruitfully extended, through comparison and contrast, to the phenomena of other "world religions."[70] Extending this comparison enabled the identification of a variety of non-Christian phenomena and texts as "religious" and, more importantly for us here, as "mystical." At the same time, a "scientific" assumption that religion and its phenomena are in some sense antithetical to reason and enlightenment pervades within the structure of this comparison.

A particular illustration of the broader dynamic that King highlights can be found in the case of "Jewish mysticism." Jewish mysticism became increasingly associated with "the Kabbalah" in the first half of the twentieth century through the works of Martin Buber and, later, Gershom Scholem.[71] The comparative approach was the methodological basis for Scholem's framing of "the Kabbalah" as an independent object of study. "Scholem recognized in the mystical foundation of Judaism the vital national force that enabled its existence in exile," explains Huss, "and which *dialectically* led to Jewish Enlightenment and Zionism."⁷² That is to say, the association between Jewish mysticism and the Kabbalah already presumes the antithetical relation between the Kabbalah and Enlightenment.

Viewed as part of a corpus of texts that are antithetical to, yet dialectically enabling of Jewish Enlightenment, the question of whether R. Nachman's stories are Kabbalistic takes on a meaning entirely tangential to the debate on Jewish mysticism. As a historiographical moment in the development of a Jewish literary modernity, the consolidation of the object the Kabbalah marks the discursive construction of a break that will be central to the understanding of modern Jewish literature as both "Jewish" and "modern," or "new."⁷³ In other words, this consolidation is part of a moment that simultaneously marked "old" Jewish literature as continuous and the end of that continuity.⁷⁴

The implication of Kabbalistic literature in questions of rupture and continuity is evident already in Buber's 1906 preface to his German translation of *The Tales of Rabbi Nachman*, which I cited in the introduction: "Rabbi Nachman of Bratzlav, who was born in 1772 and died in 1810, is perhaps the last Jewish mystic. He stands at the end of an unbroken tradition, whose beginning we do not know."⁷⁵ It is an "unbroken tradition" that is now broken, he is a rabbi who is "the last," who "stands at the end." What do these words mean with regard to the Kabbalistic aspect of R. Nachman's tales—for it is explicitly a book of *tales* that Buber introduces with these words? To call these tales Kabbalistic is to identify them as the mark of a rupture, on the other side of which "we" (Buber's readers) exist, as a discourse with which "we" maintain no continuity. Therefore, to call these tales Kabbalistic is to insist on their unreadability *as* modern literature. A critique of this assumption—and of the unnecessarily limited set of literary analytical questions applied to the study of R. Nachman's tales—will be the topic of the next chapter.

While from the perspective of the field of mysticism or religious studies, as we have seen, the term "Kabbalistic" is not broad enough to be instructive, from the perspective of the field of Literature this category is not narrow enough to be useful. In a more recent variation on the theme of "Kabbalistic stories," Don Seeman and Shaul Magid have raised the question of "the ways in which Jewish mystical texts function as literature."[76] In further unpacking their question, it becomes clear that, from the perspective of literary studies, "the mystical text's function as literature" and "the literary text's function as mysticism"—if methodologically theorizable—are practically indistinguishable.[77]

The parade of usages "Kabbalistic" receives suggests its meaning is too broad to be useful to the study of literature. For we can readily identify "mystical texts," "mystical writing," "mystical consciousness," "mystical expressions," "mystical themes," and "mystical poetics," the constellation of which ends up forming the category of "mystical literature," which is produced in turn by "mystical writers" and "mystical teachers."[78] Pierre Macherey has pointed to a moment around the turn of the eighteenth century when "literature" and "philosophy" were discursively separated.[79] The difficulty with the term "Kabbalistic stories"—at once too broad and too narrow—results from a similar discursive separation, in this case between "literature" and "mysticism," which took place around the same time. This is a separation that readers of R. Nachman in the early 1970s attempted to bridge through the category of "Kabbalistic stories." Though the attempt to think past disciplinary lines distinguishing mysticism from literature is a challenge we will here take on as well, the result of applying this particular uncritical category has proved of doubtful value for the study of R. Nachman.

To be clear, my argument is *not* that R. Nachman's stories are "literary" rather than Kabbalistic. This has as much to do with my reservations about the division of "literature" from Kabbalah as with the incoherence of the adjective "Kabbalistic." The substitution of the former for the latter would simply give us one untenable division in place of another. In this, I follow the reservations Edward Said has stated quite clearly in the opening pages of *Beginnings*, as regards

> the dissatisfaction felt at the notion that "literature" could be discussed as a completely separate genre of human activity. Related to this dissatisfaction is the positive attitude that [. . .] indeed most of the modes of writing

about men and women in history are, in fact, tangled up together, that they are often separated on professional, even epistemological grounds in order to accomplish social goals of one sort or another, and that criticism if it is to be criticism and not only the celebration of masterpieces, deals with the separations, the entanglements, the consequences of what Raymond Williams has recently entitled *Writing in Society*.[80]

Finally, beyond the difficulty of clearly denoting a genre or style of writing, the label of "Kabbalistic stories" has had profound methodological implications for the study of R. Nachman's tales. Calling them Kabbalistic locates them within a discursive field, the limits of which are presumed at the outset rather than investigated. A mere allusion by R. Nachman to something related to "the Kabbalah" suffices to activate this definition. And this definition is taken as an answer to questions regarding aesthetic decisions made by the writer. Thus, the first evidence Dan brings to support his claim that "the main materials, which serve as direct building blocks for the meaning of the tale, are taken from the world of the Kabbalah and its symbolism"[81] is that R. Nachman's disciples found such "materials" in their reading of the tales. What makes the disciples' identification all the stronger as proof of the Kabbalistic materials of the tales is that they rely on things R. Nachman himself told them about the tales.[82] The identification of these stories as Kabbalistic thus begins with their allusion to the Kabbalah. The privileging of the Kabbalistic as an interpretive lens then draws first and foremost on the auto-referential tendency of R. Nachman, who points out to his students his own allusions to works of Kabbalah. The mere fact that R. Nachman points to an allusive tendency in his own tales should not suffice to produce such allusions as "a lens" for reading the tales—and the decision to privilege this lens above aesthetic and literary questions is never fully explained by the scholars discussed above.

A properly literary engagement with the tales of R. Nachman must subsume any such Kabbalistic category under a broader consideration of aesthetic, stylistic, and narrative devices at the disposal of the storyteller. The aim of such a reading would be to ask about the aesthetic choices made by R. Nachman in the creation of his tales and the significance of such choices to the interpretation—perhaps even the interpretability—of the tales. The next chapter will focus on the questions of authorial intention and interpretive method. I will also demonstrate what I have been referring to (hopefully not too enigmatically) as a "proper literary reading" of the tales.

Chapter 7

Poetics of Intransitivity

> To begin to apprehend a text is to begin to find intention and method in it.[1]

A beginning, writes Edward Said, "not only creates but is its own method because it has intention. In short, beginning is *making* or *producing difference*."[2] So is making difference *invisible*. What would it mean to read R. Nachman from the beginning? And where might we locate the beginning in R. Nachman's writings? Said suggests that every text begins with the author's intention to write. Let us begin, then, with the statements of intention that preface R. Nachman's collection of tales. In the first edition, there are three separate statements. The first is the title page, by which the publisher introduces the book; the second is the introduction by the editor, R. Nathan Sternhartz, who explains the rationale for compiling the tales; the third is by R. Nachman regarding his tales, clearly demarcated from R. Nathan's introduction but interspersed with the latter's commentary. In the interplay of these multiple statements of intention, a method suggests itself for reading the tales.

The title page states that what is before us is a "book of tales that we have merited to hear from the mouth of our holy rabbi."[3] The paragraph that follows offers general thanks to God for providing each generation with rabbis to lead it and extols the wisdom of the rabbis who "clothe and conceal"[4] their teachings within tales. On the same title page, below a decorative graphic element, there comes in smaller font a disclaimer of sorts, which reads:

> Also, those who are wise will understand of their own accord that not like the gentiles that lived in the times of the sages of the Talmud are these gentiles in whose lands we live, for those [former] were idol worshippers [. . .] but the peoples of our times fear God and honor the Torah, do charity and justice in their lands and charity with the Jews who take refuge under their wings,[5] and far be it from us to speak or write anything so as to denigrate them, and every place in this book that it mentions a gentile, or non-Jew or nations of the world and the like the intention is to the pagans of the time of the Mishnah.[6]

Such statements were standard disclaimers at the time. The publisher would insert them to preempt and appease the government censors.[7] While the title page introduction lauds the wisdom of rabbis who "clothe and conceal" teachings within tales as a matter of theological-esoteric practice, the publisher's disclaimer on the same page marks the broader political forces underlying a text's "concealment." The main aim of the publisher's disclaimer is to excuse any unflattering representation of non-Jews in the tales that follow, and there is some tension between the formulaic language of this paragraph and the fact that the tales in this collection certainly represent non-Jews and "nations of the world" in light of very contemporary concerns, as we have already seen in our reading of "The Tale of a King Who Decreed Conversion." This theme is revisited in the third introduction, which relates a statement by R. Nachman himself:

> Before he told the first tale of this book, he said: "In the tales the world tells there are many hidden and very lofty things, but the tales have been ruined for much is missing from them, and also they have been confused and are not told in [the correct] order, for what belongs in the beginning is told at the end and vice versa, and such [confusions], but in truth there are in the tales the world tells hidden and very lofty things, and the *baal shem tov* of blessed memory was able through the telling of a tale to unite [mystical] unions, when he would

see that the heavenly channels had broken, and it was impossible to repair them through prayer, he would mend and unite them by telling a tale." And our rabbi [Nachman] spoke more about this, and then he began to tell the tale on the adjacent page.[8]

The first thing we read in this statement is an explicit reference to "the world," made in a manner that does not easily accord with the publisher's disclaimer. Subsequent lines make clear R. Nachman is not referring to tales told by "the pagans of the Mishna," but to those told by his contemporaries. And there is no distinction made between tales related by Jews and non-Jews. The mention of the *baal shem tov* is also an historical marker, indicating that the tales R. Nachman has in mind are from the years immediately after his death, when the *baal shem tov*'s ability to "tell it right" died with him.

The broad reference to "tales the world tells" underlines the political tension referenced by the disclaimer and inserts contemporary questions into the introduction of the tales. R. Nachman's opening sentence then proceeds to reintroduce the theological-esoteric question also present in the title page. In these tales, he says, "there are many hidden and very lofty things." The mention of the *baal shem tov* relates to the theological-esoteric question as well since part of what is "hidden" in these tales is their mystical power, which the *baal shem tov* knew how to bring out.

"But," continues R. Nachman, "the tales have been ruined for much is missing from them, and also they have been confused and are not told in [the correct] order, for what belongs in the beginning is told at the end and vice versa, and such." Reading the beginnings of a Jewish literary modernity in R. Nachman's tales starts by reading this "confusion" as signaling a tension he will produce and stylize in his tales, a confusion between beginning and ending. This is particularly relevant to the widespread notion in research on R. Nachman's tales, which identifies several of them as missing their ending.[9]

My suggestion in this chapter is that we read this "confusion" as relating both to the episodic order of the narrative and to the poetic presentation of the episodes. In these lines, then, R. Nachman introduces his concern with literary form into the political and theological questions already signaled. The beginning, the production of difference in R. Nachman's tales, stems from the irreducibility of his concerns to individual questions of politics, theology, or aesthetics. To "mend and unite" by retelling "the tales the world tells" is an activity that is simultaneously and irreducibly political, theological, and aesthetic. We should keep this constellation of concerns in mind throughout our reading of the tales, as we have in our readings of his teachings.

An interesting discord emerges from the introduction to the tales. On the one hand is R. Nachman's statement that he is reordering into their *proper* order tales that have gotten disordered. On the other hand is the widespread opinion in research on the tales that several of them are *missing* an ending. The implication that a missing ending forms part of the proper order of the narrative episodes is what I discuss in this chapter.

Missing the Ending

As mentioned in the previous chapter, many readers of R. Nachman have paid particular attention to what has come to be known as the "missing ending" of some of the tales. The seventh tale ("The Tale of a Fly and Spider"), for example, ends with a note informing us that the ending was not written down properly. In the case of the thirteenth tale ("The Tale of the Seven Beggars"), it seems R. Nachman did not get a chance to tell the end, and the tale was published incomplete.[10] But it is the first tale of the collection, "The Tale of the Lost Princess," that is most commonly—and most significantly—read as missing its ending.[11] Let us review the course of its narrative and then proceed to some existing interpretations of the tale.

In the exposition, a king curses his beloved and only daughter, who then mysteriously disappears. The king's assistant goes searching for her. The bulk of the tale follows the king's assistant on his quest to search for and rescue the king's daughter. The assistant locates the daughter twice. Each time, he receives instructions from her as to the method of her rescue. Both times, however, he fails to perform her instructions, and she remains in captivity. In each case, his trials and failures are described in detail, and both times, the moment of recognition and the sorrow and regret it engenders are recounted in full. After twice failing to perform what is required of him, and thus missing the opportunity of saving the king's daughter, he finally tracks her down a third time. This third time, following an arduous quest leading to the discovery of her location, the king's assistant arrives in the city-fort in which she is being held and begins to plan her rescue. The narrator explains that the king's assistant will need to plan wisely this third and most trying rescue of all. At this point the tale ends abruptly.

In his reading of R. Nachman's tales, Joseph Dan wonders why this story is missing its ending.[12] On the way to providing an answer, he distinguishes between three layers of the tales: (1) their "materials," borrowed from folktales and the broader folk culture of Eastern Europe, Jewish and non-Jewish alike;[13] (2) their "content," that is, the layer the "materials" allegorically refer to, which is comprised of the rich world of Kabbalistic symbolism. Beyond these two layers, argues Dan, there is the unique experience R. Nachman is expressing through the artistic medium of storytelling. Thus, the manner in which the plot and structure of the tales weave folk themes and Kabbalistic symbols together expresses (3) the "principal" of the story.[14] In order to solve the question of the missing ending, Dan insists, we must note the interplay between these three layers in the structuring of the tale: "In the story before us, the meaning lies in the answer to two questions, which I will try to show are really only one question: Who is the king's assistant? Why is the ending missing? We will begin with the first question, and I believe it will lead us to an answer to the second question as well."[15]

Discovering the identity of the king's assistant will answer the question of the missing ending and uncover the concealed meaning of the tale. The question Dan does not address here is how identifying the king's assistant will explain the lack of an ending. We may suggest it is precisely the allegorical nature of Dan's reading that collapses these two questions into one. He considers the possible allegorical referents of the character of the king's assistant. Dan's conclusion is that on the level of "content," he is the Messiah, while on the level of "principle," he is R. Nachman himself.[16] Along this line of Kabbalistic references, Dan also identifies the king's daughter as an allegory for the *shechina*.[17]

To further emphasize the significance of the missing ending, Dan draws attention to the fact that the final episode of R. Nachman's thirteenth tale, "The Tale of the Seven Beggars," is similar to the first tale of the collection and is similarly missing its ending.[18] The missing ending, suggests Dan, is the very same ending in both cases. He offers the interpretation that the thirteenth tale, like the first, is an account of the fall of the *shechina* and the spiritual exile of the Jewish people, and, since redemption has yet to occur, R. Nachman cannot finish the narrative.[19] Yoav Elstein affirms Dan's reading, noting that the first tale was told twice, on two separate occasions.[20] Three times, then, R. Nachman tells of the search for the king's daughter, that is, of the quest for the messianic redemption of the *shechina*, and three times he is unable to conclude the narrative, for the search is still at hand.[21] Dan's argument, then, is that because "the time of the final [. . .] implementation of the redemption on earth has not arrived yet, so the first story, as well as the last, *could not* be concluded."[22]

As further proof, Dan points out the allegorical connection of the first and second failures of the king's assistant to the Kabbalistic-symbolic characters of Adam and Noah.[23] Both biblical characters tried, and failed, to bring about the moment of redemption. Their trials are alluded to by the trials in which the king's assistant himself fails.[24] Having recognized the allegorical reading the tale supports, there is almost no need to read the account of the third and final trial. Kabbalistic convention creates the anticipation that there can be no such account because the messianic redemption has yet to come. And having recognized the allusion, Dan's reading comes to an end. As we have seen, recognizing a similar allegorical connection of R. Nachman to the Messiah is, in turn, the starting point for Caplan's reading of the seventh tale. However, while Caplan takes this connection as the starting point for his reading, he nonetheless sees this frame as posing a literary impossibility for R. Nachman: "the question therefor remains as to what Reb Nakhman would reveal in this story, and why he is *unable to do so* completely."[25]

The major implication of insisting on a Kabbalistic reading of the tales is that it limits our appreciation of their mimetic quality. It allows only a reading of the tales as a re-telling of what (presumably) was for R. Nachman a familiar "Kabbalistically" determined narrative about the reality he lived in. Thus, the narrow Kabbalistic reading enters into precisely the kind of theological assumptions Boaz Huss cautions us to avoid in the study of Jewish mysticism—an attentiveness that should certainly be extended to the study of literature as well—namely, that there *is* a (exclusive) mimetic link between the Lurianic narrative of redemption and the reality of R. Nachman's time (or any time, for that matter). "Just as a theological explanation for physical and biological phenomena that is based on [a concept of] God's will [. . .] is not admissible in academic studies of the natural sciences," argues Huss, so the same should apply "with theological explanations, according to which the cause of certain historical, social and cultural phenomena is an encounter with divinity."[26] The claim that R. Nachman *could not* finish the story because God had not yet sent the Messiah is such a claim.

Beyond the problematic literary implications of such a claim, in the case of R. Nachman's tales, this interpretative assumption is simply unjustifiable on several counts. First, R. Nachman was entirely capable of creating literary representations of the redemption, even though it had not yet occurred. As Zvi Mark observes, this is the focus of his "Scroll of Secrets,"[27] a creative and explicit narrative account of the messianic redemption. Second, regarding the thirteenth tale, R. Nathan tells of several occasions in which R. Nachman expressed his desire to tell the end of the thirteenth tale, and indeed he seems to have had the end already in mind.[28] Whether he chose not to tell it or died before he had the opportunity is not significant here. The point is that the interpretive limits of an allegorical-Kabbalistic reading are not tenable and result only in methodological constraints—the main constraint being that, upon identifying the allegory, the reader of the tales effectively stops reading.

The properly literary question that the readings surveyed above do not address is this: What does the lack of an ending produce in a story? The above reading has drawn our attention away from questions regarding the art form of storytelling and literature. Questions of this nature have already been roughly formulated by Dan ("Why is the tale missing its ending?"[29]) yet, from a literary perspective, left largely unanswered. A discussion of the endings of R. Nachman's tales must begin with a close reading of the endings themselves and the observation that he could not have chosen a more climactic moment in which to end the narrative of his first tale.

The last rescue attempt is not described, nor is it, in fact, recounted at all by R. Nachman. Only the conclusion is given: "And how he rescued her he did not tell, and, in the end, he rescued her."[30] We may notice immediately that it is not the end of the narrative that is missing. The tale and the narrative both end at the same moment—the moment in which the king's assistant rescues the princess. In the Yiddish, the first half of this concluding sentence is in parentheses, further emphasizing the narrative flow: the assistant locates the king's daughter, he finds a place to plan her rescue, and he finally rescues her. The ending is certainly provided. What is missing is the account of *how* this rescue is performed. The tale, recounting in detail the first two failures and relaying the long arduous journey of locating the king's daughter a third time, has created the anticipation of a detailed account of the hero's final success. This anticipation is entirely in line with the folkloric conventions R. Nachman is operating within.[31] Recognizing the literary effect achieved by breaking with these conventions, it becomes clear that the ending of this tale is not missing but rather provocatively anticlimactic.

Every literary expression exists within a context of literary and social conventions and derives some power of expression from its relation to these conventions. This point is neither new nor original. Regarding R. Nachman's tales, Roskies has suggested that the tales' "meaning was coded into the story's deviation from the norm."[32] This suggests that our reading of the tales must account for their adherence to the conventions that (to borrow Dan's terms) the use of "material" and "content" relates to.[33] Shmeruk makes a similar point in his own reading of R. Nachman's first tale: "The ending is unexpected; the desire for a conventional ending [relating the hero's success as part of what transpired] in the past is here replaced with a mystery."[34] I have also noted the break from folkloric convention and suggested that in poetic terms this "mystery" creates an anticlimax at the end of the narrative. What may have led readers to confuse this missing climax for a missing ending pertains, in turn, to a break from Kabbalistic conventions. With this conventional Kabbalistic priming, one may read the missing climax and confuse it for a missing ending since we are dealing with a convention that conflates *climax* with *ending* in the messianic moment of redemption.

We should certainly keep in mind the messianic overtones of the narrative. Dan and others are insightfully aware of the fact that this ending offers a commentary on redemption.[35] Yet it does not do so by reproducing the conventional Lurianic narrative. Rather, the tale breaks open the conventional narrative—separating climax and ending. Redemption here is not the *telos* of the tale but one of its literary tropes.[36] As Ora Wiskind-Elper observes, "questions of messianism and redemption are raised, less for their personal, biographical relevance than for their significance as narrative elements that invest the tales with great urgency."[37] As a trope, redemption signals the fact that R. Nachman's pressing concerns with contemporary issues find expression in the tales.

Anticlimactic endings exist in most tales of the collection, some of which have not been read as missing their ending. In fact, this seems to be the characteristic element, to some degree or another, of nearly all the endings in the collection. R. Nachman's characters are able, after years of searching, traveling, failing, and struggling, to complete their quests in a matter of a few short, fragmented sentences. We have seen this narrative element in "The Tale of a King Who Decreed Conversion" as well, where the four generations of a royal dynasty end in the span of one short fragmentary sentence: "[T]he king and his seed went, and the fire came over them, and he was burned with his seed, and they were all felled."[38] As with folkloric conventions, Kabbalah is not a binding allegorical referent that will finally "reveal a coherent meaning" in the tales.[39] Rather, it offers R. Nachman a narrative convention within which to tell his tales. Paying attention to the tales' interaction with these narrative conventions—compliance, breaks, revisions—is an important part of reading and interpreting the tales, of understanding their "proper order."

A Permanent Beginning

In conjunction with the allegorical methodology, there have been several other interpretive assumptions involved in the identification of "missing endings" in the tales. Audri Durchslag, for example, in reviewing several of the major books of the 1970s that introduced the Kabbalistic elements of R. Nachman's tales (including two English translations), states that "beginnings and ends for Nahman have to do with ontological and theological positions, not syntactic or poetic ones."[40] The irony of this statement is that it presumes such "positions" are discernable in translations of the tales (rather than R. Nachman's teachings). For the narrative art of storytelling, beginnings and ends are first and foremost a question of syntax and poetics.

At this point, I would like to proceed to a theoretical discussion of the poetics of the anticlimactic ending and insist on reintroducing those very same questions we have seen Dan pose but leave partly unanswered and Durchslag theorize as irrelevant. R. Nachman explicitly referred to beginnings and ends in the "tales the world tells"—including, by his declared intention, in his own tales—when he described them thus: "[T]hey have been confused and are not told in [the correct] order, for what belongs in the beginning is told at the end and vice versa."[41] Thus far, in pointing to the discrepancy between this statement and the assumption that some of the tales are missing their ending, I have presumed this confusion to be a matter of narrative content, of disordered episodes. But this is what I have demonstrated to be false—the claim that the *episode* we might think of as "the ending" is not in its place, at the end of the narrative. I have argued that the reason for this misidentification (or lack of identification) is the missing *poetics* we associate with such endings, namely, the climax.

While our ability to recognize an episode *as* an ending is certainly determined by the logical connections it maintains with the previous narrative flow, it is also determined by its form, by its syntax, and by its poetics. The narrative conventions R. Nachman breaks with are primarily poetic. His anticlimactic endings have caused us to rethink the relation between redemption and climax by separating the episodic redemption from the poetic climax. But they have done more. They have done away with the climax altogether—they have left the reader with an anticipation of an ending, an anticipation that will never be alleviated.

Along the lines of the allegorical interpretation of the tales, readers such as Dan and Green have identified this anticipation as an expectation of the Messiah. However, this identification ignores the fact that episodically there is no further redemption to anticipate. More importantly, however, it ignores the fact that this unalleviated anticipation is *poetically* constructed. How are we to understand this anticipation as *poetics*? Two theoretical discussions will help us here: Friedrich Schlegel's discussion of irony, and Edward Said's discussion of beginnings.

"Irony" is a term that derives from ancient Greek poetics (εἰρωνεία) and has had a longstanding presence in Western poetic traditions. But it is Schlegel who radically theorized the term, and whose thought is the touchpoint for much of the subsequent discussion of irony.[42] Born in Hanover just a few weeks before R. Nachman, Schlegel was a major thinker of German romanticism in the Prussian Empire in the same years that R. Nachman was making his mark on Hasidism in the Russian Empire. He theorized irony as that which reveals the gap between language and the world, the human spirit and human historical existence. For the present argument, I will focus on the poetic-textual aspects of this gap. In his essay "On Incomprehensibility,"[43] Schlegel enumerates the kinds of poetic irony one finds in written works of literature, concluding: "Finally, there is the irony of irony."[44] This irony of irony is the moment the awareness of the gap between language and the world, the inability of expression to capture experience, folds in upon itself—the moment the awareness of the gap loses its grip on the gap of which it is aware, and the gap again slips past the ability to express it into the very gap that expression cannot traverse. What does this look like in poetic-textual terms?

Paul de Man explains that, for Schlegel, irony is the trope that disrupts convention par excellence. It designates both a kind and an intensity of narrative break, which Schlegel terms "parabasis." Parabasis is a poetic term that denotes a pause in the narrative.

> What Schlegel refers to is the disruption of narrative illusion, the *aparté*, the aside to the audience, by means of which the illusion of the fiction is broken [. . .] The technical term for this in rhetoric, the term that Schlegel uses, is parabasis. Parabasis is the interruption of a discourse by a shift in the rhetorical register.[45]

Schlegel had already covered (and in greater detail) this taxonomy of disruptions in "On Incomprehensibility." The irony of irony—the moment expression can no longer express itself as such—is more than an aside. It is a *permanent* disruption: "Parabasis is not enough, for Schlegel. Irony is not just an interruption; it is (and this is the definition which he gave of irony), he says, the "permanent parabasis," parabasis not just at one point but at all points."[46]

R. Nachman's ending is certainly a disruption—of conventions and of narrative flow. We have already discussed this. In R. Nachman's tale, the lack of a (poetic) climax makes the suspension of the narration more of an interruption than an end. However, relating the (episodic) end moment guarantees there will be no other future end to this interruption. In this sense, ending the story with such a pause produces permanent parabasis, the indefinite postponement of any narrative horizon.

"The disruption of narrative illusion"[47] in R. Nachman's tale is also a disruption of the narrative illusion that a tale starts at a beginning and proceeds to an end. "What belongs at the beginning is told at the end and vice versa,"[48] R. Nachman has observed. This introductory statement now invites a further reflection. What would it look like to replace the beginning and end of a tale? The thought of a beginning that has been substituted for an ending should lead us to question our very (conventional) ability to distinguish between an end and a beginning. While recognizing "the end" may be based on the conventions within which we resolve to read a tale, identifying a beginning involves assumptions about our relationship to writing that precede our encounter with a particular narrative. "Writing is the unknown, or the beginning from which reading imagines and from which it departs,"[49] states Said. Here is the argument about R. Nachman's "correction" of the tales the world tells: replacing beginnings and ends creates narratives that (episodically) end at the (poetic) beginning, at the unknown from which the reader departs—must depart, and yet cannot depart.

Said's differentiation between two types of beginnings can help us further. Most beginnings are transitive, he explains. That is, they are beginnings *of* something, the departure from which leads *to* something. This transitivity also relates to the intention ascribed (or presumed) at the beginning.

> The concept "beginning" is associated in each case with an idea of precedence and/or priority [. . .] In short, the designation of a beginning generally involves also the designation of a consequent *intention* [. . .] I introduce a second sort of beginning, one that has no intention other than simply to be a beginning in the sense of being first.[50]

The second sort of beginning Said introduces is what he calls an "intransitive beginning." The fact of calling that-which-is-first a "beginning" already assumes transitivity and attempts to recognize in it an intention. To differentiate being first from such transitivity, Said posits an intransitive beginning as "one that has no intention other than simply to be a beginning in the sense of being first."[51] These two sorts of beginnings cannot be isolated from one another and are in fact two "aspects" of any point of departure. The interplay of these two is where Said's interests lie.

> The point of departure [. . .] has two aspects that animate one another. One leads to the project being realized: this is the transitive aspect of the beginning—that is, beginning with (or for) an anticipated end, or *at least expected continuity*. The other aspect retains for the beginning its identity as radical starting point: the intransitive and conceptual aspect, that which has no object but its own constant clarification.[52]

Certainly, it is hard to distinguish being first from being the beginning of what follows, unless, of course, nothing follows, because we are, in fact, at the end—an end that has been replaced with a beginning. The poetics of R. Nachman's tale destabilizes the relation of Redemption to "ending" in the same way Said's project attempts to destabilize the relation of origin to "beginning."

Disrupting the Lurianic narrative convention would throw the reader into the redemptive moment, the moment that is conventionally maintained as the unattainable horizon of the narrative. This, we have argued, could take two forms: episodic and poetic. The episodic option would be to narrate the episode that "cannot" (to borrow Dan's word) be narrated, that is, the postmessianic moment. R. Nachman did this in his "Scroll of Secrets."[53] No such effort marks the tales collected in *Sippurey Ma'asiyot*. Instead, tales such as "The Tale of the Lost Princess" throw the reader into a moment of poetic uncertainty, transforming the question "How is this going to end?" into an intransitive beginning.[54]

The poetic endings produced by R. Nachman's "correct" ordering of ends and beginnings can be understood in terms of a "permanent parabasis," at which point the narrative illusion of redemption-as-ending is irreparably broken and redemption has arrived, but only (and permanently) episodically. The disruption of this narrative illusion ends the tale at the beginning moment of redemption—an intransitive beginning, with no discernible horizon or intention, and no clear possibility of departure. And yet, what if one knew there was no "at least expected continuity"[55] to hope for, and nonetheless had no choice but to depart, to begin? This is the challenge in the next pair of tales we will read, which explore the narrative limits of R. Nachman's "poetics of intransitivity."

Poetics of Intransitivity

Our initial discussion of R. Nachman's introduction to *Sippurey Ma'asiyot* outlined the constellation of political, theological, and aesthetic concerns in his tales. In discussing the first tale and the anticlimactic ending, I have dealt with its theology and poetics. I return now to a discussion of R. Nachman's sociopolitical concerns. Two stories, "The Parable of the Wheat" and "The Parable of the Turkey," will serve to demonstrate the way these latter concerns are represented through R. Nachman's poetics of intransitivity.[56]

As we have seen, R. Nachman's life coincided with a tumultuous period in European history. In the West were the French Revolution and the Napoleonic conquests, with the forced emancipation they promised. In the East were the three divisions of the Polish-Lithuanian Commonwealth that carved out the Pale of Settlement, followed by the Russian tsarist reforms. Kings were subjected to human, social conventions and had to answer to the emerging entity of "the people." The people, in turn, were subjected to the Enlightenment demands of progress through education. The latter is exemplified by the 1804 statute, while the former can be seen in two historical events—the execution of Louis XVI and the madness of George III. These were by no means discreet occurrences. The emancipation of the people was accompanied by new forms of constraint and a reorganization of the social limits that determined inclusion and exclusion.

In the following tales, R. Nachman engages with contemporary questions regarding the widespread social changes he was witnessing. In his representation of such changes, he employs the metaphor of madness. This is not an arbitrary metaphor. As Michel Foucault argues in his analysis of the changing ideas of madness from "the great confinement" to the "moral treatment," the shifting attitudes, rethinking of its definition and novel treatments, were all parts of a process intimately linked to the emergence of those new limits that constituted the emancipated society.[57]

What would remain after the reorganization of social limits and ideologies? Returning to the beginnings of Hebrew and Yiddish literary modernity, R. Nachman leaves us finally with the question: What if one knew there was no "at least expected continuity"[58] to hope for, and yet had no choice but to depart, nonetheless to begin? I'd like to end (or begin) the present study by highlighting this question with "The Parable of the Wheat" and "The Parable of the Turkey."

"The Parable of the Wheat" certainly relates R. Nachman's anxieties about the transition from the traditionalist society he grew up in to the social order sweeping the Europe of his time. But this aspect of the tale is not what I want to focus on here. I have already discussed it, and I hope we will hear resonances of this anxiety as we proceed. What I want to do here is to read this tale as a parable of the beginnings of literary modernity.

Reconceiving "madness" was only one symptom of a broader and quite forceful epistemic shift that was taking place during R. Nachman's life.[59] The shift led to a new order of representation, one that would paradigmatically reconfigure the relation between the monarchy and "the people." In "The Parable of the Wheat," R. Nachman tells the tale of a king, "the people," and an approaching madness. Here is the text in full:

> That once the king said to his beloved viceroy: "When I gaze in the stars I see that all the wheat that will grow

this year, whoever eats from it will go mad.[60] Therefore advise me what we should do."

The viceroy answered: "Therefore we should prepare wheat in advance, so that we don't have to eat from the maddening wheat."

And the king answered: "If so, when we alone don't go mad, and the entire world will go mad, then it will be the opposite, that we will be the madmen, [and we cannot prepare enough for everyone,] therefore we will certainly have to eat from the wheat as well, just this that we should make a mark on our forehead so that we know in any event that we are mad. So that when I see your forehead and you see my forehead we will know by the mark that we are mad."

The king and his viceroy are the characters at the center of the narrative, and their peculiar conversation is its main event. But while the narrative is concentrated on this (present) conversation, there are two other events in the tale as well. In the past, there is the event of the king's stargazing and prediction, and in the future, there is the impending madness. The king feels he must prepare for this bizarre future event and seeks his viceroy's advice.

The viceroy's answer is sensible. He suggests the king stockpile food, so they don't have to eat from the maddening wheat. For the viceroy, there are only two characters in this tale—the king and himself. And there are only two events with which he must engage—the king's prediction and the present conversation. The viceroy's answer is not even that of the old regime: "Let them eat cake, or maddening wheat, it's of no consequence to us," he might have said. But there seems to be no "them" that he is aware of.

For the king, however, there is another character in this tale—"them," "the entire world," everyone, all those who will eat the wheat—and they cannot be ignored. The impending madness is also the impending emergence of this third character *as* a character. In *Short Voyages to the Land of the People*, Jacques Rancière samples the emergence of the new character "the people" in the literature of some of R. Nachman's best-known non-Jewish contemporaries.[61]

He suggests that this period sees the emergence of a new order of representation. What characterizes this new order is a form of relativity that reconfigures the limits of social inclusion in such a way that a group of peasants might be consolidated politically as "the people" and in literature as a character.[62]

For the king of R. Nachman's tale, too, the maddening wheat (through which "those that have eaten from it" will emerge as a new character) is not only the herald of an age of madness but of a new social and representational order, an order in which the king might find himself on the outside. It is worth pausing for a moment to consider the relation of this particular tale *about* the emergence of "the entire world" as the character *of* a tale to the broader project of storytelling that R. Nachman introduced with the declaration of his intention to "correct" the tales that "the world" tells. The "correction" is broader than a rearrangement of episodes; broader still than the poetic substitution of beginnings for endings; it is the project of retelling the familiar folkloric and Kabbalistic narratives of the age of monarchic order (social and representational), of "translating" them into a new order of representation—the order of "the people," which he (like the king) sees emerging. "The tales the world tells" must be reconfigured into an order that represents their teller *as* their main character, as "the world." In that sense, the present tale is also a parable of the beginnings of literary modernity.

This project is invested with some urgency, as the impending order cannot be avoided. One cannot avoid eating the new wheat, concludes the king. The madness is impending, the new character is emerging, and with it a new social order in which "everyone" determines the borders. The king realizes what Louis XVI might have realized under the guillotine, or George III under the watchful eye of his physician. Namely, in this age of madness and social emancipation, the borders have shifted, and no one can afford to ignore "the people." A moment before this new order emerges, the king wishes to prepare, and this is where R. Nachman's innovative thought is most clearly expressed. It is the idea that one might be able to prepare for such a coming age.

But how does one prepare for such an age? "We will certainly have to eat from the wheat as well," answers the king. Those who have eaten from it will soon become the main character. Those who have not will be excluded as mad. The king's advantage in this tale lies in this very capacity to prepare. "The people" do not share the king's premonitory stargazing knowledge. They have no part in the tale's past events, since it precedes their emergence *as part* of the tale. It seems they will not know they have all gone mad, since they will not have existed *as* "the people" prior to that moment. The king's foreknowledge is what allows him to prepare, and it is the only difference from his (present) world that may have any bearing upon the new order.

In poetic terms, this tale in which the king is the main character is headed toward a conclusion similar to that of "The Tale of the Lost Princess." The narrative leads toward a climax, the very realization of which would undo its climactic nature, turning "the end" into an inaccessible past moment, and throwing "the world" into its beginning. The foreseeable future of the tale ends at the reordering (socially and representationally) of the world. The shift between orders of representation, which is coming "at the end," is the end. It cannot be reversed. It irreparably breaks the illusion of the narrative in which the king is the main character. This narrative reaches permanent parabasis.

And yet there is a "point of departure" in view,[63] a point of departure that is defined by the inaccessibility of a prior moment, from which one cannot imagine a beginning, but from which one must begin. It is the intransitive beginning of a narrative that has not yet begun, that cannot begin from this tale's order of representation, a narrative in which "the people" are the main character. This future narrative as a point of departure, its *transitive* beginning as *"producing difference,"*[64] is first and foremost the production of a difference from itself *as* beginning.

The preparation the king suggests is as strange as the rest of the circumstances: "We should make a mark on our forehead so that we know in any event that we are mad," he suggests. The nature of the mark is unclear. It certainly invokes several possibilities from Jewish textual sources. It may refer to the mark of Cain[65] or to phylacteries.[66] However—like the wise man facing the riddle of ox and lamb in "The Tale of a King Who Decreed Conversion" or the one we will encounter shortly in "The Parable of the Turkey"—what I want to emphasize here goes beyond the ambiguity of the mark or its possible textual referents. What the king's solution signals is the possibility of a shared knowledge between two people, even in the midst of madness. The madman may not know he is mad, but he will still be able to look at another (mad) person and recognize that they have something in common.

R. Nachman gives no clue as to the content of the sign, thus placing his readers in the same position as the postmadness king will find himself. He will no longer identify any meaning *in* the sign. As a madman, he may not even remember how it was created or that it ever had a beginning. The king will understand nothing more than that he shares it with another, and that is precisely the importance of the sign. The king's suggestion is thus a poetic one: to mark the inaccessibility of a prior moment *at* the beginning, *as* the beginning. This inaccessibility of a prior moment *is* the beginning of the next story we will read, where R. Nachman explores the proposition of creating shared knowledge and mutual recognition in a reality of madness.

Here is the text of "The Parable of the Turkey" in full:

> Once a prince went mad, and believed he was a turkey [called *Hindik*[67]], and that he had to sit naked under the table and drag pieces of bread and bones like a turkey. And all the doctors gave up hope of helping him and curing him of this, and the king was very distressed.
>
> One day a wise man came and said: "I take it upon myself to cure him." And he stripped himself naked as well and sat under the table by the prince, and also dragged pieces of bread and bones.
>
> The prince asked him: "Who are you and what are you doing here?"
>
> And the wise man answered: "And what are you doing here?"
>
> The prince said: "I'm a turkey."
>
> The wise man responded: "I'm a turkey too."
>
> They sat together thus for a time until they grew accustomed to each other. Then the wise man gestured and they were thrown shirts, and the wise man-turkey said to the prince: "Do you think a turkey can't wear a shirt? You can wear a shirt and still remain a turkey." And they both put on shirts.

Some time later the wise man gestured and they were thrown pants. And he said the same thing again: "Do you think a turkey can't wear pants? Etc." And they both put on pants. And so he did with the other items of clothing.

Then he gestured and they were thrown human food from the table, and he said: "Do you think that if one eats good food, that one is no longer a turkey? You can eat and still remain a turkey." And so they ate. Then he said: "Do you think a turkey must remain under the table? You can be a turkey and sit at the table."

And so he treated him until he cured him completely.

This tale begins with an event of "going mad." The king's son goes mad and believes he is a turkey. Reading the two tales of madness in conjunction, we may immediately signal the ambiguity of the opening scene of the second. There is no mention of any event anterior to that of the prince going mad. With no past to refer to, the reader (unlike the previous king) is unable to prepare for this madness. Keeping in mind the previous king's sensitivity, we must recognize the ambiguity of a situation in which one man is perceived as mad by "everyone" and ask: Has the prince really gone mad, or has "everyone" except for him gone mad? Has an entire kingdom of turkeys eaten from some maddening wheat and begun thinking they are all human? Is the mad prince in the very situation the king from the previous tale wished to avoid?

We cannot know. For the tale to begin, we must presume a past moment in which the prince was not mad but accept that such a moment is inaccessible from within the narrative. Its mark as such is the point of departure for the tale. With a blink of the reader's eye, across the blank space on the page that separates these two tales in the book, an intransitive beginning has been demarcated. Between the going-mad that is to come and a going-mad that has already passed, there is the intransitive space of a permanent beginning. The inaccessibility of a moment after and the inaccessibility of a moment before converge between stories. It is the point of departure that cannot be articulated, only demarcated by a poetics of intransitivity.

Yet, with the opening line of the second story, we have already departed. A voyage into the order of "the people" has set forth. It has landed the reader under a table, by a prince who sits naked, behaving like a turkey. All the king's doctors are unable to cure him, and then a wise man shows up and takes it upon himself to do so. The wise man's behavior is surprising. Instead of approaching the prince from a position of authority (the way a doctor may be expected to do) he undresses himself and joins the price under the table. To the prince's surprise, the wise man introduces himself as a fellow turkey.

A note is in order at this point in our reading regarding the depiction of madness in these tales. To be clear, this is not the madness discussed by Mark,[68] which is used to fashion the *baal shem tov*'s character in his hagiography *Shivchei HaBesht*.[69] It is not one that can be cured by doctors or driven out by exorcists. This madness is not in competition with spiritual authorities, the way madmen in *Shivchei HaBesht* compete with the *baal shem tov* to provide supernatural services to the community.[70] This is also not the madness used in R. Nachman's teachings to depict ecstatic spiritual accomplishments. Mark characterizes the spiritual achievements depicted as madness in R. Nachman's teachings as related to a lack of reason that enables ecstasy.[71] In this tale, it is through the retention of the faculty of reason that the wise man is able to "reason" with the prince and cure him. The wise man's surprising behavior implies both a power dynamic and a conception of madness much closer to Philippe Pinel's "moral treatment" than to any demonological understanding.[72]

In this tale, madness is depicted as lack of a shared knowledge, as the prince's inability to recognize the possibility of having something in common with "everyone." This is the point at which the wise man's treatment begins—establishing the proposition that there is something in common between himself and the prince. Building on the stability of this shared knowledge ("we are both turkeys"), the prince is less wary of the possibility of a shared commonality with "everyone." He slowly agrees to dress like everyone, eat like everyone, come out from under the table like everyone, and so on until he is cured completely.

The question remains: In what sense did the wise man "cure" the prince? It seems the prince still believes he is a turkey and that he will remain a turkey indefinitely despite his commonality with everyone. The wise man's lesson is double edged. On the one hand, he shows the prince that the possibility of having something in common with everyone is not threatening. In that sense, the way out of the prince's madness (or into everyone else's madness) is to embrace this possibility. On the other hand, the knowledge the prince comes to share with the wise man is that no matter what form they take, these commonalities will never change the fact that they are turkeys. In the ambiguous reality of madness, the cure seems to lie as much in strengthening the prince's sense of turkey-self as in weakening his aversion to a collective norm. The prince and the wise man form the relation proposed by the previous king, they come to share the knowledge of their madness. Through the shared knowledge that they are turkeys (and will remain so), they are able to adapt to the collective madness of a society that believes they are all humans.

But, we might object, the wise man doesn't really believe he is a turkey. Nor did he "really" cure the prince. These objections hit upon the central question R. Nachman's tales of madness raise. What *would* count as "curing" the prince? If the only acceptable answer is the mentally invasive procedure of altering the prince's thoughts about himself, of getting him to "really" no longer believe he is a turkey, then this depiction of madness is indeed, as Mark suggests, a turning point in the history of madness in Jewish society, as much so and through the same considerations as Pinel's "moral treatment" was a turning point in the history of madness in the age of Enlightenment. However, in that it postulates the madness of the prince as *opposed* to that of "everyone" rather than as part of it, this answer falls short of appreciating the reciprocal links R. Nachman's parables depict between moments of social reorganization and the ambiguous distinction between individual and collective.

Here is also the beginning of a reply to the former objection. Whether or not the wise man believes he is a turkey is irrelevant to his cure. The ambiguity of the situation is also that of the wise man's sense of self. For the purpose of curing the prince, he may as well have been a turkey too. The narrator certainly never explicitly resolves this question. But moreover, within these tales' effort to apprehend the relativity of this situation, we may propose that answering the following question—Did the wise man really cure the prince, or did he only fool everyone else into thinking the prince was cured?—is impossible to answer. And this impossibility is what allows this depiction of madness to capture the logic of the new order of "the whole world" which R. Nachman is concerned with. In that sense, the wise man's solution was never meant to be a cure for madness. It is a solution for existing within the age of madness predicted by the previous king, for living within the new order of representation. It is both a literary-critical depiction of the impossibility of determining (within this age) between one king's madness and "everyone" else's madness and a proposal for coping with this impossibility.

Conclusion

Reading outside Modernity

By way of conclusion, let us recall the 1906 preface to Martin Buber's German translation of *The Tales of Rabbi Nachman*, in which he introduced the storyteller thus: "Rabbi Nachman of Bratzlav, who was born in 1772 and died in 1810, is perhaps the last Jewish mystic. He stands at the end of an unbroken tradition, whose beginning we do not know."

As we have now seen, Buber's concern with ends and beginnings in R. Nachman's position vis-à-vis tradition is, in part, informed by his self-positioning "at the edge" in statements such as: "Here we are now at the limit and edge of Israel where the limit of Israel ends, for everything has a limit and an end."[1] To make sense of such self-positioning, we have considered the temporal aspect of "the edge," which Buber clearly implies. We have also considered the spatial sense that R. Nachman here alludes to and develops more comprehensively in Teaching I:64. And yet, for Buber and his contemporaries (and up to our present day), this positioning is taken uncritically to designate R. Nachman as that from which Buber and "we" have broken. Meanwhile, R. Nachman's investment in discursively producing the contours and possibilities of just such a break has been ignored.[2]

His discursive effort is bifurcated. He negotiates an opening of "the edge" onto an "in-between" position, while constructing his own position "at the edge" as an intransitive point of departure. This discursive effort takes place in both the social and the aesthetic terms of European Jewish thinkers at the turn of the eighteenth century. In reading R. Nachman, the words "in-between" and "edge" are triggers for recurring and persistent questions about position, identification, and difference. For R. Nachman, this is a complex position, equally geographical and social, discursive and political, aesthetic and literary—an edge that is being discovered, an in-between that is still in the making. A century later, however, his very position was cast as the "tradition" from which a departure was to take place.

Let us briefly return to the historiographical frame with which this book began. The "May Laws" of 1882 heralded the disintegration of the Pale of Settlement as it had been consolidated by Alexander I in the 1804 "Statute Concerning the Organization of the Jews." But what exactly "disintegrated," in *aesthetic* terms, in terms of the representation of difference, in the period between 1881 and 1905? The poetic emergence of a modern Hebrew and Yiddish Eastern European literature involved rethinking the question of representing invisible differences and inaugurating a "new" aesthetic order. But it also involved determining a break from that previous aesthetic order inaugurated by R. Nachman. This break would be introduced (at least discursively) by the writers of modern Hebrew and Yiddish literature at the turn of the nineteenth century, in order to constitute themselves as modern.

The aesthetic order that R. Nachman had inaugurated a century earlier was deliberately broken with by the makers of what we now call "modern literature," whose authors—all having read R. Nachman's tales—desired to see in that very order, the "far shore" of their constitutive break. This break takes the form of narrating the postmadness king or the "cured" turkey-prince as both a "position" that cannot be sustained and as a "location" from which a departure path is clear and unavoidable. What kind of difference would be made visible through its literary representation? Reconfiguring literary representation of the invisibility of confessional differences at the turn of the nineteenth century largely fell into one of the two options. R. Nachman has already outlined both for us in Teaching I:61. The choice was between overrepresentation and complete omission.

Two canonical characters of modern Hebrew and Yiddish literature clearly mark this departure. First is Abramovitsh's hero in *Benjamin the Third*. He and his companion Sendryl are turkeys that wander out from under their tables but cannot suppress their mad behavior. Benjamin and Sendryl go out as fools among the nations, overrepresenting their difference from the nations to parodic extents, only to finally discover that they will never "be cured."[3] Second, the turkey-prince himself can no longer keep it together, emerging at the turn of the nineteenth century as the new literary character of the *talush*, the rootless man detached from society.[4] Desperately seeking out his place in the world, overwhelmed by a feeling of "the difference between [himself] and the nations," for which (as opposed to Benjamin the Third) he can find *no* representation in his surroundings, he eventually goes mad—nostalgically turns to fantasizing about his old spot under the table. The paradoxical nature of seeing tradition as a series of breaks, or seeing a series of breaks as the cumulation of a tradition, comes to this: for modern Hebrew and Yiddish writers at the turn of the nineteenth century, by discursively breaking with R. Nachman they end up imitating the very same discursive departure he had already outlined a century before.

In this book, I have attempted to sketch the map of this departure. However, the very necessity of having a map, of developing a model for modernity or in-betweenness attests, as Pierre Bourdieu notes, to the observer's distance from the topography being navigated. The map is "the analogy which occurs to an outsider who has to find his way around in a foreign landscape and who compensates for his lack of practical mastery, the prerogative of the native, by the use of a model of all possible routes."[5] R. Nachman never had a full view of all the possible roads in the moment of choosing one. He did not yet know what lay beyond this or that mountain, past this or another turn. He should be read, in this sense, not as elaborating a "Jewish model of modernity or revival" (a proposal which would not be so different from the anachronistic title of "Jewish Intellectual"), but as providing the reflections of a wayfarer who turns a corner only to discover an edge he had not expected to find and sets out to explore beyond it. His position precedes the map that will articulate it.

Every turn the wayfarer takes, every social change coming into view, reveals unexpected locations. Mendes-Flohr states that the "detachment of the present from its moorings in the past—and its elevation as an autonomous category of experience and an independent sphere of meaning—is often regarded as the ultimate hallmark of the secularization inaugurated with the advent of modernity [. . .] The founding sensibility of modernity, hence, entails a self-conscious discontinuity with the past."[6] Certainly, such detachment from the past is characteristic of thinkers such as Buber, who discursively produce this discontinuity. However, as opposed to Buber, who finds himself on the far side of a break he did not initiate, R. Nachman was able to discursively produce a break that he himself would not ultimately transgress. Thus, R. Nachman's effort to articulate his position precedes the vocabulary of the map I have drawn.

Where does this leave us as far as "positioning" R. Nachman? If we are reading him along the lines of a literary historiography that is presumed to lead to "modern Jewish literature" then we will glimpse his figure only on the "far shore" of a departure from which (we must convince ourselves) we cannot return. In conclusion, I want to offer a more optimistic note for the student of Hebrew and Yiddish literature who is taken with R. Nachman's writing but uncertain what to make of it. I want to suggest the possibility of not reading him as a writer "outside modernity," as it were. Or, more precisely, not allowing this exteriority—a constitutive assumption of our own concept of modern literature—to deter us from reading him as an integral constituent of what we think of more broadly as Hebrew and Yiddish literary modernity. In order to read him as just such an integral actor, we need to recognize R. Nachman's position in a modernity outside of our own. While this may be a modernity we have broken with, he is nonetheless its key figure, a figure whose writing was part of structuring and stylizing that very break *as* a departure.

This study has attempted to read outside modernity in several senses: first, in the sense of reading outside of a project defined by privileging a single constitutive break—which turns out to have been constituted as much by that which was "broken away from" as by one's discovery of having departed; second, as a way of reading R. Nachman that—if successful—would undermine the very privileged concept of "break" in the constitution of our notions of tradition, literature, and modernity; and last, as reading "outside modernity" also in the sense of a modernity that is not "inside" the vessel that has departed. In R. Nachman's voice, we can discern both the outline of the "far shore" and the possibility of departure. Finding himself drawn to the limit, R. Nachman inscribes his voice—associative, staccato, perhaps anticlimactic—at the limit, opening the limit onto an in-between space—vacant, treacherous with heresy, and uncharted.

Notes

Introduction

1. In the final decade of the eighteenth century, the habitation of Jews in the newly annexed regions to the west of Russia was regulated, and the term "Pale of Settlement" (in Russian: "Черта оседлости") was used to designate the region.

2. Eli Lederhendler makes a similar point about unsatisfactory explanations for how Jewish political groups emerged following the 1882 pogroms. He suggests analysis must address the structural considerations within which the individuals in question act. See Eli Lederhendler, *The Road to Modern Jewish Politics* (New York: Oxford University Press, 1989).

3. For one influential example, see Hans-Georg Gadamer, *Truth and Method* (London: Bloomsbury Academic, 2014).

4. See Gil Anidjar, "Literary History and Hebrew Modernity," *Comparative Literature Studies* 42, no. 4 (2005). This statement is largely true of other "Jewish literatures" beyond Eastern Europe. However, this book is focused on Nachman of Braslav, and so it strives to contextualize his life and work within an admittedly narrower set of scholarly and historical frames pertaining largely to his contemporary Eastern European historical moment.

5. Martin Buber, ed., *The Tales of Rabbi Nachman* (Atlantic Highlands, NJ: Humanities Press International, 1988), 3.

6. Without anticipating too much of the discussion in the coming pages, a note is in order on our subject's appellation. Before asking if he was an intellectual, an innovation, or even the Messiah (as the table of contents proposes), we must ask a far more basic question: Was Nachman of Braslav a "Rabbi?"

This purportedly linguistic question begins with two Yiddish terms—"Reb," which would be used for an adult male Jew similar to the term "mister" in English, and the Hebraicized "Rav" (or "ha-Rav"), which would indicate the charge of rabbinic Jewish communal leadership. In Hebrew, the distinction at hand would be between the term "Rabi," commonly referring to a Hasidic leader, and "Rav" (or "ha-Rav") which would be the honorific title by which an ordained rabbi would be introduced. In English, of course, there is no term for an adult male Jew, while the term "Rabbi" is used for rabbis. The question at hand is thus in part the result of a slippage between the Hebrew, Yiddish, and English terms—a "Rabi" is not a rabbi, and a "Rabbi" is not just any adult male Jew. This confusion is exacerbated by the Hebrew and Yiddish abbreviation "R." which indeterminately serves to abbreviate "Rabi," "Reb" and "Rav." In fact, in much of the Hebrew and Yiddish scholarship on Nachman of Braslav, he is referred to as "R. Nachman." Since the term "Rabi" is not commonly used in contemporary Hebrew, in reference to any contemporary figure this abbreviation would imply they are a Hasidic leader. But if used in reference to figures from a time when the terms "Rabi," "Reb" and "Rav" were in use in Hebrew and Yiddish respectively, this abbreviated R. must be treated with more circumspection, particularly because the manner in which one might unpack this abbreviation is markedly ideological as well.

So which "R." was "R. Nachman"? In the contemporary sense of a figure charged with religious communal leadership, he was certainly the religious and social leader of a small community of students and followers. However, in the sense of having been ordained to a position of religious authority by a line of transmission that passed this authority down from one generation to the next, he was not a "rabbi" in the (lowercase) orthodox sense of the term. In fact, the Hasidic movement was at odds with this orthodox model of leadership from its very beginnings. By the first half of the nineteenth century, a patrilineal model of Hasidic leadership had developed. Yet there was still no "ordination" in the orthodox sense of the term. R. Nachman was an unordained leader, a figure of religious authority not invested by orthodoxy yet more important to his followers than any "rabbi" at the time.

The convention in Hebrew language scholarship refers to him rather consistently as R. Nachman. This is consistent from the earlier works of Joseph Weiss and Mendel Piekarz, all the way to more contemporary works by Zvi Mark and Roee Horen. This is true in translation as well. For example, Chani Haran Smith's English-language book *Tuning the Soul: Music as a Spiritual Process in the Teachings of Rabbi Nahman of Bratzlav* has him as "Rabbi Nachman" already in the title, whereas the Hebrew translation of the same book has him as "R. Nachman." This is not the case in Hebrew editions of the tales, where he may appear as "R. Nachman," "Rabi Nachman," or "ha-Rav Nachman." Nor is this the case among his disciples—neither in his lifetime nor among contemporary Braslav followers today—where he is conventionally referred to as "ha-Rav" in acronyms such as *Moharan*: moreinu ha-Rav Nachman. However, my current dilemma has to do with representing the subject of my study in an academic work, so I will not survey the variety of appellations he has received by the many editors and adherents who have brought his works to print in Hebrew. There are certainly Hasidic leaders referred to as "rabbi" (and at times "holy rabbi") by their students in many citations discussed throughout the present study.

Yiddish-language scholarship from Haim Liberman to Chone Shmeruk also predominantly refers to him as "R. Nachman," whereas Yiddishists writing in English, such as David Roskies and Mark Caplan, use the Yiddish appellation "Reb." Disciplinary-linguistic conventions largely hold firm in Hebrew, Yiddish, and among Yiddishists writing in English. The problem begins when one turns to scholarship about Nachman of Braslav in English.

In English, he is referred to as "Rabbi Nahman" already in the 1940s by Gershom Scholem, as well as in Martin Buber's edition of the tales (both in its English translation and in the original German). Arthur Green's title has him as "Rabbi Nahman," while the text of the book has him mostly as "Nachman," and so too Shaul Magid's book *Hasidism Incarnate*. Joseph Dan has him in Hebrew as "R. Nachman" and in English as "Rabbi Nachman," in his preface to Arnold Band's translation of the tales as well as later publications. Yet Dan himself refers to our subject as "R. Nahman" in his own English-language review of Green's book. The title of Band's translation of the tales has him as "Nahman of Braslav," while the introduction by Band has him as "Nahman" until the bottom of page 30, at which point the text begins referring to him as "Rav Nahman," "Rabbi Nahman," and "Nahman" inconsistently. Influenced by the Yiddishist convention, Ora Wiskind-Elper refers to him consistently as "Reb Nahman" in her English language monograph on the tales.

More recently, scholars such as Shaul Magid, Ken Frieden, and others have been largely consistent in referring to him as "R. Nachman." I welcome this decision to avoid explicit implications about his "holiness" in favor of a less determined appellation that echoes the Hebrew and Yiddish conventions. In order to both echo this ambiguity and avoid an ideological determination unwarranted in a scholarly study, I will refer to him as "R. Nachman" for the remainder of this book. However, when citing works that do not use this same designation, I will accurately cite the designations used by the sources at hand. This practice may result in some apparent inconsistencies, as there is much variety among determinations used by scholars in the field.

Here is a concentrated list of citations for all authors and works mentioned above. Most of these references will appear repeatedly throughout the present study:

For examples of Hebrew language scholarship, see Joseph Weiss, *Mehkarim Ba-Hasidut Braslav* (Yerushalayim: Mosad Byalik, 1974); Mendel Piekarz, *Hasidut Braslav: Perakim Be-Haye Meholeleha Uvi-Khetaveha* (Yerushalayim: Mosad Byalik, 1972); Zvi Mark, *Mistikah Ve-Shigaon Bi-Yetsirat R. Nahman Mi-Breslav* (Tel Aviv: 'Am 'oved, 2003); Roee Horen, ed., *Ha-Hayim Ke-Ga'Agu'A: Keriot Hadashot Be-Sipure Ha-Ma'Asiyot Shel R. Nahman Mi-Breslev* (Tel-Aviv: Yedi'ot aharonot: Sifre hemed, 2010); Joseph Dan, *Ha-Sipur Ha-Hasidi* (Yerushalayim: Bet Hotsa'ah Keter Yerushalayim, 1975).

For translated scholarship, see Chani Haran Smith, *Tuning the Soul: Music as a Spiritual Process in the Teachings of Rabbi Nahman of Bratzlav* (Leiden; Boston: Brill, 2010); Buber, *The Tales of Rabbi Nachman*.

For Yiddish-language scholarship, see Haim Liberman, "R. Nachman Breslaver Und Die Umener Maskilim," *YIVO Bleter* XXIX (1947); Chone Shmeruk, *Prokim Fun Der Yidisher Literatur-Geshikhte* (Tel-Aviv; Yerusholaim: Farlag Y. L. Perets; Yidish-opteylung, der Hebraisher universitet in Yerusholaim, 1988).

For Yiddishists writing in English, see David G. Roskies, *A Bridge of Longing: The Lost Art of Yiddish Storytelling* (Cambridge, MA: Harvard University Press, 1995); Marc Caplan, *How Strange the Change Language, Temporality, and Narrative Form in Peripheral Modernisms* (Stanford, CA: Stanford University Press, 2011).

For scholarship in English using various appellations, see Gershom Gerhard Scholem, *Major Trends in Jewish Mysticism* (New York: Schocken Books, 1995); Arthur Green, *Tormented Master: The Life and Spiritual Quest of Rabbi Nahman of Bratslav* (Woodstock, VT: Jewish Lights, 1992); Joseph Dan, "Rabbi Nahman's Third Beggar," in *History and Literature: New Readings of Jewish Texts in Honor of Arnold J. Band*, ed. William Cutter and David C. Jacobson (Providence, RI: Program in Judaic Studies, Brown University, 2002); Arnold J. Band, *Nahman of Bratslav: The Tales* (New York: Paulist, 1978); Ora Wiskind-Elper, *Tradition and Fantasy in the Tales of Reb Nahman of Bratslav* (Albany: State University of New York Press, 1998); and Shaul Magid, *Hasidism Incarnate: Hasidism, Christianity, and the Construction of Modern Judaism* (Stanford, CA: Stanford University Press, 2015).

For scholarship in English using "R. Nachman," see "Through the Void: The Absence of God in R. Nahman of Bratzlav's 'Likkutei Moharan,'" *The Harvard Theological Review* 88, no. 4 (1995); Ken Frieden, *Travels in Translation: Sea Tales at the Source of Jewish Fiction* (Syracuse, NY: Syracuse University Press, 2016).

7. For more on Buber's readers and the context in which he represents R. Nachman as the marker of a break from tradition, see Martina Urban, *Aesthetics of Renewal: Martin Buber's Early Representation of Hasidism as Kulturkritik* (Chicago: University of Chicago Press, 2008). Scholem too represents the moment of this break, but more broadly, in the title of his ninth lecture "Hasidism, the Final Phase," in Scholem, *Major Trends in Jewish Mysticism*.

8. Urban, *Aesthetics of Renewal: Martin Buber's Early Representation of Hasidism as Kulturkritik*, 4.

9. Two recent examples of rethinking the conventional historiographical narrative: Jonatan Meir has done so by reading the importance of Jewish Enlightenment (*haskala*) writing for subsequent "modern" literary production and the *haskala* writers' debt to Hasidic writing. See, for example: Jonatan Meir, *Hasidut Medumah: 'Iyunim Bi-Khetavav Ha-Satiriyim Shel Yosef Perl [Imagined Hasidism: The Anti-Hasidic Writings of Joseph Perl]* (Jerusalem: Mosad Bialik, 2013); Yonatan Meir, *Literary Hasidism: The Life and Works of Michael Levi Rodkinson* (2016). Ken Frieden has noted the impact of R. Nathan Sternhartz's style of travel-writing on his contemporary *haskala* writers and identifies an important effect R. Nathan had in the innovation of Hebrew and Yiddish prose style (in non-Hasidic writing). See Frieden, *Travels in Translation: Sea Tales at the Source of Jewish Fiction*.

10. See Ben-Zion Dinur, "Reshitah Shel Ha-Hasidut Ve-Yesodoteha Ha-Sotsialiyim Ve-Hameshichiyim," in *Studies in Hasidism*, ed. Avraham Rubinstein (Jerusalem: Zalman Shazar Center; Historical Society of Israel, 1977); Immanuel Etkes, *Tnuat Ha-Hasidut Be-Reshitah* (Tel-Aviv: Misrad habitahon, 1998).

11. See Israel Bartal, *The Jews of Eastern Europe, 1772–1881* (Philadelphia: University of Pennsylvania Press, 2005); Ada Rapoport-Albert, "Hasidism after 1772: Structural Continuity and Change," in *Hasidism Reappraised*, ed. Ada Rapoport-Albert (London: Littman Library of Jewish Civilization, 1996); Gershon David Hundert, *Jews in Poland-Lithuania in the Eighteenth Century: A Genealogy of Modernity* (Berkeley: University of California Press, 2004); Glenn Dynner, *Men of Silk: The Hasidic Conquest of Polish Jewish Society* (New York: Oxford University Press, 2006). This observation also exists outside of the study of the Hasidic movement, in broader Jewish studies scholarship on the turn of the eighteenth century in Eastern Europe. For example, see Eliyahu Stern, *The Genius Elijah of Vilna and the Making of Modern Judaism* (New Haven: Yale University Press, 2013).

12. Marc Caplan, "Watch the Throne: Allegory, Kingship and Trauerspiel in the Stories of Der Nister and Reb Nakhman," in *Uncovering the Hidden: The Works and Life of Der Nister*, ed. Gennady Estraikh, Kerstin

Hoge, and Mikhail Krutikov, Studies in Yiddish (Cambridge: Legenda, 2014), 101.

13. I allude here to the early work of Jürgen Habermas on the public sphere. While I depart sharply from the Habermasian perception of modernity—by insisting that "crisis" is a critically productive term for understanding certain transformations that took place in the aesthetic sphere—my frame largely adopts his historical periodization, locating a significant moment for the transformations of Hebrew literature in the late eighteenth and early nineteenth centuries. Having valorized the critical utility of "crisis," I must equally stress my departure from the kind of sharp separation between the social sphere and the political sphere, between crisis-as-political and "the public"-as-social, outlined by Reinhart Koselleck. My argument is that political crisis is centrally operative in the social public sphere, albeit in importantly *aesthetic* terms, hence my criticism of the lack of discussion relating particularly to the *representation* of historical moments by those who live through and report on them. See Jürgen Habermas, *The Structural Transformation of the Public Sphere: An Inquiry into a Category of Bourgeois Society*, trans. Thomas Burger (Cambridge: Polity, 1989); Reinhart Koselleck, *Critique and Crisis: Enlightenment and the Pathogenesis of Modern Society* (Cambridge, MA: MIT Press, 1988).

14. Nathan Sternhartz, *Chayey Moharan* (Lemberg, 1874), 264.

15. I allude here to the work of Edward Said that will be integral to the discussion in chapter 7. See Edward W. Said, *Beginnings: Intention and Method* (New York: Basic Books, 1975).

16. Yakov Travis, "Adorning the Souls of the Dead," in *God's Voice from the Void Old and New Studies in Bratslav Hasidism*, ed. Shaul Magid (Albany: State University of New York Press, 2002), 156.

17. Nathan Sternhartz was R. Nachman's closest disciple and scribe. Most of the Braslav literature that exists is the result of his collection and compilation of R. Nachman's teachings and tales. His autobiography, *Yemei Moharnat* (published posthumously in 1876), offers an account of his relationship with R. Nachman beyond what appears in R. Nathan's biography of R. Nachman, *Chayey Moharan* (published posthumously in 1874). Note that the same appellation "R." applies to R. Nathan as well, and with similar slippage to what I have discussed above in ff. 5. See Nathan Sternhartz, *Sefer Yemei Moharnat* (Lemberg 1876); *Chayey Moharan*.

18. For a comprehensive discussion of the process by which R. Nachman's tales were documented and published, as well as the methodology for enumerating the tales told by R. Nachman and other important bibliographic references, see the introduction to Zvi Mark, ed. *Kol Sipure Rabi Nahman Mi-Braslav: Ha-Ma'Asiyot, Ha-Sipurim Ha-Sodiyim, Ha-Halomot*

Veha-Hezyonot (Jerusalem, Israel: Mosad Bialik; Yedi'ot Sefarim; Bayit—Yetsirah Ivrit, 2014), 17–111.

19. In the preceding pages, I have made an effort to avoid any linguistic determination of the "modern" literary corpus, in relation to which I seek to position the writing of R. Nachman. While contemporary disciplinary divisions allow one to easily distinguish between Yiddish literature and Hebrew literature in "modern" literary production, this distinction was not as self-evident to R. Nachman. In fact, these disciplinary divisions echo the later moment of "language wars" at the turn of the nineteenth century. For reasons beyond the scope of the current study, it became increasingly important for authors of that later moment to choose one language in which to write. This choice related to their broader ideological and political affiliations and would determine their reception (or lack thereof) among various groups of readers. In the language in which R. Nachman spoke and taught, as in the language in which he chose to have his tales published, it is clear that for R. Nachman there is no such choice to be made. He simply cannot imagine a monolingual Jewish literary mode of expression. This is a problematic that pervades the current study. This also explains my methodology of comparing the Yiddish and Hebrew versions of the tales at certain points. Completely avoiding the theoretical slippage between "Hebrew," "Yiddish," and "Jewish" literature is impossible. In part, this is because I am informed by existing scholarship from both fields of Hebrew literature and Yiddish literature in my discussion of R. Nachman's tales. More deliberately, however, the impossibility of distinguishing between the "modernities" of Jewish literature at the turn of the eighteenth century is part of the broader theoretical frame for my argument about R. Nachman's relevance to the study of Eastern European Jewish literature. Rather than resolve or avoid this problematic, I hope the present book will suggest further nuance to our appreciation of this question about literary language. For an historical and textual analysis of R. Nachman's use of Hebrew and Yiddish languages, see Piekarz, *Hasidut Braslav: Perakim Be-Haye Meholeleha Uvi-Khetaveha*, ch. 1. For more on the question of diglossia in the context of Hasidic writing, see Hannan Hever, "The Politics of the Hebrew Hassidic Tale in the Russian Empire," in *Languages of Modern Jewish Cultures*, ed. Joshua Miller and Anita Norich (Ann Arbor: University of Michigan Press, 2016).

20. See Roskies, *A Bridge of Longing: The Lost Art of Yiddish Storytelling*; Band, *Nahman of Bratslav, the Tales*.

21. Rabbi Yitzhak Luria (1534–1572) was the major figure of the Safed circle of Kabbalists in the sixteenth century. For more on his innovative contributions to the Jewish mystical tradition, see Scholem, *Major Trends*

in Jewish Mysticism, ch. 7. For a thesis on R. Luria's influence on Jewish storytelling (including the Hasidic story), see Dan, *Ha-Sipur Ha-Hasidi*.

22. Mark, *Kol Sipure Rabi Nahman Mi-Braslav: Ha-Ma'Asiyot, Ha-Sipurim Ha-Sodiyim, Ha-Halomot Veha-Hezyonot*, 52.

23. Ibid., 28.

24. Shmeruk, *Prokim Fun Der Yidisher Literatur-Geshikhte*, ch. 6.

25. Yisra'el ben Eliezer (c. 1695–1760), who came to be known as the *baal shem tov* (literally "of the good name"), is recognized in Hasidic historiography and hagiography as the founder of the movement circa 1740. This identification is debated in scholarship, both with regards to the earliest possible identification of Hasidism as a "movement" and with regards to R. Yisra'el Baal Shem Tov's role in the early years of Hasidism. For more on the identification of Hasidism as a movement, see Rapoport-Albert, "Hasidism after 1772: Structural Continuity and Change." For more on the historical figure of the *baal shem tov*, see Murray Jay Rosman, *Founder of Hasidism: A Quest for the Historical Ba'al Shem Tov* (Berkeley: University of California Press, 1996).

26. Shmeruk, *Prokim Fun Der Yidisher Literatur-Geshikhte*, 243.

27. Such works were already circulating in R. Nachman's vicinity. In 1813, Dov Ber (a Maskil of Uman, with whom R. Nachman spent the final months of his life) published the Yiddish translation of Defoe's *Robinson Crusoe*. And, in 1817, Chaikel Horowitz (another Maskil of Uman) published the Yiddish book *Tsofnat Pa'ane'ach* on Columbus's discovery of the Americas. That is to say, the "news of the world" of imperial expansion projects was readily available to R. Nachman but, more importantly, so were the fictions and fantasies of this expansion.

28. Sternhartz, *Chayey Moharan*, no. 216.

29. For more on aerial advances and ballooning in France, see Charles Coulston Gillispie, *The Montgolfier Brothers and the Invention of Aviation, 1783–1784* (Princeton, New Jersey: Princeton University Press, 2014). In Britain, see Clare Brant, *Balloon Madness: Flights of Imagination in Britain, 1783–1786* (2017).

30. Avraham Eliezer Tshingal, ed. *Sefer Siach Sarfei Kodesh* (Yerushalayim: Agudat Meshekh ha-Nachal, 1988), no. 501.

31. Cited in ibid.

32. Roskies, *A Bridge of Longing: The Lost Art of Yiddish Storytelling*, 25.

33. Ibid., 27.

34. Caplan, *How Strange the Change Language, Temporality, and Narrative Form in Peripheral Modernisms*, 12.

35. Ibid.

36. Ibid.

37. Travis, "Adorning the Souls of the Dead," 156.

38. See Weiss, *Mehkarim Ba-Hasidut Braslav*.

39. Zvi Mark, "Why Did R. Moses Zvi of Savran Persecute R. Nathan of Nemirov and Bratslav Hasidim?," *Zion* 69, no. 4 (2004).

40. Simon Dubnow, *Toldot Ha-Hasidut*, 3 vols. (Tel-Aviv: Devir, 1944), 307.

41. For more on these biases see Israel Bartal, "The Imprint of Haskalah Literature on the Historiography of Hasidism," in *Hasidism Reappraised*, ed. Ada Rapoport-Albert (London: Littman Library of Jewish Civilization, 1996). For more on the internal Hasidic conflicts R. Nachman was involved in see Piekarz, *Hasidut Braslav: Perakim Be-Haye Meholeleha Uvi-Khetaveha*; Weiss, *Mehkarim Ba-Hasidut Braslav*. For a broader overview and context of some of the major internal conflicts see David Asaf, *Ne'eḥaz Ba-Sevakh: Pirḳe Mashber U-Mevukhah Be-Toldot Ha-Ḥasidut* (Jerusalem: Merkaz Zalman Shazar le-Toldot Yiśra'el, 2006).

42. Though it is clear this was a significant relationship for R. Nachman in his later years, the nature and motivation of this relationship remains an issue of debate. The two most extensive surveys of this relationship are Liberman, "R. Nachman Breslaver Und Die Umener Maskilim,"; Piekarz, *Hasidut Braslav: Perakim Be-Haye Meholeleha Uvi-Khetaveha*, ch. 2.

43. Some recent examples of research in this direction include Hannan Hever, "The Politics of Form of the Hassidic Tale," *Dibur Literary Journal*, no. 2 (2016); "The Politics of the Hebrew Hassidic Tale in the Russian Empire."

44. R. Nachman's collected teachings were published in two volumes titled *Likkutei Moharan* (literally "collections of our rabbi Nachman") in 1808 and 1811.

45. Shaul Magid sees "bechina" as a "meta-midrashic literary trope." See Shaul Magid, "Associative Midrash: Reflections on a Hermeneutical Theory in Rabbi Nachman of Braslav's *Likkutei Moharan*," in *God's Voice from the Void: Old and New Studies in Bratslav Hasidism*, ed. Shaul Magid (Albany: State University of New York Press, 2002), 16. The term "trope" may be out of place here, since the essential point about *bechina* is neither its figurative use nor its recurrence as a theme. In fact, the semantic denotation of *bechina* is too vast and vague for it to be of use to the reader navigating R. Nachman's thoughts. Nor, on the other hand, are the formal relations of the two elements being linked by the word properly definable. To the extent that such a definition would be coterminous with a typology of association as such, *bechina* points to a type of relationship that lies beyond definition. It connotes the making of an imaginative, freely associative link.

Chapter 1

1. Rapoport-Albert, "Hasidism after 1772: Structural Continuity and Change," 76.

2. For more on this apparent paradox of "consolidating a decentralized movement," and the significance of the events of 1772 in Hasidic history more broadly, see ibid.

3. The Council was officially disbanded in 1764, but it wasn't until the Polish-Lithuanian Commonwealth—the political structure under which it operated—fell apart that the effects of the vacuum of leadership spread so fiercely throughout the Jewish community. For more on Eastern European Jewish History in this period, see Hundert, *Jews in Poland-Lithuania in the Eighteenth Century a Genealogy of Modernity*; Simon Dubnow, *History of the Jews in Russia and Poland, from the Earliest Times until the Present Day*, trans. Israel Friedlaender, 3 vols., vol. 1 *From the beginning until the death of Alexander I* (1825) (Philadelphia: Jewish Publication Society of America, 1916). See also Bartal, *The Jews of Eastern Europe, 1772–1881*. For more on the Hasidic expansion in Eastern Europe, see Dynner, *Men of Silk: The Hasidic Conquest of Polish Jewish Society*.

4. For more on the conflict between Hasidism and the Mitnagdim, see Mordecai Wilensky, *Hasidim U-Mitnagdim: Le-Toldot Ha-Pulmus She-Benehem* (Yerushalayim: Mosad Byalik, 1970). See also Simon Dubnow, *A History of Hasidism*, trans. Lederer Helen (Cincinnati 1970).

5. Rapoport-Albert, "Hasidism after 1772: Structural Continuity and Change," 76.

6. This ideology venerates the charismatic *zadik* as a link between the faithful and God. It was most notably elaborated by R. Elimelech of Leżajsk, see Elimelech of Leżajsk, *Sefer No'am Elimelech* (Lemberg1787). In counterdistinction, the ideology of "eruditism," the social-hierarchical superiority of a traditionally educated elite was firmly represented by the Mitnagdim of Vilna. For a discussion of the mediating function of the *zadik*, see Moshe Idel, *Hasidism between Ecstasy and Magic* (Albany: State University of New York Press, 1995).

7. I'm referring here to the books of R. Yakov Yosef of Polnoie, beginning with Jaakov Joseph of Polnoie, *Sefer Toldot Ya'Akov Yosef* (1780).

8. See David B. Siff, "Shifting Ideologies of Orality and Literacy in Their Historical Context: Rebbe Nahhman of Bratslav's Embrace of the Book as a Means for Redemption," *Profftexts* 30 (2010).

9. Yiddish for "a Lithuanian"; this term is used to refer to orthodox Jews to this day. We should mention the third archetypal figure, the Galicianer (Yiddish for "a person from Galicia"), which refers to the Jews

of Galicia who had been annexed to the Austro-Hungarian Empire with the first partition of the Polish-Lithuanian Commonwealth.

10. Shneur Zalman of Lyadi, *Tanya, Ve-Hu, Sefer Likute Amarim* (n.a.: Defus Dov Ber ben Yisrael ve Dov Ber ben Pesach, 1796).

11. In 1798, the Mitnagdim approached the Russian authorities and accused R. Shneur Zalman of sending money to the Ottoman Empire in support of Russia's major enemy. They knew of course that this money was meant to support a Hasidic community living in Tiberias and not the Ottoman Empire. R. Shneur Zalman was able to convince the authorities of this and was released after two months in jail. In 1801, he was accused by the Mitnagdim of being an anarchist. His book *Tanya*, so they argued, expressed his opposition to the empire and put him in the same subversive anarchist category as the Freemasons' Association. R. Shneur Zalman was able to convince the authorities of his innocence again and was released. For more on the first arrest, see Yehosha Mondshein, *Ha-Ma'asar Ha-Rishon* (Israel: Hish-Hafatsat ha-Ma'ayan, 2012).

12. The following account of R. Nachman's travels is based on this episode of his biography, as recounted by his student and scribe R. Nathan. See Nathan Sternhartz, *Shivchei Haran* (Ostroh 1816). I have added Gregorian dates and other relevant historic context related to the Napoleonic campaign. Much work has been done on the significance of R. Nachman's journey to the Holy Land. See, for example, the discussion in Green, *Tormented Master: The Life and Spiritual Quest of Rabbi Nahman of Bratslav*. For a discussion of the textual sources of this journey, see Ada Rapoport-Albert, "Shnei Mekorot Le-Te'ur Nesi'ato Shel Rabi Nachman Mi-Braslav Le-Eretz Yisrael," *Kiryat Sefer* 46 (1971).

13. R. Nachman's experience in the Holy Land and his encounter with the geopolitical struggles in the region certainly endowed his historical awareness with a sense of urgency. Moreover, debates within the Hasidic movement as to whom the better ruler might be for the Jewish community—Alexander I or Napoleon—were a central theme during the years that followed. However, the figure of Napoleon would emerge most notably in R. Nachman's writing only in 1809, with the surrender of the Austro-Hungarian Empire to Napoleon and French forces nearing the borders of his native Podolia. For more on the Hasidic debate, both ideological and pragmatic, over support for Napoleon or Alexander I, see Hillel Levine, "'Should Napoleon Be Victorious': Politics and Spirituality in Early Modern Jewish Messianism," *Jerusalem Studies in Jewish Thought* 16–17 (2001). And, in the context of Chabad Hasidism, see Immanuel Etkes, *Rabbi Shneur Zalman of Liady: The Origins of Chabad Hasidism*, trans. Jeffrey M. Green (Waltham, MA: Brandeis University Press, 2015).

14. For more on this conflict and its seminal role in R. Nachman's thought, see Weiss, *Mehkarim Ba-Hasidut Braslav*. See also Piekarz, *Hasidut Braslav: Perakim Be-Haye Meholeleha Uvi-Khetaveha*.

15. Ilia Lurie, ed., *History of the Jews of Russia*, 3 vols., vol. 2 (Jerusalem: Zalman Shazar Center for Jewish History, 2012), 15.

16. Vitaly Charny, "1804 Russian Set of Laws Concerning Jews," http://www.jewishgen.org/belarus/1804_laws.htm. I have translated as "governorate" the term "gubernia" that appears in Charny's translation of the statute.

17. For more on these processes, see Bartal, *The Jews of Eastern Europe, 1772–1881*.

18. Sternhartz, *Chayey Moharan*, 1:1. It is not entirely clear which "Emperor" is referred to here. While Catherine the Great was the ruler during the partitions that annexed the Kingdom of Poland to the Russian Empire, Paul I acceded soon after and was notably less interested in his mother's modernizing efforts. R. Nathan's intention here is clearly not to offer a historical account of the *"punktin,"* but rather of the context in which R. Nachman's thought and teaching developed.

19. Lurie, *History of the Jews of Russia*, 18. One such delegate was the early Eastern European Maskil Mendel Lefin of Satanów (1749–1826). His involvement with the committee is discussed in Nancy Sinkoff, *Out of the Shtetl Making Jews Modern in the Polish Borderlands* (Providence, RI: Brown Judaic Studies, 2008), 106–12. See also Israel Halpern, *Yehudim VE-Yahadut Be-Mizraḥ Eropah: MehḲArim Be-Toldotehem* (Jerusalem: Hebrew Univeristy Magnes Press, 1968), 345.

20. While the dating of this assembly is in question, its purpose of discussing the tsar's modernizing efforts and their effect on the Jewish community has been convincingly argued for by Rapoport-Albert and others. See Rapoport-Albert, "Hasidism after 1772: Structural Continuity and Change," 120–21, and references therein. (The possibility mentioned by Rapoport-Albert that this meeting actually took place in 1809 does not detract from the fact that Eastern European modernization processes were an important point of reference for R. Nachman [and should be for his readers too]. It just postdates an account of R. Nachman's broader communitywide engagement with these questions to a later period.)

21. It is possible that Mendel Lefin was also present at the 1802/3 meeting in Berdichev. See Abraham Baer Gottlober, *Zikhronot U-Masaot* (Yerushalayim: Mosad Bialik, 1976), 173–78.

22. Sternhartz, *Chayey Moharan*, 1:6.

23. Ofer Dynes has brought to my attention the existence of a partial Yiddish translation of the statute produced in 1804 in Vilna. The purpose and circulation of this document remains to be determined, but it is pos-

sible that such local translations were produced in other governorates as well. Much work remains to be done in understanding the events and processes of this formative period in Eastern European Jewish history. I thank Ofer Dynes for sharing this information with me and look forward to his work on the matter.

24. As we will see later in this study, R. Nachman explicitly addresses policy matters that appear in the statute in some of his teachings as well as addressing them implicitly in some of his tales.

25. Charny, "1804 Russian Set of Laws Jews" (introduction).

26. Dubnow, *History of the Jews in Russia and Poland, from the Earliest Times until the Present Day*, 1 *From the beginning until the death of Alexander I* (1825), X.2.

27. While nationalism is an anachronistic term to employ here, differences in language, region, and religion, as well as in historical affiliations—some of the non-Jewish population was annexed from the Kingdom of Poland, others from the Grand Duchy of Lithuania, and still others from smaller regions—did determine broader group affiliations.

28. Charny, "1804 Russian Set of Laws Concerning Jews," I.1–3.

29. Ibid., I.6.

30. Ibid., I.8.

31. Ibid., I.9.

32. Ibid., II. C. & D. 28.

33. Ibid., III.31.

34. Dubnow, *History of the Jews in Russia and Poland, from the Earliest Times until the Present Day*, 1 *From the beginning until the death of Alexander I* (1825), 343. For more on the significance of alcohol sale licenses (and the Jewish monopoly on the sale of grain alcohol in the Polish-Lithuanian Commonwealth) for the Jewish community during the Council of the Four Lands, see Adam Teller, *Money, Power, and Influence in Eighteenth-Century Lithuania: The Jews on the Radziwill Estates* (Stanford, California: Stanford University Press, 2017).

35. Dubnow, *History of the Jews in Russia and Poland, from the Earliest Times until the Present Day*, 1 *From the beginning until the death of Alexander I* (1825), 346.

36. A notable bureaucrat involved in drafting the statute was Michael Speransky, whose own biography tracks much of the ups and downs of this empirewide process. See Marc Raeff, *Michael Speransky: Statesman of Imperial Russia, 1772–1839* (Hague: M. Nijhoff, 1957).

37. Charny, "1804 Russian Set of Laws Concerning Jews," IV.42.

38. The similarities of "demographic rule" to the colonial administrative system of "indirect rule" are worth mentioning here, though discussion is obviously beyond our present scope. For more on "legal

pluralism" and "indirect rule," see Lauren A. Benton, *Law and Colonial Cultures Legal Regimes in World History, 1400–1900* (Cambridge; New York: Cambridge University Press, 2002); Lauren A. Benton and Richard Jeffrey Ross, eds., *Legal Pluralism and Empires, 1500–1850* (New York: New York University Press, 2013). See also Mahmood Mamdani, *Define and Rule: Native as Political Identity* (Cambridge, MA: Harvard University Press, 2012).

39. This was the case in all types of law, even capital offences. There are rare instances of documented application of capital punishment by the council, in cases of Jews murdering other Jews. For more on the council's functions in Jewish life, see Dubnow, *History of the Jews in Russia and Poland, from the Earliest Times until the Present Day*, 1 *From the beginning until the death of Alexander I* (1825). On the utilization of its mechanisms by the Mitnagdim in their conflict against Hasidim, see *A History of Hasidism*; Wilensky, *Hasidim U-Mitnagdim: Le-Toldot Ha-Pulmus She-Benehem*.

40. What the opposite of "public" was in this context is a question we will see R. Nachman take up in the next chapter.

41. Charny, "1804 Russian Set of Laws Concerning Jews," V.52. The statute does not distinguish between Hasidic leaders and ordained (orthodox) rabbis, referring to all Jewish community leadership as "rabbis."

42. Ibid., V.51.

43. See Dubnow, *History of the Jews in Russia and Poland, from the Earliest Times until the Present Day*, 1 *From the beginning until the death of Alexander I* (1825). In particular ch. 10.

44. Charny, "1804 Russian Set of Laws Concerning Jews," V.53.

45. For more on the implications of this legislation for the conflict, see Wilensky, *Hasidim U-Mitnagdim: Le-Toldot Ha-Pulmus She-Benehem*, 16.

46. For more on the various "phases" of Hasidism, see Dubnow, *A History of Hasidism*.

47. The conflict erupted in full force only in 1815, five years after R. Nachman's death, but he was close to the Maskilim in his region, and his friendship with them was the source of considerable criticism, even from his own disciples. For more on this conflict, see Refa'el Mahler, *Hasidism and the Jewish Enlightenment: Their Confrontation in Galicia and Poland in the First Half of the 19th Century* (Philadelphia: Jewish Publication Society of America, 1985). For the effects of this conflict on the historiography of Hasidism, see Bartal, "The Imprint of Haskalah Literature on the Historiography of Hasidism." For more on R. Nachman's relations with the Maskilim, see Liberman, "R. Nachman Breslaver Und Die Umener Maskilim."

48. Ronald Schechter, *Obstinate Hebrews: Representations of Jews in France, 1715–1815* (Berkeley: University of California Press, 2003), 3. For

a discussion of foreshadowing and the possibility of "backshadowing" in Jewish literary historiography, see Michael Bernstein, *Foregone Conclusions: Against Apocalyptic History* (Berkeley: University of California Press, 1994).

49. Schechter, *Obstinate Hebrews: Representations of Jews in France, 1715–1815*, 3.

50. For a fictional depiction of this moment, see Martin Buber, *Gog and Magog: A Novel*, trans. Ludwig Lewisohn (Syracuse, NY: Syracuse University Press, 1999). For accounts of this difference of opinion, see Paul R. Mendes-Flohr and Jehuda Reinharz, *Jew in the Modern World: Documentary History* (Oxford: Oxford University Press, 1995), 137–38.

51. Quoted in Levine, "'Should Napoleon Be Victorious . . .': Politics and Spirituality in Early Modern Jewish Messianism," 65. For a full account of the ideological and pragmatic motivations behind R. Shneur Zalman of Lyadi's position, see Etkes, *Rabbi Shneur Zalman of Liady: The Origins of Chabad Hasidism*, ch. 9.

52. In the two decades following R. Nachman's death, the Russian Empire rolled back some of the policy decisions presented in the statute. Following the death of Alexander I and the accession of Nicholas I, further changes occurred in the Russian Empire's attitude toward the Jewish population of the Pale. One such example is the clothing decrees, which were not fully enforced until the 1850s. However, R. Nachman does not live to see these processes, so any knowledge we have of the future histories of these decrees and modernization ideologies must be bracketed. Our effort is to understand R. Nachman's response to his moment, in the context of that very same moment. For more on the implementation of the clothing decrees, see Glenn Dynner, "The Garment of Torah: Clothing Decrees and the Warsaw Career of the First Gerer Rebbe," in *Warsaw. The Jewish Metropolis: Essays in Honor of the 75th Birthday of Professor Antony Polonsky*, ed. Glenn Dynner, Francois Guesnet, and Antony Polonsky, Ijs Studies in Judaica (Leiden; Boston: Brill, 2015). For more on the rule of Nicholas I, see Michael Stanislawski, *Tsar Nicholas I and the Jews: The Transformation of Jewish Society in Russia, 1825–1855* (Philadelphia: Jewish Publication Society of America, 1983). For more on the history of the Russian Empire and its Jewish population over the course of the nineteenth century, see Dubnow, *History of the Jews in Russia and Poland, from the Earliest Times until the Present Day*, Vol. 1: *From the beginning until the death of Alexander I* (1825). See also Bartal, *The Jews of Eastern Europe, 1772–1881*, and Lurie, *History of the Jews of Russia*.

53. See Mark, *Kol Sipure Rabi Nahman Mi-Braslav: Ha-Ma'Asiyot, Ha-Sipurim Ha-Sodiyim, Ha-Halomot Veha-Hezyonot*.

54. R. Nachman of Braslav, *Sippurei Maasiyot* (Lemberg, 1815).

Chapter 2

1. Some prominent examples include Dubnow, *History of the Jews in Russia and Poland, from the Earliest Times until the Present Day, 1 From the beginning until the death of Alexander I* (1825); Bartal, *The Jews of Eastern Europe, 1772–1881*; Hundert, *Jews in Poland-Lithuania in the Eighteenth Century a Genealogy of Modernity*; Dynner, *Men of Silk: The Hasidic Conquest of Polish Jewish Society.*

2. R. Nachman of Braslav, *Likkutei Moharan*, vol. 2 (Mohilev, 1811), no. 28.

3. For more on this word and its uses in R. Nachman's texts, see the discussion of translation challenges in the final paragraphs of the introduction to this book and the discussion in note 45 of the introduction.

4. R. Nachman of Braslav, *Likkutei Moharan*, 2, no. 28.

5. See Isadore Twersky, *Introduction to the Code of Maimonides: (Mishneh Torah)* (New Haven: Yale University Press, 2010).

6. See Moses Mendelssohn, *Jerusalem, or, on Religious Power and Judaism*, trans. Allan Arkush (Hanover: Published for Brandeis University Press by University Press of New England, 1983), 102–03.

7. Charny, "1804 Russian Set of Laws Concerning Jews." (Emphasis added.)

8. The tsar-mandated German and/or Polish dress, which served as part of an effort to forcefully modernize the Jews of the Pale of Settlement, became the hallmark of ultra-orthodox Jewish communities everywhere. The clothing that marked public invisibility of confessional difference at the turn of the eighteenth century came to mark its utmost visibility by the midtwentieth century. The irony (if that's what it is) of this transition should not be lost on us.

9. R. Nachman of Braslav, *Likkutei Moharan*, 2, no. 28. Beyond the confusion between Jew and non-Jew, R. Nachman's teaching seems to imply the possibility of confusing between the affiliations of non-Jews as well. There is no presumption of a stable discernable difference between the "several nations," among which the "man of Israel" stands. But this line of questioning is not elaborated in the teaching. In that at the end of the teaching "Jewish difference" is seen as an "advantage" for the "man of Israel," it seems R. Nachman is privileging this difference over the differences that exist between non-Jewish "nations."

10. On the removal of markers of difference from the public sphere, see, for example, Michel Foucault, *History of Madness*, trans. Jean Khalfa (New York: Routledge, 2006). See also *Discipline and Punish: The Birth of the Prison*, 1st American ed. (New York: Pantheon Books, 1977); Jacques

Rancière, *The Politics of Aesthetics: The Distribution of the Sensible* (London; New York: Continuum, 2006).

11. R. Nachman of Braslav, *Likkutei Moharan*, 2, no. 28.

12. Ibid. (Emphasis added.)

13. In this, among other elements, R. Nachman's teaching echoes Mendelssohn's project in *Jerusalem*—arguing for the compatibility of Judaism with the new Enlightenment concept of an emancipated public sphere, as differently interpreted and implemented in Prussia and Russia. For more on Mendelssohn's argument, see the introduction to Mendelssohn, *Jerusalem, or, on Religious Power and Judaism*.

14. Here is the language of the statute: "Beginning on January 1, 1807, no Jew in the big or small villages of the governorates of Astarkhanskaya, Kavakazskaya, Malorossia and Novorossia, nor in the other governorates beginning on January 1, 1808, can keep any leases, taverns, or inns under their own or somebody else's name nor sell their alcohol nor even live there." See Charny, "1804 Russian Set of Laws Concerning Jews," Sec. 3, Article 33.

15. The Hebrew title reads: *Ma'aseh mi-Melech she-Gazar Shmad*—a tale of a king who decreed *shmad* (conversion). The original 1815 edition did not title the stories, but the first line of the tale (cited below) already contains all the allusions mentioned. For dating see Mark, *Kol Sipure Rabi Nahman Mi-Braslav: Ha-Ma'Asiyot, Ha-Sipurim Ha-Sodiyim, Ha-Halomot Veha-Hezyonot*, 228.

16. The Hebrew word "anusim" could be translated as "Marranos," "New Christians" or Conversos. Based on the depiction of this group in the story, their hidden practices of Judaism and concern for repealing the "decree," R. Nachman's use of the term points to Marranism. However, we cannot be sure of R. Nachman's understanding of the differences between these groups. I have thus avoided a determination by leaving the word untranslated or by referring to the minister as a "Marrano." For more on the differences between these groups, see Yirmiyahu Yovel, *The Other Within: The Marranos: Split Identity and Emerging Modernity* (Princeton, N.J.: Princeton University Press, 2009).

17. R. Nachman of Braslav, *Sippurei Maasiyot*, 20b. Unless otherwise indicated, the translations of R. Nachman's texts are my own. I have consulted the fine work of translation done by Marianne Schleicher. While my own rendering is fairly similar to hers, I have maintained differences I believe are significant. I therefore do not make note of every difference between our translations. The reader is invited to consult her work in Marianne Schleicher, *Intertextuality in the Tales of Rabbi Nahman of Bratslav a Close Reading of Sippurey Maasiyot* (Leiden; Boston: Brill, 2007).

18. Among those relevant to our subject matter, see Gershom Gerhard Scholem, *Major Trends in Jewish Mysticism* (New York: Schocken Books, 1961). See also Martin Buber, *Hasidism* (New York: Philosophical Library, 1948); Dan, *Ha-Sipur Ha-Hasidi*.

19. See *Ha-Sipur Ha-Hasidi*.

20. R. Nachman of Braslav, *Sippurei Maasiyot*, 20b.

21. See "Redemption through Sin," in Gershom Gerhard Scholem, *The Messianic Idea in Judaism and Other Essays on Jewish Spirituality* (New York: Schocken Books, 1971), 78–141; *Sabbatai Sevi; the Mystical Messiah, 1626–1676* (Princeton, NJ: Princeton University Press, 1973).

22. That is, unless one believes R. Nachman was himself a Sabbatian. No scholarly argument has been made that he belonged to these movements or interacted with members of these movements. However, influences of Sabbatian and Frankist thought are clearly evident in R. Nachman's writing. His engagement with these movements' theologies and ideologies, on an intellectual and spiritual level, was at times very intense. In fact, he saw himself as continuing the efforts of the *baal shem tov* to redeem the sins of these movements, which in part meant taking account of their views and seriously engaging them. For more on R. Nachman's engagement with Sabbatian and Frankist ideas, see Joseph Weiss, "Torat Ha-Dialektika Ve-Ha-Emuna Le-Rabi Nachman Mi-Braslav" (Hebrew University of Jerusalem, 1951), ch. 3. See also Yehuda Liebes, "R. Nahman of Bratslav's "Hattikkun Hakkelali" and His Attitude towards Sabbatianism," *Zion* 45, no. 3 (1980); Noam Zadoff and Jonathan Meir, "The Empty Space, Sabbateanism and Its Melodies—Joseph Weiss's Reading of Liqqutei Moharan 64," *Kabbalah: Journal for the Study of Jewish Mystical Texts* 15 (2006).

23. R. Nachman of Braslav, *Sippurei Maasiyot*, 21a.

24. Pirkei Avot 3:2.

25. It is worth noting that this text, as so many other canonical Jewish texts, was composed under Roman imperial rule. For more on this context, see Seth Schwartz, *Imperialism and Jewish Society: 200 B.C.E. To 640 C.E.* (Princeton: Princeton University Press, 2009).

26. *Parrhesia* is a Greek word meaning free speech, which comes to represent the space that is open to everyone. It has a long Talmudic history in which it denotes a public sphere. For more on this term in Jewish tradition, see Mordechai Arad, *Mehalel Shabat Be-Farhesya: Munah Talmudi U-Mashma'Uto Ha-Historit* (New York; Yerushalayim: Jewish Theological Seminary, 2009). For more on this term in Western thought, see Michel Foucault, *Fearless Speech* (Los Angeles: Semiotext(e), 2001).

27. R. Nachman of Braslav, *Sippurei Maasiyot*, 20b. The parenthetical material reads: "Tsin'ah (deheinu far borgin) [. . .] parrhesia (deheinu far leit)." R. Nachman vowels the Yiddish word "farborgen" a bit differently, and spells it as two words.

28. Ibid., 21a.
29. Ibid.
30. Ibid.
31. Ibid., 21b.
32. Wiskind-Elper, *Tradition and Fantasy in the Tales of Reb Nahman of Bratslav*, 156.
33. R. Nachman of Braslav, *Sippurei Maasiyot*, 21b.
34. Daniel 2:32.
35. R. Nachman of Braslav, *Sippurei Maasiyot*, 21b.
36. Ibid.
37. This also alludes to the *Urim and Tummim*, the semiprecious stones that adorn the high priest's breastplate in the Bible and that glow in oracular response to Moses's questions (according to Talmudic legend).
38. For more on this, see Yovel, *The Other Within: The Marranos: Split Identity and Emerging Modernity*.
39. R. Nachman of Braslav, *Sippurei Maasiyot*, 22a.
40. Ibid.
41. Ibid.
42. Ibid.
43. Ibid., 22a–22b. R. Nachman calls the zodiac signs "ox and lamb," to fit with the earlier symbols, but he refers, of course, to Taurus and Aries. In Hebrew, *taleh* is the name for Aries.
44. R. Nachman of Nachman of Braslav, *Likkutei Moharan*, vol. 1 (Ostroh1808), 61:3.
45. *Sippurei Maasiyot*, 23a. What this iron rod refers to is not clear. Braslav interpreters see it as an allusion to Psalms 2:9. Arnold Band (and Schleicher follows his interpretation) notes the double meaning of the Hebrew word *shevet*, which means both "rod" and "tribe" and suggests that it is an allusion to the Jews themselves, as an "iron tribe." There is a didactic redundancy in the tale according to this moralistic interpretation, however, since the kings are already walking with the Jews of their kingdom on the path toward the rod.
46. Ibid.
47. Ibid.
48. Ibid.
49. Ibid.
50. R. Nachman of Braslav, *Likkutei Moharan*, 2, no. 28.

Chapter 3

1. The sermon was delivered on October 3–4, 1807, and is published as Teaching I:61 of *Likkutei Moharan*. For the dating of this teaching, see Sternhartz, *Chayey Moharan*, no. 59.

2. R. Nachman of Braslav, *Likkutei Moharan*, 2, no. 28.
3. *Sippurei Maasiyot*, 23a.
4. Ibid., 21b.
5. Ibid., 22b.
6. Ibid., 21b.
7. Ibid., 22b. It should be noted that in both the king's and the wise man's accounts, R. Nachman consistently portrays typical rabbinic and medieval concepts of astronomy. This is reflected in the enumeration of seven planets—a characteristic of pre-Copernican and rabbinic astronomy, in which the sun was included among the planets. It is also reflected in the description of the "courses of the sun," which depicts a geocentric model in which it is the sun that takes its full "course" (or orbit) around the earth over the course of 365 days. For more on early Jewish astronomy, see Robert R. Stieglitz, "The Hebrew Names of the Seven Planets," *Journal of Near Eastern Studies* 40, no. 2 (1981). For more on the history of astronomy in general, see Anton Pannekoek, *A History of Astronomy* (New York: Dover, 1989).
8. R. Nachman uses the rather idiosyncratic Hebrew word *mazri'ach* (להזריח), which stands out among the recurring usages of the word *me'ir* (להאיר) in the description of the planets and their corresponding metals.
9. R. Nachman of Braslav, *Sippurei Maasiyot*, 23a.10; ibid., 22b.
11. R. Nachman of Braslav, *Likkutei Moharan*, 2, no. 28. (Emphasis added.)
12. *Sippurei Maasiyot*, 23a.
13. R. Nachman is citing a line from BT Eruvin 21b, where Ecclesiastes 12:12 is creatively misread. The verse reads: "And furthermore, my son, be admonished: of making many books there is no end; and much study [*lahag*] is a weariness of the flesh." The word *lahag* (study) is misread as *la'ag*, meaning "mockery." The citation of a biblical verse admonishing excessive book publication will soon tie into the theme from Teaching II:28 that I discussed previously.
14. R. Nachman of Braslav, *Likkutei Moharan*, 1, 61:1.
15. Ibid., 61:2.
16. Ibid.
17. Ibid. R. Nachman quotes here from Proverbs 149:20. Another pun exists in the Hebrew plural form of *ketav*, which means both script and writings.
18. Charny, "1804 Russian Set of Laws Concerning Jews."
19. R. Nachman of Braslav, *Likkutei Moharan*, 1, 61:3.
20. Ibid. What R. Nachman identifies as the secret of Jewish wisdom is the knowledge of astrology.
21. Ibid.
22. R. Nachman of Braslav, *Sippurei Maasiyot*, 22b.

23. Ibid., 23a.
24. Ibid.
25. Ibid.
26. R. Nachman of Braslav, *Likkutei Moharan*, 2, 28.

27. The word translated as "your fetishes" is *giluleichem*. There is an alliterative similarity R. Nachman is playing on here between the words *gilulim* (idolatrous fetish) and *gelalim* (feces, droppings).

28. The biblical episode referenced here is that of Moses hitting the rock, for which he was forbidden to enter the promised land. *Meribah* is the name of the water well that emerged from the rock and means literally "argument, quarrel."

29. The Hebrew word for a channel of water is *peleg*. R. Nachman is playing with the alliterative similarity of this word to the Aramaic word for division or disagreement, *plugta*.

30. R. Nachman of Braslav, *Likkutei Moharan*, 1, 61:5.
31. Ibid., 61:6.
32. Ibid.

Chapter 4

1. Band, *Nahman of Bratslav, the Tales*, 31.
2. Roskies, *A Bridge of Longing: The Lost Art of Yiddish Storytelling*, 27.
3. Yehuda Liebes, "The Novelty of Rabi Nahman of Bratslav," *Daat: A Journal of Jewish Philosophy & Kabbalah* 45 (2000): 92.

4. Liebes's insistence on "confining" R. Nachman to a traditionalist Hasidic movement may not reflect the consensus understanding of Hasidism as a rather innovative movement in its early years. However, despite Liebes's over-pronounced conservatism in this matter, the "confines" within which R. Nachman is read by other scholars are akin to the "confines" Liebes would like to demarcate around R. Nachman's own intellectual scope. See, for example, Ada Rapoport-Albert, "'Katnut,' 'Pshitut' Ve-'Eini Yode'a' Shel Rabi Nachman Mi-Braslav," in *Studies in Jewish Religious and Intellectual History*, ed. Siegfried Stein and Raphael Loewe (Institute of Jewish Studies, London and the University of Alabama Press, 1979).

5. Band, *Nahman of Bratslav, the Tales*, xiii.

6. Whether "Jewish mysticism" is a subdiscipline of "Jewish thought" or its own field is not germane to the argument I am making since R. Nachman is only rarely (and not always productively) studied in terms of his "mysticism." Nonetheless, in chapter 6, I will attend to the question of mysticism and Kabbalah more explicitly.

7. See Louis Jacobs, "Hasidism and the Dogma of the Decline of the Generations," in *Hasidism Reappraised*, ed. Ada Rapoport-Albert (London: Littman Library of Jewish Civilization, 1996).

8. See Anidjar, "Literary History and Hebrew Modernity."

9. Pierre Macherey, *The Object of Literature* (Cambridge [England]; New York: Cambridge University Press, 1995), 3–5. On the modern sense of the term "literature," Macherey states: "The moment occurred between 1760, when Lessing began to publish his journal *Briefe die neueste Literature betreffend*, and 1800, which saw the appearance of Mme. de Staël." Ibid., 3, note 9. Here, Macherey is referring to Germaine de Staël, *Politics, Literature, and National Character*, trans. Morroe Berger (New Brunswick, NJ; London: Transaction, 2000).

10. I thank Dan Miron for drawing my attention to the fact that the pervasive resignification of "literature" across several European languages at this time did not pass over the Hebrew language.

11. The roots of these conceptions of innovation are also those from which emerges a prevalent contemporary ideological formation, which animates the slippage between questions of innovation and questions of discipline.

12. Howard Schwartz, "Rabbi Nachman of Bratslav: Forerunner of Modern Jewish Literature," *Judaism* 31, no. 2 (1982).

13. See the debate between Yehuda Liebes, Ada Rapoport-Albert, and Yehoshua Mondshein in *Zion*: Liebes, "R. Nahman of Bratslav's 'Hattikkun Hakkelali' and His Attitude towards Sabbatianism"; Ada Rapoport-Albert, "Concerning Y. Liebes' Article (Zion Xlv, 1980, Pp. 201–245)," ibid., 46, no. 4 (1981); Yehoshua Mondshine, "On 'R. Nahman of Bratzlav's "Hattikun Hakkelali" and His Attitude towards Sabbataianism,'" ibid. 47, no. 2 (1982); Yehuda Liebes, "Tendencies in the Research of Bratslav Hasidism: A Reply to Y. Mondshine," ibid.

14. "The Novelty of Rabi Nahman of Bratslav."

15. See Wiskind-Elper, *Tradition and Fantasy in the Tales of Reb Nahman of Bratslav*, 124–25; Band, *Nahman of Bratslav, the Tales*, 29; Roskies, *A Bridge of Longing: The Lost Art of Yiddish Storytelling*, 27.

16. Arthur Green, "Early Hasidism: Some Old/New Questions," in *Hasidism Reappraised*, ed. A. Rapoport-Albert (London: Littman Library of Jewish Civilization, 1996).

17. Ibid., 443. (Emphasis added.)

18. Jacobs, "Hasidism and the Dogma of the Decline of the Generations," 108. See also Green, "Early Hasidism: Some Old/New Questions."

19. Jacobs, "Hasidism and the Dogma of the Decline of the Generations," 210.

20. The major polemics against the movement in fact *emphasizes* Hasidic innovation. See Wilensky, *Hasidim U-Mitnagdim: Le-Toldot Ha-Pulmus She-Benehem*.

21. Sternhartz, *Chayey Moharan*, 264.

22. Ibid., 392.

23. Ibid., 247. (Emphasis added.)

24. A reticent attitude toward innovation not only was a feature in post-Napoleonic Hasidism but also is a major component in the emergence of ultra-orthodoxy. See Michael Silber, "The Emergence of Ultra-Orthodoxy: The Invention of a Tradition," in *The Uses of Tradition: Jewish Continuity in the Modern Era*, ed. Jack Wertheimer (New York; Cambridge, MA: Jewish Theological Seminary of America, distributed by Harvard University Press, 1992).

25. See Siff, "Shifting Ideologies of Orality and Literacy in Their Historical Context: Rebbe Nahhman of Bratslav's Embrace of the Book as a Means for Redemption."

26. Band, *Nahman of Bratslav, the Tales*, 30.

27. Roskies, *A Bridge of Longing: The Lost Art of Yiddish Storytelling*, 25.

28. Ibid., 27.

29. Wiskind-Elper, *Tradition and Fantasy in the Tales of Reb Nahman of Bratslav*, 5.

30. See Zvi Mark, *The Scroll of Secrets: The Hidden Messianic Vision of R. Nachman of Breslav*, trans. Naftali Moses (Brighton, MA: Academic Studies, 2010). See also Dan, *Ha-Sipur Ha-Hasidi*.

31. R. Yisroel of Rodzin was known to fabulate first-person events as part of his sermons. See Rivka Dvir-Goldberg, *Ha-Tsadik Ha-Hasidi Ve-Armon Ha-Livyatan: 'Iyun Be-Sipure Ma'Asiyot Mi-Pi Tsadikim* (Tel-Aviv: ha-Kibuts ha-meuhad, 2003).

32. R. Nachman of Braslav, *Sippurei Maasiyot*, 2a.

33. Ibid., 2b.

34. Sternhartz, *Chayey Moharan*, no. 5.

35. R. Nachman of Braslav, *Likkutei Moharan*, 1, 21:4. For "free will," R. Nachman uses a phrase that literally means "the power to choose."

36. Ibid.

37. Ibid.

38. See Weiss, *Mehkarim Ba-Hasidut Braslav*, 148–49.

39. Weiss elaborates further on the notion of doubt as paradoxical faith. See ibid., ch. 8.

Chapter 5

1. Nachman-Nathan Rapoport was the Jewish Enlightenment scholar in Uman in whose home R. Nachman lived when he first arrived in Uman in early 1810. The strange symbolism of this Maskil having both the same name as R. Nachman of Braslav and the name of his scribe R. Nathan

Sternhartz did not escape their attention. See Liberman, "R. Nachman Breslaver Und Die Umener Maskilim."

2. Weiss, *Mehkarim Ba-Hasidut Braslav*, 62. On R. Nachman's relations with the Maskilim of his day, see Liberman, "R. Nachman Breslaver Und Die Umener Maskilim." R. Nachman's words are cited in Sternhartz, *Chayey Moharan*, 195.

3. Weiss, *Mehkarim Ba-Hasidut Braslav*, 99.

4. Paul R. Mendes-Flohr, *Divided Passions: Jewish Intellectuals and the Experience of Modernity* (Detroit: Wayne State University Press, 1991), 14.

5. In the past half century, there have been studies that have indicated doubt in this seemingly straightforward characterization of the Jewish Enlightenment project. To the extent that rationalism was recognized as its hallmark by the Hasidic movement, it should be noted that this is, in fact, a noncritical acceptance of the Maskilim's self-presentation on the part of Hasidic thinkers. Furthermore, the characterization of early Maskilim as heretics is as much an indication of the traditionalist mindset of the accusers as it is of any deviance from tradition on the part of the Maskilim. See Lois Dubin, "The Social and Cultural Context: Eighteenth-Century Enlightenment," in *History of Jewish Philosophy*, ed. Daniel H. Frank and Oliver Leaman (London; New York: Routledge, 2007). For more on the Haskalah movement and the conflicts surrounding it, see Mahler, *Hasidism and the Jewish Enlightenment: Their Confrontation in Galicia and Poland in the First Half of the 19th Century*. It is questionable whether the Maskilim reciprocated with a noncritical acceptance of the Hasidim's self-presentation. They did take Hasidism at its word, understanding it as a religious movement. But they also doubted Hasidic claims to be looking out for the Jewish masses. Maskilic literature largely depicts Hasidic leaders, against their own self-representation, as corrupt and exploitative. For a discussion of the Haskalah imprint on the study of Hasidism, see Bartal, "The Imprint of Haskalah Literature on the Historiography of Hasidism."

6. Weiss, *Mehkarim Ba-Hasidut Braslav*, 64–65. "Investigators"—in Hebrew, *mechakrim*—is the term R. Nachman uses for scholars of the Jewish Enlightenment.

7. See ibid. Weiss's work is the most critically astute reading of Braslav ideology to date and an indispensable backdrop to my own argument. However, as I will make clear in the coming pages, the present argument departs from Weiss's in both disciplinary scope and concern for the broader sociopolitical implications of Teaching I:64.

8. In R. Nachman of Braslav, *Likkutei Moharan*, 1.

9. George B. de Huszar, ed. *The Intellectuals: A Controversial Portrait* (Glencoe, IL: Free Press, 1960), 8.

10. Staël, *Politics, Literature, and National Character*.

11. For the French context, see Alexis de Tocqueville, *The Old Regime and the French Revolution* (Garden City, NY: Doubleday, 1955). For the British context, see Raymond Williams, *Culture and Society, 1780–1950* (New York: Columbia University Press, 1958). For a discussion of the extent to which politics and letters blended in this process, see Sophia Rosenfeld, "Writing the History of Censorship in the Age of Enlightenment," in *Postmodernism and the Enlightenment: New Perspectives in Eighteenth-Century French Intellectual History*, ed. Daniel Gordon (New York: Routledge, 2001). Huszar's edited volume offers a comprehensive view of the political role of eighteenth- and early nineteenth-century intellectuals in the United States and Russia. See Huszar, *The Intellectuals: A Controversial Portrait*.

12. See *The Intellectuals: A Controversial Portrait*, 3.

13. Ibid., 8.

14. On religious strands in the French intellectual thought of the time, see Albert Salomon, "The Messianic Bohemians," in *The Intellectuals: A Controversial Portrait*, ed. George B. de Huszar (Glencoe, IL: Free Press, 1960); in contemporary Russian intellectual thought, see Hugh Seton-Watson, "The Russian Intellectuals," ibid.; in the later Russian intellectual context, see Sydney Hook, "Communism and the Intellectual," ibid. On Mendelssohn, see Allan Arkush, *Moses Mendelssohn and the Enlightenment* (Albany: State University of New York Press, 1994).

15. In fact, much of the Maskilic literature against the Hasidic movement satirizes the *zadik* to the point of presenting him as the very antithesis of the modern intellectual Maskil. For more on the bias of early documentations of Hasidism see Bartal, "The Imprint of Haskalah Literature on the Historiography of Hasidism." For more on Maskilic satire against Hasidism, see Jonatan Meir, *Imagined Hasidism: The Anti-Hasidic Writings of Joseph Perl* (Yerushalayim: Mosad Bialik, 2013).

16. Such invocations are constitutive of "the intellectual" in definitions by figures ranging from Julian Benda and Antonio Gramsci to Edward Said and Paul Mendes-Flohr. See Julien Benda, *The Treason of the Intellectuals (La Trahison Des Clercs)* (New York: Norton, 1969); Antonio Gramsci, *A Gramsci Reader: Selected Writings, 1916–1935* (New York: New York University Press, 2000); Edward W. Said, *Representations of the Intellectual: The 1993 Reith Lectures* (New York: Pantheon Books, 1994); Mendes-Flohr, *Divided Passions: Jewish Intellectuals and the Experience of Modernity*.

17. See, for example, Thorstein Veblen, "The Intellectual Pre-Eminence of Jews in Modern Europe," *Political Science Quarterly* 34, no. 1 (March 1919).

18. Interesting push-backs against this are the Marranos of Spain and Portugal. Some have identified in these early examples the origins of the same in-between position we are discussing. See Yovel, *The Other Within: The Marranos: Split Identity and Emerging Modernity*.

19. Mendes-Flohr, *Divided Passions: Jewish Intellectuals and the Experience of Modernity*, 15.

20. R. Nachman of Braslav, *Likkutei Moharan*, 1, 64:5. R. Nachman is referencing Babylonian Talmud, Tractate Hagiga 15.

21. Antonio Gramsci, "The Intellectuals," in *Selections from the Prison Notebooks of Antonio Gramsci* (New York: International, 1971), 8.

22. Caplan, *How Strange the Change Language, Temporality, and Narrative Form in Peripheral Modernisms*.

23. Gramsci, "The Intellectuals," 10. Gramsci goes on to distinguish between urban and rural intellectuals. However, the towns and shtetls in which R. Nachman and the Maskilim operated do not fall neatly into this largely postindustrialization dichotomy.

24. Caplan, *How Strange the Change Language, Temporality, and Narrative Form in Peripheral Modernisms*, 47.

25. Ibid., 275, ff. 52.

26. Prime examples of such institutional figures follow a generation later. Joseph Perl, for example, a staunch critic of Hasidism, was employed by the Russian imperial bureaucracy as a censor overseeing the publication of Jewish books. For more on Perl, see Meir, *Imagined Hasidism: The Anti-Hasidic Writings of Joseph Perl*. See also the introduction to Dov Taylor, ed., *Joseph Perl's Revealer of Secrets: The First Hebrew Novel* (Boulder, Colo: Westview Press, 1997).

27. Gramsci, "The Intellectuals," 8.

28. See Weiss, *Mehkarim Ba-Hasidut Braslav*, ch. 8; Zadoff and Meir, "The Empty Space, Sabbateanism and Its Melodies—Joseph Weiss' Reading of Liqqutei Moharan 64." Other readings of Teaching I:64 include: Zvi Mark, *Mysticism and Madness: The Religious Thought of Rabbi Nachman of Bratslav* (London; New York; [Jerusalem]: Continuum; Shalom Hartman Institute, 2009), ch. 8; Magid, "Through the Void: The Absence of God in R. Nahman of Bratzlav's 'Likkutei Moharan.'"

29. The investigator is a character largely ignored by previous readings. I do not see this teaching as describing the purely experiential aspect of religious faith (be it mystical, as in Mark, *Mysticism and Madness: The Religious Thought of Rabbi Nachman of Bratslav* or existential as in Magid, "Through the Void: The Absence of God in R. Nahman of Bratzlav's 'Likkutei Moharan'").

30. For R. Nachman's disciples and readers of the time, this brief reference to familiar themes and Kabbalistic ideas would have been a summary, meant only as an exposition to his subsequent elaboration on the theme. To the interested reader for whom these brief passages are anything but a "recap," I would suggest following up on the references in the following footnotes, especially Scholem, *Major Trends in Jewish*

Mysticism and Gershom Scholem, *On the Kabbalah and Its Symbolism* (New York: Schocken Books, 1965).

31. Referred to as *Tzimtzum* in Hebrew.

32. Referred to as *Chalal HaPanui* in Hebrew.

33. R. Nachman of Braslav, *Likkutei Moharan*, 1, 64:1. My additions for purposes of clarification will be marked with brackets.

34. *Etz HaChaim* is the major book of Lurianic Kabbalah. It contains the teachings of R. Luria collected by his student R. Chaim Vittal in Safed in the early 1570s.

35. This implication of Lurianic Kabbalah is the source of the classical (yet simplistic) opposition between immanence and transcendence in Kabbalah. The former paradigmatically expressed in the *Zohar's* system of God's ten emanations, and the latter expressed in the Lurianic idea of God's withdrawal. For further discussion of this, as well as accounts of the *Zohar* and Luria in Kabbalah, see Scholem, *Major Trends in Jewish Mysticism*; Moshe Idel, *Kabbalah New Perspectives* (New Haven: Yale University Press, 1988).

36. The *baal shem tov*, "founder" of Hasidism c. 1740, made this verse from Isaiah [6:3] an integral part of his innovative teaching.

37. See Weiss, *Mehkarim Ba-Hasidut Braslav*, ch. 6.

38. The principle of logic that stipulates that if *A* is true, then its opposite (*not-A*) cannot also be true.

39. R. Nachman of Braslav, *Likkutei Moharan*, 1, 64:1.

40. R. Nachman describes the futility of rational investigation in *Likkutei Moharan*, 2, 7:8. He argues that rational investigation proposes to answer questions, only to eventually fortify the question by providing the very logical conditions that are to be doubted in posing the question in the future.

41. *Likkutei Moharan*, 1, 64:2.

42. Zadoff and Meir, "The Empty Space, Sabbateanism and Its Melodies—Joseph Weiss' Reading of Liqqutei Moharan 64," 221.

43. *Ethics of the Fathers*, 2:17.

44. Weiss, *Mehkarim Ba-Hasidut Braslav*, 129.

45. R. Nachman of Braslav, *Likkutei Moharan*, 1, 64:2.

46. Zadoff and Meir, "The Empty Space, Sabbateanism and Its Melodies—Joseph Weiss' Reading of Liqqutei Moharan 64," 221.

47. Weiss further maps this distinction onto the Lurianic distinction between "shells" and "sparks" (*klipot* and *nitzotzot*) within the created world, but this is beyond our scope.

48. Weiss is not the only one to have focused on the experience of faith and doubt. Green and Magid, in their respective readings of Teaching I:64, also proceed from the epistemological to the existential question. See

Green, *Tormented Master: The Life and Spiritual Quest of Rabbi Nahman of Bratslav*; Magid, "Through the Void: The Absence of God in R. Nahman of Bratzlav's 'Likkutei Moharan.'" None of the abovementioned readers pays sufficient attention to the character of the "investigator," the Jewish Enlightenment "heretic" whom R. Nachman is centrally concerned with "recuperating" in this teaching. R. Nachman's preoccupation with "recuperating" these "heretics" is what launches his speculation into the nature of the Vacant Space in the first place. The social questions this concern opens are a focus of my reading here.

49. R. Nachman of Braslav, *Likkutei Moharan*, 1, 64:2.

50. Ibid.

51. Weiss, *Mehkarim Ba-Hasidut Braslav*, 133. By "does not hold true for itself," Weiss means to insert the law of noncontradiction as the "A" of the law. That is, within the epistemology of the Vacant Space, the two statements (1) "A and not-A *cannot* both be true" and (2) "A and not-A *can* both be true," *can* both be true.

52. Magid, "Associative Midrash: Reflections on a Hermeneutical Theory in Rabbi Nachman of Braslav's Likkutei Moharan," 18.

53. See Liberman, "R. Nachman Breslaver Und Die Umener Maskilim."

54. It should be noted that the "heresy" R. Nachman associates with the Maskilim of his day is a projection of his own traditionalist position as much as it is a description of their ideology. Most of the Eastern European Jewish Enlightenment figures were fairly traditional in their religious practices. The "surprise" is not so much that they attended Rosh Hashana prayers, but that they did so in a Hasidic setting. Their persistent depiction as "heretics" speaks as much to R. Nachman's self-perception as a "religious" individual. References to this from R. Nathan's biography of R. Nachman (see Sternhartz, *Chayey Moharan*) and later sources (see Avraham Hazan, *Sefer Sippurim Nifla'im* [Jerusalem: H. Zukerman, 1935]) have been collected in Liberman, "R. Nachman Breslaver Und Die Umener Maskilim."

55. "R. Nachman Breslaver Und Die Umener Maskilim," 208. Hirsch Ber Hurwitz (1785–1857) was a young Maskil in Uman and one of the first in Eastern Europe. In 1825, he moved to England, converted to Christianity, and changed his name to Herman Hedwig Bernard. He served as a professor of Oriental languages in Cambridge until his death. See ibid., 211 cf. 37, appendix 4 (18–19).

56. I am alluding to Dan Miron's conceptualization in Dan Miron, *From Continuity to Contiguity toward a New Jewish Literary Thinking* (Stanford, CA: Stanford University Press, 2010).

57. Bruno Bosteels, "Borges as Antiphilosopher," *Vanderbilt e-journal of Luso-Hispanic studies* 3 (2006).

58. Weiss, *Mehkarim Ba-Hasidut Braslav*, 129.

59. Bosteels, "Borges as Antiphilosopher," 1.

60. Ibid., 2.

61. Ibid.

62. The second "clue," that of the historical and cultural contingency of knowledge, is expressed by R. Nachman in other teachings, which I will not discuss here. See, for example, Braslav, *Likkutei Moharan*, 1, 29.

63. This is an allusion to the *Sefer Yetzirah*, one of the earliest Jewish mystical texts, which begins by recounting that "God created the Universe in thirty-two mysterious paths of wisdom [. . .] Ten *sefirot* are its firmament, and twenty-two letters its foundation" (my paraphrasing). *Sefirot* refers here both to the ten basic mathematical digits and to the ten emanations of God. For more on *Sefer Yetzirah*, see Scholem, *Major Trends in Jewish Mysticism*.

64. R. Nachman of Braslav, *Likkutei Moharan*, 1, 64:3.

65. Ibid.

66. Bosteels, "Borges as Antiphilosopher," 4.

67. R. Nachman refers here to scholars of Jewish tradition, but this term could be understood more broadly as well.

68. R. Nachman of Braslav, *Likkutei Moharan*, 1, 64:4.

69. Bosteels, "Borges as Antiphilosopher," 6.

70. In paraphrase, the Hebrew reads "Sing ye praises *maskil*," which is also the term for a Jewish Enlightenment scholar.

71. R. Nachman of Braslav, *Likkutei Moharan*, 1, 64:5.

72. The place of music in R. Nachman's thought is a fascinating topic but beyond the scope of our present concerns. The interested reader may find the following references helpful. In R. Nachman's teachings, see *Likkutei Moharan*, 1, 3, 65, 282; Braslav, *Likkutei Moharan*, 2, 63. In research, see Weiss, *Mehkarim Ba-Hasidut Braslav*, ch. 5; Mark, *Mysticism and Madness: The Religious Thought of Rabbi Nachman of Bratslav*, ch. 4; Magid, "Through the Void: The Absence of God in R. Nahman of Bratzlav's 'Likkutei Moharan.'" A fascinating and wonderfully insightful discussion of the theme can be found in Smith, *Tuning the Soul: Music as a Spiritual Process in the Teachings of Rabbi Nahman of Bratzlav*.

73. R. Nachman of Braslav, *Likkutei Moharan*, 1, 64:5.

74. Ibid.

75. Ibid.

76. In line with the emergent Hasidic doctrine of Zadikism, R. Nachman develops in his teachings an entire hierarchy of *zadiks*. There is "the

true *zadik*" who stands in opposition to "the false *zadiks*," and there is "the *zadik* of the generation" who stands above all other *zadiks* in terms of charisma and spiritual ability. This *"zadik* of the generation" is *bechina* of Moses and also of the Messiah. There is broad consensus within the scholarship cited throughout this study that these figures R. Nachman develops are intended to refer to himself and speak to his self-perceived position in the Hasidic movement (and perhaps in the world). In the next chapter, we will ask about R. Nachman's self-perceived messianic role and whether it should matter to a reader of literature. Further references to this issue can be found in the notes to chapter 6.

77. Mendes-Flohr, *Divided Passions: Jewish Intellectuals and the Experience of Modernity*, 25.

Chapter 6

1. The most significant readers of Braslav literature all agree on this point. See Band, *Nahman of Bratslav, the Tales*; Dan, *Ha-Sipur Ha-Hasidi*; Yoav Elstein, *Pa'Ame Bat Melekh: Hikre Tokhen Ve-Tsurah Be-Sipuro Ha-Rishon Shel R. Nahman Mi-Braslav* (Ramat-Gan: Bar-Ilan University, 1984); Green, *Tormented Master: The Life and Spiritual Quest of Rabbi Nahman of Bratslav*; Zvi Mark, *Megilat Setarim: He-Hazon Ha-Meshihi Ha-Sodi Shel R. Nahman Mi-Braslav* (Ramat-Gan: Bar-Ilan University, 2006); Piekarz, *Hasidut Braslav: Perakim Be-Haye Meholeleha Uvi-Khetaveha*. Caplan, "Watch the Throne: Allegory, Kingship and Trauerspiel in the Stories of Der Nister and Reb Nakhman."

2. The possibility that R. Nachman's tales are not fictional but rather allegorical references to very present metaphysical realities has been raised by many of the readers already referenced. Not being a mystic, my own access to this (somewhat oxymoronic) "metaphysical reality" is rather limited. I suspect the same is true of the readers I have mentioned as well. For more on this point, see Yitzhak Lewis, "Revealing and Concealing as Literary Devices in the Tales of Rabbi Nachman, or, the Case of the Missing Ending" (MA Thesis, Columbia University, 2010).

3. Band, *Nahman of Bratslav, the Tales*, 30.

4. See Schwartz, "Rabbi Nachman of Bratslav: Forerunner of Modern Jewish Literature."

5. Band, *Nahman of Bratslav, the Tales*, 29.

6. See Buber, *The Tales of Rabbi Nachman*.

7. See Eliezer Malkiel, *Hokhmah U-Temimut: Perush Le-Khamah Torot Ve-Sipurim Shel Rabi Nahman Mi-Breslav* (Tel-Aviv: Yedi'ot aharonot: Sifre hemed, 2005). See also Mark, *Mysticism and Madness: The Religious Thought of Rabbi Nachman of Bratslav*. For example, Mark's reading of the sixth tale

(ch. 12), which we will read later as well, focuses almost exclusively on its folkloric exemplification of the concept of negative theology.

8. See Green, *Tormented Master: The Life and Spiritual Quest of Rabbi Nahman of Bratslav*.

9. See Yoav Elstein, *Maaseh Hoshev: Iyunim Ba-Sipur Ha-Hasidi* (Tel Aviv: Eked, 1983); Dan, *Ha-Sipur Ha-Hasidi*.

10. See Henie Haidenberg and Michal Oron, *Me-'Olamo Ha-Misti Shel R. Nahman Mi-Braslav/: 'Iyunim Be-Shishah Mi-Sipure Ha-Ma'Asiyot Shel R. Nahman Mi-Braslav* (Tel-Aviv: Papirus, 1986).

11. See Dan, "Rabbi Nahman's Third Beggar"; Arnold J. Band, "The Function of the Enigmatic in Two Hasidic Tales," in *Studies in Jewish Mysticism: Proceedings of Regional Conferences Held at the University of California, Los Angeles, and Mcgill University in April, 1978*, ed. Joseph Dan and Talmage Frank (Cambridge, MA: Association for Jewish Studies, 1982).

12. Among those who discuss this question are Dan, *Ha-Sipur Ha-Hasidi*; Band, *Nahman of Bratslav, the Tales*; Elstein, *Maaseh Hoshev: Iyunim Ba-Sipur Ha-Hasidi*; Green, *Tormented Master: The Life and Spiritual Quest of Rabbi Nahman of Bratslav*; Roskies, *A Bridge of Longing: The Lost Art of Yiddish Storytelling*.

13. The Greek *allegoría*, "to speak otherwise," and *symbolon*, "to put together," imply opposite orientations in the production of meaning. The former separates the meaning from the text that "speaks otherwise" than the words it presents. The latter combines the meaning and the text into one object. Perhaps the most influential and insightful theorization of the tense relation between symbol and allegory belongs to Walter Benjamin. See Walter Benjamin, *The Origin of German Tragic Drama*, trans. John Osborne (London; New York: Verso, 2003). For an intellectual history of allegory, see Theresa M. Kelley, *Reinventing Allegory* (Cambridge: Cambridge University Press, 1997). For a "classic" and comprehensive study of the symbol, see Tzvetan Todorov, *Theories of the Symbol*, trans. Catherine Porter (Ithaca, NY: Cornell University Press, 1984).

14. Arguably, the two most influential literary theorists of the twentieth century to discuss these terms were Walter Benjamin and Paul de Man. See Benjamin, *The Origin of German Tragic Drama*; Paul De Man, *Allegories of Reading: Figural Language in Rousseau, Nietzsche, Rilke, and Proust* (New Haven: Yale University Press, 1979); *The Rhetoric of Romanticism* (New York: Columbia University Press, 1984).

15. The correspondence between them has been published in Walter Benjamin and Gershom Scholem, *The Correspondence of Walter Benjamin and Gershom Scholem, 1932–1940* (Cambridge, MA: Harvard University Press, 1992). Their thought has been studied comparatively in Eric Jacobson, *Metaphysics of the Profane: The Political Theology of Walter Benjamin and Gershom Scholem* (New York: Columbia University Press, 2003).

16. For an example, see Elstein, *Maaseh Hoshev: Iyunim Ba-Sipur Ha-Hasidi*, ch. 5. Such allegorical readings are mostly concerned with Zoharic and Lurianic Kabbalah. Idel's critique of the narrow focus on these Kabbalistic traditions in the study of the Hasidic movement is worth mentioning in this context. See Moshe Idel, *Messianic Mystics* (New Haven: Yale University Press, 1998).

17. See Elstein, *Maaseh Hoshev: Iyunim Ba-Sipur Ha-Hasidi*, ch. 6.

18. See Dan, *Ha-Sipur Ha-Hasidi*, 141. I will discuss this example in more detail in the following part of the book.

19. See De Man, *Allegories of Reading: Figural Language in Rousseau, Nietzsche, Rilke, and Proust*.

20. Walter Benjamin, *The Work of Art in the Age of Its Technological Reproducibility, and Other Writings on Media*, trans. Michael W. Jennings (Cambridge, MA: Belknap Press of Harvard University Press, 2008), 175.

21. Ibid. Benjamin's discussion of allegory and symbol is extremely rich, and I cannot do it justice in the scope of this discussion. However, it illuminates the dialectical aspects within allegorical reference as well as between allegory and symbol, which I will return to later in the book.

22. Benjamin, *The Work of Art in the Age of Its Technological Reproducibility*, 175.

23. Weiss, *Mehkarim Ba-Hasidut Braslav*, 152.

24. In his reading of the ninth and eleventh tales, Green proposes that R. Nachman is both the prince *and* the pauper, the wise man *and* the simple man. Green, *Tormented Master: The Life and Spiritual Quest of Rabbi Nahman of Bratslav*, 347.

25. Benjamin, *The Origin of German Tragic Drama*, 160.

26. Green, *Tormented Master: The Life and Spiritual Quest of Rabbi Nahman of Bratslav*, 353.

27. Benjamin, *The Origin of German Tragic Drama*, 160.

28. Roskies, *A Bridge of Longing: The Lost Art of Yiddish Storytelling*, 27. Less explored is the connection between romanticism and R. Nachman's critique of rationalism.

29. However, as with any dialectical relationship, they do contain some tension, which is interestingly exhibited in a debate between Piekarz and Green. See Piekarz, *Hasidut Braslav: Perakim Be-Haye Meholeleha Uvi-Khetaveha*, ch. 9; Arthur Green, "Le'bikorto Shel M. Piekarz Le'sifri 'Ba'al Ha'yissurim,'" *Tarbitz* 51 (1982).

30. See Scholem's discussion of these two modes in Scholem, *Major Trends in Jewish Mysticism*, 25–32. See also Paul Mendes-Flohr, *Gershom Scholem: The Man and His Work* (Albany; Jerusalem: State University of New York Press; Israel Academy of Sciences and Humanities, 1994), 3–6.

31. See Walter Benjamin, *The Origin of German Tragic Drama* (London: NLB, 1977).

32. Scholem never published on R. Nachman, but the Scholem Archives at the Israeli National Library do contain his extensive personal collection of Braslav material. I thank Dr. Zvi Leshem, head librarian of the Scholem Archives, for drawing my attention to this unstudied collection.

33. Weiss, *Mehkarim Ba-Hasidut Braslav*, 168.

34. Zvi Mark picks up on this line of interpretation in his *Hitgalut Ve-Tikun: Bi-Khetavav Ha-Geluyim Veha-Sodiyim Shel R. Nahman Mi-Breslav* (Yerushalayim: Magnes Press, Hebrew University, 2011).

35. Dan, *Ha-Sipur Ha-Hasidi*, 138.

36. Although this suggestion integrates both the allegorical and the symbolic frameworks, the exclusivity implied by the allegorical identification of "materials" as Kabbalistic "symbols" pulls Dan's reading of the tales strongly toward allegorical interpretation. This is apparent in his reading of the first tale, which I will soon discuss in more detail.

37. Caplan, "Watch the Throne: Allegory, Kingship and Trauerspiel in the Stories of Der Nister and Reb Nakhman."

38. Ibid., 97.

39. Ibid., 99.

40. Weiss, *Mehkarim Ba-Hasidut Braslav*, 168.

41. De Man, *Allegories of Reading: Figural Language in Rousseau, Nietzsche, Rilke, and Proust*, 173.

42. Caplan, "Watch the Throne: Allegory, Kingship and Trauerspiel in the Stories of Der Nister and Reb Nakhman," 104.

43. R. Nachman's inability to finish the first tale (allegorically a tale of redemption) so long as redemption had not occurred implies precisely this commitment to an expression of Kabbalistic convention and will be discussed shortly.

44. In the case of the first tale, for example, Dan's assumption that knowing the allegorical referent of a particular character will unlock the meaning of the entire tale presumes the emergence of meaning from the recognition of individual references.

45. See the introduction in Green, *Tormented Master: The Life and Spiritual Quest of Rabbi Nahman of Bratslav*, particularly the discussion of the source material relevant to a psychobiography of R. Nachman.

46. Ibid., 7.

47. Ibid., 9–14.

48. For the most comprehensive among these textual studies of R. Nachman's tales, see Schleicher, *Intertextuality in the Tales of Rabbi Nahman of Bratslav a Close Reading of Sippurey Maasiyot*.

49. This is as true of the earliest academic research into the tales of R. Nachman as it is of the most contemporary studies. See Dan, *Ha-Sipur*

Ha-Hasidi; Elstein, *Maaseh Hoshev: Iyunim Ba-Sipur Ha-Hasidi*; Schleicher, *Intertextuality in the Tales of Rabbi Nahman of Bratslav a Close Reading of Sippurey Maasiyot.*

50. *Intertextuality in the Tales of Rabbi Nahman of Bratslav: A Close Reading of Sippurey Maasiyot.*

51. Ibid., 1.

52. Ibid., 2. (Emphasis added.)

53. R. Nachman is not the only one who maintains such a reference. The narratives surrounding the life of Shabtai Zvi and the *baal shem tov* do so as well. See Dan, *Ha-Sipur Ha-Hasidi*, ch. 1.

54. See Dan, *Ha-Sipur Ha-Hasidi*, ch. 1. Dan follows the lead of Scholem here, as do all other readers who find the end "missing." See Scholem, *Major Trends in Jewish Mysticism*, esp. lecture 7; Scholem, *The Messianic Idea in Judaism and Other Essays on Jewish Spirituality.*

55. It was not only R. Nachman who was branded "Kabbalistic." An interest in the "Kabbalistic" nature of stories by writers such as Jorge Luis Borges and Franz Kafka also gained popularity in the early 1970s. On Borges, see Jaime Alazraki, "Borges and the Kabbalah," *TriQuarterly* 25 (1972); Saúl Sosnowski, *Borges Y La Cábala: La Búsqueda Del Verbo* (Buenos Aires: Ed. Hispamérica, 1976). For a critique of "Kabbalistic" readings of Borges, see Yitzhak Lewis, "Writing the Margin: Rabbi Nachman of Braslav, Jorges Luis Borges and the Question of Jewish Writing" (Doctoral Dissertation, Columbia University, 2016). On Kafka, see David Biale, "Gershom Scholem's Ten Unhistorical Aphorisms on Kabbalah: Text and Commentary," *Modern Judaism* 5, no. 1 (1985); Karl-Erich, Grözinger, *Kafka and Kabbalah*, trans. Susan Hecker Ray (New York: Continuum, 1994). For a critique of this "Kabbalistic" reading of Kafka, see Moshe Idel, "Hieroglyphs, Keys, Enigmas: On G. G. Scholem's Vision of Kabbalah: Between Franz Molitor and Franz Kafka," in *Arche Noah: Die Idee Der "Kultur" Im Deutsch-Jüdischen Diskurs*, ed. Bernhard Greiner and Christoph Schmidt (Freiburg: Rombach Verlag, 2002).

56. There are other adjectives that have been discussed in relation to R. Nachman's stories: "Hebrew" and "Yiddish," "printed," but none of these is as prominent as "Kabbalistic," and none implies a methodological framework the way the latter does. For a discussion of the influence of print technology on Braslav ideology, see Siff, "Shifting Ideologies of Orality and Literacy in Their Historical Context: Rebbe Nahhman of Bratslav's Embrace of the Book as a Means for Redemption."

57. See Green, *Tormented Master: The Life and Spiritual Quest of Rabbi Nahman of Bratslav*, ch. 6 and Excursus II.

58. Dan, "Rabbi Nahman's Third Beggar," 41–42.

59. Band, *Nahman of Bratslav, the Tales*, xvii. (Emphasis added.)

60. This is evident in the references provided and the assumptions made about the textuality and canonicity of "the Kabbalah."

61. Both of whom, it is important to note, mark a departure from Scholem's view of "the Kabbalah." This debate does not take place directly between Huss and Wolfson. I have constructed it out of their respective writings to illustrate my point about the limitations of the adjective "Kabbalistic" in the context of R. Nachman's tales.

62. Elliot Wolfson, *Through a Speculum That Shines: Vision and Imagination in Medieval Jewish Mysticism* (Princeton, NJ: Princeton University Press, 1994), 52.

63. Ibid., 55.

64. Boaz Huss, "The Mystification of the Kabbalah and the Myth of Jewish Mysticism," *Pe'amim*, no. 110 (2007): 13. See also "Contemporary Kabbalah and Its Challenge to the Academic Study of Jewish Mysticism," in *Kabbalah and Contemporary Spiritual Revival*, ed. Boaz Huss, the Goldstein-Goren Library of Jewish Thought (Beer-Sheva: Ben-Gurion University of the Negev, 2011).

65. For a critique of "the Kabbalah" from a perspective closer to literary studies, see Gil Anidjar's discussion of the rhetorical construction of the field of Jewish mysticism and Kabbalah—and most centrally Scholem's role in it—in Gil Anidjar, *"Our Place in Al-Andalus": Kabbalah, Philosophy, Literature in Arab Jewish Letters* (Stanford, CA: Stanford University Press, 2002), esp. ch. 3. See also "Jewish Mysticism Alterable and Unalterable: On *Orient*ing Kabbalah Studies and the 'Zohar of Christian Spain,'" *Jewish Social Studies* 3, no. 1 (1996).

66. Even Zvi Mark, who argues that R. Nachman *had* ecstatic mystical experiences—and documented them (albeit esoterically) in his writings—interestingly shies away from the most canonical tales in his discussion. See Mark, *Hitgalut Ve-Tikun: Bi-Khetavav Ha-Geluyim Veha-Sodiyim Shel R. Nahman Mi-Breslav*.

67. Huss, "The Mystification of the Kabbalah and the Myth of Jewish Mysticism," 13. See also "Contemporary Kabbalah and Its Challenge to the Academic Study of Jewish Mysticism."

68. Such as the *Zohar* and *Etz HaChayim* (the major work of the Lurianic school).

69. See Huss, "The Mystification of the Kabbalah and the Myth of Jewish Mysticism."

70. King criticizes both the "implicit monotheism" of this understanding of mysticism and its privileging of the category of experience. See Richard King, *Orientalism and Religion: Postcolonial Theory, India and "the Mystic East"* (London; New York: Routledge, 1999), 8.

71. See Huss, "The Mystification of the Kabbalah and the Myth of Jewish Mysticism." It is important to note that, while claiming there *is* such a coherent object as Jewish mysticism, Scholem too recognizes the contingency of the phenomena he studies. But he attributes this contingency to differences between "religious systems," thus keeping the discussion squarely within the study of religion rather than the sociohistorical and political contexts Huss is promoting in the study of Kabbalah. See Scholem, *Major Trends in Jewish Mysticism*, 15–18. For a broader critique of the category of "religion" as an equally discursively produced object, see Talal Asad, *Genealogies of Religion: Discipline and Reasons of Power in Christianity and Islam* (Baltimore: Johns Hopkins University Press, 1993). For a critique of assumptions underlying "comparative religion," see Tomoko Masuzawa, *The Invention of World Religions: Or, How European Universalism Was Preserved in the Language of Pluralism* (Chicago: University of Chicago Press, 2007).

72. Huss, "The Mystification of the Kabbalah and the Myth of Jewish Mysticism," 23. (Emphasis added.) For more on the relation between Scholem's conception of Kabbalah and his political thought, see David Biale, *Gershom Scholem: Kabbalah and Counter-History* (Cambridge, MA: Harvard University Press, 1979).

73. For a discussion of the constitutive role of this break, see Anidjar, "Literary History and Hebrew Modernity."

74. I am, of course, drawing upon Dan Miron's recent suggestion to think beyond "continuity" as the organizing (or disrupting) principle of the object that is "Jewish literature." See Miron, *From Continuity to Contiguity toward a New Jewish Literary Thinking*.

75. Buber, *The Tales of Rabbi Nachman*, 3.

76. Don Seeman and Shaul Magid, "Mystical Poetics: The Jewish Mystical Text as Literature," *Prooftexts* 29, no. 3 (2009): 317.

77. "The former is largely a question about how (and to what extent) models that have been developed for the study of literature might be applied to the specialized texts of Jewish mysticism; the latter asks, in addition, how literary and other features of such texts relate to culture and the phenomenology of religion" (ibid.).

78. Ibid., 317–18, 20.

79. See Macherey, *The Object of Literature*. Likewise, Gil Anidjar has discussed the separations of "Muslim from Christian Spain, Jews from Arabs, Kabbalah from literature, literature from philosophy, and text from context" in the study of Arab Jewish letters (Anidjar, *"Our Place in Al-Andalus": Kabbalah, Philosophy, Literature in Arab Jewish Letters*, 6). The moments I am discussing here form, in a sense, later links in a chain of discursive separations that include: (1) the turn of the eighteenth cen-

tury—the moment these discourses fashion *as* a break, and themselves as having emerged *from*—and (2) the midtwentieth century—the moment these discourses are cemented into the discrete field of Jewish mysticism.

80. Said, *Beginnings: Intention and Method*, xiv. Here, Said refers to Raymond Williams, *Writing in Society* (London: Verso, 1983).

81. Dan, *Ha-Sipur Ha-Hasidi*, 137.

82. Ibid.

Chapter 7

1. Said, *Beginnings: Intention and Method*, 59.
2. Ibid., xvii.
3. R. Nachman of Braslav, *Sippurei Maasiyot*, 1a.
4. Ibid.
5. Alluding to Psalms 91:4.
6. R. Nachman of Braslav, *Sippurei Maasiyot*, 1a.
7. Readers of R. Nachman's day would likely skip over it the way contemporary readers skip over the copyright page with the Library of Congress reference information in current publications. For more on the development and content of cover pages in the history of Hebrew print, see Yaakov Shmuel Spiegel, *Chapters in the History of the Jewish Book*, 3 vols., vol. 3, *BeSha'arei HaDefus* (Ramat-Gan: Bar-Ilan University, 2014).
8. R. Nachman of Braslav, *Sippurei Maasiyot*, 1a–1b.
9. Among those who discuss the question of the missing ending, see Dan, *Ha-Sipur Ha-Hasidi*; Band, *Nahman of Bratslav, the Tales*; Elstein, *Maaseh Hoshev: Iyunim Ba-Sipur Ha-Hasidi*; Green, *Tormented Master: The Life and Spiritual Quest of Rabbi Nahman of Bratslav*; Roskies, *A Bridge of Longing: The Lost Art of Yiddish Storytelling*.
10. See Nathan Sternhartz, *Sichot Haran* (Jerusalem: Even Shtiya, 2011 [1850]), 154.
11. The most significant readers of Braslav literature all agree on this point (with the exception of Mark, who does not discuss this tale.) See Band, *Nahman of Bratslav, the Tales*; Dan, *Ha-Sipur Ha-Hasidi*; Elstein, *Pa'Ame Bat Melekh: Hikre Tokhen Ve-Tsurah Be-Sipuro Ha-Rishon Shel R. Nahman Mi-Braslav*; Green, *Tormented Master: The Life and Spiritual Quest of Rabbi Nahman of Bratslav*; Piekarz, *Hasidut Braslav: Perakim Be-Haye Meholeleha Uvi-Khetaveha*.
12. Dan, *Ha-Sipur Ha-Hasidi*, 140.
13. While much research has been dedicated to identifying Kabbalah references in R. Nachman's tales, little attention has been given to the folkloric sources from which these tales clearly borrow, and of which they

clearly form a part. Notable exceptions are Sh. Pitrushka's comparison of the first tale to an early modern Polish folktale, see Sh. Pitrushka, "Makor Polani Le-"Sippurei Ma'asiyot" Shel Rabi Nachman Mi-Braslav," *Ketuvim* 42, no. 91 (1928). See also Yoav Elstein's discussion of the motif of "the princess locked in the tower," which mentions R. Nachman's first tale, though it is a broader study of Jewish folklore. See Yoav Elstein and Avidav Lipsker, eds., 3 vols., *Entsiklopedyah Shel Ha-Sipur Ha-Yehudi: Sipur 'Okev Sipur* (Ramat Gan: Bar Ilan University, 2004).

14. See Dan, *Ha-Sipur Ha-Hasidi*, 136–40.

15. Ibid., 140.

16. This conclusion (along with several other elements in Dan's reading) is also based on statements by R. Nachman's followers—R. Nathan Sternhartz and R. Nachman of Tscheherin—about the meaning of this tale. It relates to other claims they make about R. Nachman's messianic role, which he perceived himself as fulfilling in his generation. See Green, *Tormented Master: The Life and Spiritual Quest of Rabbi Nahman of Bratslav*.

17. The *shechina* is a Kabbalistic symbol for the feminine aspect of divinity, which is God's presence in the world and, in Lurianic terms, has been exiled along with the Jewish people. Unlike the "split" assistant, the king's daughter refers to the *shechina* on the levels of both "content" and "principle" (Dan, *Ha-Sipur Ha-Hasidi*, 141). For more on the *shechina*, see Scholem, *On the Kabbalah and Its Symbolism*.

18. Dan, *Ha-Sipur Ha-Hasidi*, 167–71. This episode is the story told by the sixth beggar. The episode ends the thirteenth tale, since R. Nachman died before completing it.

19. This is true of both the first and the thirteenth tales, he claims (ibid., 171). As noted above, there is a report by R. Nathan, according to which R. Nachman intended to finish the tale but died before doing so (Sternhartz, *Sichot Haran*, 154).

20. This story was told on two separate occasions in 1806, and also (as Dan has pointed out) repeated with some variation in the account of the sixth beggar, told in 1809. For a chronology of tales and teachings around the time of the first tale, see Elstein, *Maaseh Hoshev: Iyunim Ba-Sipur Ha-Hasidi*, ch. 6.

21. This inability persists despite significant changes in R. Nachman's own experience from 1806 to 1809, particularly as far as his messianic aspirations were concerned. See Green, *Tormented Master: The Life and Spiritual Quest of Rabbi Nahman of Bratslav*, ch. 5–6.

22. Dan, "Rabbi Nahman's Third Beggar," 42. (Emphasis added.)

23. *Ha-Sipur Ha-Hasidi*, 141.

24. In the first trial, like Adam in Eden, the assistant eats a forbidden fruit that causes the failure of his efforts. In the second, like Noah after

the flood, he falls asleep after drinking wine, which frustrates his attempt at rescuing the king's daughter.

25. Caplan, "Watch the Throne: Allegory, Kingship and Trauerspiel in the Stories of Der Nister and Reb Nakhman," 97. (Emphasis added.)

26. Huss, "The Mystification of the Kabbalah and the Myth of Jewish Mysticism," 14.

27. See Mark, *The Scroll of Secrets: The Hidden Messianic Vision of R. Nachman of Breslav*.

28. R. Nathan's remarks refer to the end of the broader narrative of the thirteenth tale, not to the sixth beggar's account of the search for the king's daughter. See Sternhartz, *Sichot Haran*, 154.

29. Dan, *Ha-Sipur Ha-Hasidi*, 140.

30. R. Nachman of Braslav, *Sippurei Maasiyot*, 6b.

31. Conventional structural components of folk literature, such as a hero facing a challenge three times and succeeding on the third and most difficult, are famously discussed by: Vladimir Propp, *Morphology of the Folktale*, trans. Laurence Scott (Austin: University of Texas Press, 1968).

32. Roskies, *A Bridge of Longing: The Lost Art of Yiddish Storytelling*, 27.

33. For a study of the conventions of "the ending" in modern Hebrew literature, see Michal Arbel, *Tam Ve-Nishlam?: 'Al Darkhe Ha-Siyum Ba-Siporet* (Tel-Aviv: ha-Kibuts ha-meuhad: Keren Yehoshu'a Rabinovits le-omanuyot, 2008).

34. Shmeruk, *Prokim Fun Der Yidisher Literatur-Geshikhte*, 251.

35. For the clearest discussion of this allegorical layer, see discussions of the tale in Band, *Nahman of Bratslav, the Tales*; Dan, *Ha-Sipur Ha-Hasidi*.

36. Green, for example, has suggested that the tales were meant to prepare for the advent of the Messiah. See Green, *Tormented Master: The Life and Spiritual Quest of Rabbi Nahman of Bratslav*, ch. 6.

37. Wiskind-Elper, *Tradition and Fantasy in the Tales of Reb Nahman of Bratslav*, 6.

38. R. Nachman of Braslav, *Sippurei Maasiyot*, 23a.

39. Schleicher, *Intertextuality in the Tales of Rabbi Nahman of Bratslav a Close Reading of Sippurey Maasiyot*, 1.

40. Audri Durchslag, "Rabbi Nahman and His Readers," *Prooftexts* 2, no. 2 (1982): 224. Durchslag's review includes Arthur Green and Arnold Band's books, which I mentioned previously, as well as Adin Steinsaltz's book. See Adin Steinsaltz, *Beggars and Prayers: Adin Steinsaltz Retells the Tales of Rabbi Nachman of Bratslav*, trans. Yehuda Hanegbi (New York: Basic Books, 1979).

41. R. Nachman of Braslav, *Sippurei Maasiyot*, 1a.

42. See Johann Pillai, "Irony, Romantic," in *Encyclopedia of the Romantic Era, 1760–1850*, ed. Christopher John Murray (London: Routledge, 2003).

43. Friedrich Schlegel, *Friedrich Schlegel's Lucinde and the Fragments*, trans. Peter Firchow (Minneapolis: University of Minnesota Press, 1971).

44. Ibid., 267.

45. Paul De Man, "The Concept of Irony," in *Aesthetic Ideology*, ed. Andrzej Warminski (Minneapolis; London: University of Minnesota Press, 1997), 178.

46. Ibid., 178–79. De Man references "permanent parabasis" as " 'Die Ironie ist eine permanente Parekbase.—'; Schlegel, 'Zur Philosophic' (1797), Fragment 668, in *Philosophische Lehrjahre I* (1796–1806), ed. Ernst Behler, in K.A. (Paderborn-Vienna-Munich: Verlag Ferdinand Schoningh, 1963), 18:85" (ibid., 179, ff. 20).

Schlegel is a major theorist of German romanticism who has been widely discussed in studies from Hegel to Hamacher. My admittedly narrow interest in irony in the present discussion lies in the idea of "permanent parabasis" and the poetic *mise-en-abyme* it is able to capture between the limits of expression and the expression of limits. See Werner Hamacher, *Premises: Essays on Philosophy and Literature from Kanat to Celan* (Stanford, CA: Stanford University Press, 2000). For a bibliography of critical sources on Schlegel, see Allen Speight, "Friedrich Schlegel," in *The Stanford Encyclopedia of Philosophy*, ed. Edward N. Zalta (2011).

47. De Man, "The Concept of Irony," 178.

48. R. Nachman of Braslav, *Sippurei Maasiyot*, 1a.

49. Said, *Beginnings: Intention and Method*, 74.

50. Ibid., 4–5.

51. Ibid.

52. Ibid., 72–73. (Emphasis added.)

53. See Mark, *The Scroll of Secrets: The Hidden Messianic Vision of R. Nachman of Breslav*. This imaginative and highly speculative text deserves its own literary analysis, which is well beyond the scope of the present project.

54. In Lurianic terms, the archetypal end is the redemption, which is always unknown. (See Dan, *Ha-Sipur Ha-Hasidi*, ch. 1.) "The archetypal unknown is the beginning," Said might retort (Said, *Beginnings: Intention and Method*, 78).

55. *Beginnings: Intention and Method*, 72.

56. Mark, *Kol Sipure Rabi Nahman Mi-Braslav: Ha-Ma'Asiyot, Ha-Sipurim Ha-Sodiyim, Ha-Halomot Veha-Hezyonot*, 409–11. Regarding the attribution of these short parables to R. Nachman, see ibid., 40–45.

57. See Foucault, *Discipline and Punish: The Birth of the Prison; History of Madness*. See also *The History of Sexuality*, 1st American ed. (New York: Pantheon Books, 1978).

58. Said, *Beginnings: Intention and Method*, 72.

59. "The clearest available example of such epistemic violence is the remotely orchestrated, far flung, and heterogeneous project to constitute the colonial subject as Other. This project is also the asymmetrical obliteration of the trace of that Other in its precarious Subjectivity. It is well known that Foucault locates epistemic violence, a complete overhaul of the episteme, in the redefinition of sanity at the end of the European eighteenth century. But what if that particular redefinition was only a part of the narrative of history in Europe as well as in the colonies? What if the two projects of epistemic overhaul worked as dislocated and unacknowledged parts of a vast two-handed engine?" Gayatri Chakravorty Spivak, "Can the Subaltern Speak?," in *Marxism and the Interpretation of Culture*, ed. Cary Nelson and Lawrence Grossberg (Urbana: University of Illinois Press, 1988), 280–81.

60. This narrative is a familiar trope in folklore, though usually it tells of a poisoned well rather that wheat. The differences between various versions of this trope will not interest us here. A student of folklore may find interest in tracking the course along which this trope reached R. Nachman.

61. Jacques Rancière, *Short Voyages to the Land of the People* (Stanford, CA: Stanford University Press, 2003).

62. "We the People," the speaking subject of the US Declaration of Independence is a particularly notable moment in the emergence of this character.

63. Cited above and in Said, *Beginnings: Intention and Method*, 60.

64. Ibid., xvii.

65. See Genesis 4:15.

66. See Deuteronomy 6:8.

67. This is the word for "turkey" in Yiddish.

68. Mark, *Mysticism and Madness: The Religious Thought of Rabbi Nachman of Bratslav*.

69. First published the same year as R. Nachman's tales (1815), *Shivchei HaBesht* is the hagiography of R. Yisra'el Baal Shem Tov, the "founder" of Hasidism.

70. See Mark, *Mysticism and Madness: The Religious Thought of Rabbi Nachman of Bratslav*, ch. 1. R. Nachman too expresses views of madness as reprehensible social deviance in his teachings: "For one who transgresses is mad, as our sages have said (Sota 3): One does not transgress unless he is possessed by a spirit of foolishness. And just as the mad need to be beaten and treated with amulets, so the Torah is like sticks and amulets, with which one beats and subdues evil inclination, and drives out madness and the spirit of foolishness" (R. Nachman of Braslav, *Likkutei Moharan*, 1,

1:1). All the more so should we regard the contrast between this rather medieval notion of "cure," whereby the madman is beaten and treated with amulets, and the notion of "cure" expressed in the present tale.

71. See Mark, *Mysticism and Madness: The Religious Thought of Rabbi Nachman of Bratslav*, ch. 2. While Mark is observant in pointing out R. Nachman's identification of a lack of reason with madness, R. Nachman more readily offers physiological (rather than mystical) accounts of the latter: "And when there are no oils in the body, the mind cannot light up with observation, and that is how madmen come to be, that the humors of the body dry up, and that ruins the brain, for it does not have oils to burn" (Braslav, *Likkutei Moharan*, 1, 60:3).

72. For more on Pinel and the "moral treatment," see Foucault, *History of Madness*. For more on demonological understandings of madness in the Jewish Traditions, see Mark, *Mysticism and Madness: The Religious Thought of Rabbi Nachman of Bratslav*.

Conclusion

1. Sternhartz, *Chayey Moharan*, 195.

2. This is a unique point of agreement between Buber and Scholem (who otherwise dispute the significance of the Hasidic movement)—Buber seeing R. Nachman as "the last" and Scholem seeing Hasidism as "the final stage." See Scholem, *Major Trends in Jewish Mysticism*. For Scholem's comments on Buber's understanding of Hasidism, see Gershom Scholem, "Martin Buber's Hasidism," *Commentary* 1961. For a discussion of the debate between the two, see Claire Sufrin, "On Myth, History, and the Study of Hasidism: Martin Buber and Gershom Scholem," in *Encountering the Medieval in Modern Jewish Thought*, ed. James Diamond and Aaron Hughes (Leiden and Boston: Brill, 2012). For a contemporary collection of literary and other readings of R. Nachman's tales, see Roee Horen, ed., *Life of Yearning: New Interpretation to the Tales of Reb Nachman of Breslov* (Tel Aviv: Miskal, 2010).

3. See S. Y. Abramovitsh, *Tales of Mendele the Book Peddler: Fishke the Lame and Benjamin the Third*, trans. Hillel Halkin (New York: Schocken Books, 1996). For an analysis of Abramovitsh's story, see Dan Miron and Anita Norich, "The Politics of Benjamin the Third," in *The Field of Yiddish*, ed. Marvin I Herzog et al. (Philadelphia: Institute for the Study of Human Issues, 1980).

4. For more on the figure of the *talush* in modern Hebrew literature, see Dan Miron, "Bodedim Be-Mo'Adam: Li-Deyoknah Shel Ha-Republikah Ha-Sifrutit Ha-'Ivrit Bi-Tehilat Ha-Meah Ha-'Esrim" (1987). For a recent

comparative work on "diaspora" and "native" rootlessness, see Heddy Shait, *The Evolution of Rootlessness in Twentieth Century Hebrew Literature* (Ramat-Gan: Bar-Ilan University Press, 2015).

5. Pierre Bourdieu, *Outline of a Theory of Practice* (Cambridge, UK; New York: Cambridge University Press, 1977), 2.

6. Mendes-Flohr, *Divided Passions: Jewish Intellectuals and the Experience of Modernity*, 54.

Bibliography

Abramovitsh, S. Y. *Tales of Mendele the Book Peddler: Fishke the Lame and Benjamin the Third*. [in English] Translated by Hillel Halkin. New York: Schocken Books, 1996.

Alazraki, Jaime. "Borges and the Kabbalah." [in English] *TriQuarterly* 25 (1972).

Anidjar, Gil. "Jewish Mysticism Alterable and Unalterable: On *Orient*ing Kabbalah Studies and the 'Zohar of Christian Spain.'" *Jewish Social Studies* 3, no. 1 (1996): 89–157.

———. "Literary History and Hebrew Modernity." *Comparative Literature Studies* 42, no. 4 (2005): 277–96.

———. *"Our Place in Al-Andalus": Kabbalah, Philosophy, Literature in Arab Jewish Letters*. [in English] Stanford, CA: Stanford University Press, 2002.

Arad, Mordechai. *Mehalel Shabat Be-Farhesya: Munah Talmudi U-Mashma'Uto Ha-Historit*. [in Hebrew] New York; Yerushalayim: Jewish Theological Seminary, 2009.

Arbel, Michal. *Tam Ve-Nishlam?: 'Al Darkhe Ha-Siyum Ba-Siporet*. [in Hebrew] Tel-Aviv: ha-Kibuts ha-meuhad: Keren Yehoshu'a Rabinovits le-omanuyot, 2008.

Arkush, Allan. *Moses Mendelssohn and the Enlightenment*. [in English] Albany: State University of New York Press, 1994.

Asad, Talal. *Genealogies of Religion: Discipline and Reasons of Power in Christianity and Islam*. [in English] Baltimore: Johns Hopkins University Press, 1993.

Asaf, David. *Ne'eḥaz Ba-Sevakh: Pirḳe Mashber U-Mevukhah Be-Toldot Ha-Ḥasidut*. [in Hebrew] Jerusalem: Merkaz Zalman Shazar le-Toldot Yiśra'el, 2006.

Band, Arnold J. "The Function of the Enigmatic in Two Hasidic Tales." In *Studies in Jewish Mysticism: Proceedings of Regional Conferences Held at the University of California, Los Angeles, and Mcgill University in April, 1978*, edited by Joseph Dan and Talmage Frank, 185–209. Cambridge, MA: Association for Jewish Studies, 1982.

———. *Nahman of Bratslav, the Tales.* [translation of *Sipure ma'asiyot*] New York: Paulist Press, 1978.

Bartal, Israel. "The Imprint of Haskalah Literature on the Historiography of Hasidism." In *Hasidism Reappraised*, edited by Ada Rapoport-Albert. London: Littman Library of Jewish Civilization, 1996.

———. *The Jews of Eastern Europe, 1772–1881.* [translated from the Hebrew by Chaya Naor] Philadelphia: University of Pennsylvania Press, 2005.

Benda, Julien. *The Treason of the Intellectuals (La Trahison Des Clercs).* [in English] New York: Norton, 1969.

Benjamin, Walter. *The Origin of German Tragic Drama.* [in English] Translated by John Osborne. London; New York: Verso, 2003.

———. *The Origin of German Tragic Drama.* [in English] London: NLB, 1977.

———. *The Work of Art in the Age of Its Technological Reproducibility, and Other Writings on Media.* Translated from the German by Thomas Y. Jephcott E. F. N. Cambridge, M: Belknap Press of Harvard University Press, 2008.

Benjamin, Walter, and Gershom Scholem. *The Correspondence of Walter Benjamin and Gershom Scholem, 1932–1940.* [in translation of Walter Benjamin/Gershom Scholem Briefwechsel 1933–1940] Cambridge, MA: Harvard University Press, 1992.

Benton, Lauren A. *Law and Colonial Cultures Legal Regimes in World History, 1400–1900.* [in English] Cambridge; New York: Cambridge University Press, 2002.

Benton, Lauren A., and Richard Jeffrey Ross, eds. *Legal Pluralism and Empires, 1500–1850.* New York: New York University Press, 2013.

Bernstein, Michael. *Foregone Conclusions: Against Apocalyptic History.* [in English] Berkeley: University of California Press, 1994.

Biale, David. *Gershom Scholem: Kabbalah and Counter-History.* Cambridge, MA: Harvard University Press, 1979.

———. "Gershom Scholem's Ten Unhistorical Aphorisms on Kabbalah: Text and Commentary." *Modern Judaism* 5, no. 1 (1985): 67–93.

Bosteels, Bruno. "Borges as Antiphilosopher." [in English] *Vanderbilt e-journal of Luso-Hispanic studies* 3 (2006).

Bourdieu, Pierre. *Outline of a Theory of Practice.* [in translation with revisions of *Esquisse d'une thÈorie de la pratique*] Cambridge, UK; New York: Cambridge University Press, 1977.

Brant, Clare. *Balloon Madness: Flights of Imagination in Britain, 1783–1786.* [in English] 2017.

Buber, Martin. *Gog and Magog: A Novel.* [in English] Translated by Ludwig Lewisohn. Syracuse, NY: Syracuse University Press, 1999.

———. *Hasidism*. [in English] New York: Philosophical Library, 1948.
———, ed. *The Tales of Rabbi Nachman*. Atlantic Highlands, NJ: Humanities Press International, 1988.
Caplan, Marc. *How Strange the Change Language, Temporality, and Narrative Form in Peripheral Modernisms*. [in English] Stanford, CA: Stanford University Press, 2011.
———. "Watch the Throne: Allegory, Kingship and Trauerspiel in the Stories of Der Nister and Reb Nakhman." In *Uncovering the Hidden: The Works and Life of Der Nister*, edited by Gennady Estraikh, Kerstin Hoge, and Mikhail Krutikov. Studies in Yiddish. Cambridge: Legenda, 2014.
Charny, Vitaly. "1804 Russian Set of Laws Concerning Jews." http://www.jewishgen.org/belarus/1804_laws.htm.
Dan, Joseph. *Ha-Sipur Ha-Hasidi*. [in Hebrew] Yerushalayim: Bet Hotsa'ah Keter Yerushalayim, 1975.
———. "Rabbi Nahman's Third Beggar." In *History and Literature: New Readings of Jewish Texts in Honor of Arnold J. Band*, edited by William Cutter and David C. Jacobson. Providence, RI: Program in Judaic Studies, Brown University, 2002.
De Man, Paul. *Allegories of Reading: Figural Language in Rousseau, Nietzsche, Rilke, and Proust*. [in English] New Haven: Yale University Press, 1979.
———. "The Concept of Irony." In *Aesthetic Ideology*, edited by Andrzej Warminski, 163–84. Minneapolis; London; London: University of Minnesota Press, 1997.
———. *The Rhetoric of Romanticism*. [in English] New York: Columbia University Press, 1984.
Dinur, Ben-Zion. "Reshitah Shel Ha-Hasidut Ve-Yesodoteha Ha-Sotsialiyim Ve-Hameshichiyim." In *Studies in Hasidism*, edited by Avraham Rubinstein. Jerusalem: The Zalman Shazar Center; The Historical Society of Israel, 1977.
Dubin, Lois. "The Social and Cultural Context: Eighteenth-Century Enlightenment." In *History of Jewish Philosophy*, edited by Daniel H. Frank and Oliver Leaman. London; New York: Routledge, 2007.
Dubnow, Simon. *A History of Hasidism*. [in English] Translated by Lederer Helen. Cincinnati 1970.
———. *History of the Jews in Russia and Poland, from the Earliest Times until the Present Day*. [in English] Translated by Israel Friedlaender. 3 vols. Vol. 1 *From the beginning until the death of Alexander I (1825)*, Philadelphia: Jewish Publication Society of America, 1916.
———. *Toldot Ha-Hasidut*. [in Hebrew] 3 vols. Tel-Aviv: Devir, 1944.
Durchslag, Audri. "Rabbi Nahman and His Readers." *Prooftexts* 2, no. 2 (1982): 221–26.

Dvir-Goldberg, Rivka. *Ha-Tsadik Ha-Hasidi Ve-Armon Ha-Livyatan: 'Iyun Be-Sipure Ma'Asiyot Mi-Pi Tsadikim.* [in Hebrew] Tel-Aviv: ha-Kibuts ha-meuhad, 2003.

Dynner, Glenn. "The Garment of Torah: Clothing Decrees and the Warsaw Career of the First Gerer Rebbe." In *Warsaw. The Jewish Metropolis: Essays in Honor of the 75th Birthday of Professor Antony Polonsky,* edited by Glenn Dynner, Francois Guesnet and Antony Polonsky. Ijs Studies in Judaica. Leiden; Boston: Brill, 2015.

———. *Men of Silk: The Hasidic Conquest of Polish Jewish Society.* [in English] New York, NY: Oxford University Press, 2006.

Elstein, Yoav. *Maaseh Hoshev: Iyunim Ba-Sipur Ha-Hasidi.* [in Hebrew] Tel Aviv: Eked, 1983.

———. *Pa'Ame Bat Melekh: Hikre Tokhen Ve-Tsurah Be-Sipuro Ha-Rishon Shel R. Nahman Mi-Braslav.* [in Hebrew] Ramat-Gan: Universitat Bar-Ilan, 1984.

Elstein, Yoav, and Avidav Lipsker, eds. 3 vols., *Entsiklopedyah Shel Ha-Sipur Ha-Yehudi: Sipur 'Okev Sipur.* Ramat Gan: Bar Ilan University, 2004.

Etkes, Immanuel. *Rabbi Shneur Zalman of Liady: The Origins of Chabad Hasidism.* [in English] Translated by Jeffrey M. Green. Waltham, MA: Brandeis University Press, 2015.

———. *Tnuat Ha-Hasidut Be-Reshitah.* [in Hebrew] Tel-Aviv: Misrad habitahon, 1998.

Foucault, Michel. *Discipline and Punish: The Birth of the Prison.* 1st American ed. New York: Pantheon Books, 1977.

———. *Fearless Speech.* [in English] Los Angeles: Semiotext(e), 2001.

———. *History of Madness.* Translated by Jean Khalfa. New York: Routledge, 2006.

———. *The History of Sexuality.* 1st American ed. New York: Pantheon Books, 1978.

Frieden, Ken. *Travels in Translation: Sea Tales at the Source of Jewish Fiction.* [in English] Syracuse, New York: Syracuse University Press, 2016.

Gadamer, Hans-Georg. *Truth and Method.* [translated from the German] London: Bloomsbury Academic, 2014.

Gillispie, Charles Coulston. *The Montgolfier Brothers and the Invention of Aviation, 1783–1784.* [in English] Princeton, New Jersey: Princeton University Press, 2014.

Gottlober, Abraham Baer. *Zikhronot U-Masaot.* [in Hebrew] Yerushalayim: Mosad Bialik, 1976.

Gramsci, Antonio. *A Gramsci Reader: Selected Writings, 1916–1935.* [in English] New York: New Yrok University Press, 2000.

———. "The Intellectuals." Translated by Quintin Hoare and Geoffrey Nowell-Smith. In *Selections from the Prison Notebooks of Antonio Gramsci.* New York: International, 1971.

Green, Arthur. "Early Hasidism: Some Old/New Questions." In *Hasidism Reappraised*, edited by A. Rapoport-Albert. London: Littman Library of Jewish Civilization, 1996.

———. "Le'bikorto Shel M. Piekarz Le'sifri 'Ba'al Ha'yissurim.'" [in Hebrew] *Tarbitz* 51 (1982): 508–09.

———. *Tormented Master: The Life and Spiritual Quest of Rabbi Nahman of Bratslav.* [in English] Woodstock, VT: Jewish Lights, 1992.

Grözinger, Karl-Erich. *Kafka and Kabbalah.* Translated by Susan Hecker Ray. New York: Continuum, 1994.

Habermas, Jürgen. *The Structural Transformation of the Public Sphere: An Inquiry into a Category of Bourgeois Society.* [in English] Translated by Thomas Burger. Cambridge: Polity, 1989.

Haidenberg, Henie, and Michal Oron. *Me-'Olamo Ha-Misti Shel R. Nahman Mi-Braslav/: 'Iyunim Be-Shishah Mi-Sipure Ha-Ma'Asiyot Shel R. Nahman Mi-Braslav.* [in Hebrew] Tel-Aviv: Papirus, 1986.

Halpern, Israel. *Yehudim VE-Yahadut Be-Mizraḥ Eropah: MeḥḲArim Be-Toldotehem.* Jerusalem: Hebrew Univeristy Magnes Press, 1968.

Hamacher, Werner. *Premises: Essays on Philosophy and Literature from Kanat to Celan.* [translated by Peter Fenves] Stanford, CA: Stanford University Press, 2000.

Hazan, Avraham. *Sefer Sippurim Nifla'im.* Jerusalem: H. Zukerman, 1935.

Hever, Hannan. "The Politics of Form of the Hassidic Tale." *Dibur Literary Journal*, no. 2 (2016).

———. "The Politics of the Hebrew Hassidic Tale in the Russian Empire." In *Languages of Modern Jewish Cultures*, edited by Joshua Miller and Anita Norich. Ann Arbor: University of Michigan Press, 2016.

Hook, Sydney. "Communism and the Intellectual." In *The Intellectuals: A Controversial Portrait*, edited by George B. de Huszar. Glencoe, IL: Free Press, 1960.

Horen, Roee, ed. *Ha-Hayim Ke-Ga'Agu'A: Keriot Hadashot Be-Sipure Ha-Ma'Asiyot Shel R. Nahman Mi-Breslev.* Tel-Aviv: Yedi'ot aharonot: Sifre hemed, 2010.

———, ed. *Life of Yearning: New Interpretation to the Tales of Reb Nachman of Breslov.* Tel Aviv: Miskal, 2010.

Hundert, Gershon David. *Jews in Poland-Lithuania in the Eighteenth Century a Genealogy of Modernity.* [in English] Berkeley: University of California Press, 2004.

Huss, Boaz. "Contemporary Kabbalah and Its Challenge to the Academic Study of Jewish Mysticism." In *Kabbalah and Contemporary Spiritual Revival*, edited by Boaz Huss. Goldstein-Goren Library of Jewish Thought, 357–73. Beer-Sheva: Ben-Gurion University of the Negev, 2011.

———. "The Mystification of the Kabbalah and the Myth of Jewish Mysticism." [in Hebrew] *Pe'amim*, no. 110 (2007): 9–30.

Huszar, George B. de, ed. *The Intellectuals: A Controversial Portrait*. Glencoe, IL: Free Press, 1960.

Idel, Moshe. *Hasidism between Ecstasy and Magic*. [in English] Albany: State University of New York Press, 1995.

———. "Hieroglyphs, Keys, Enigmas: On G. G. Scholem's Vision of Kabbalah: Between Franz Molitor and Franz Kafka." In *Arche Noah: Die Idee der "Kultur" im deutsch-jüdischen Diskurs*, edited by Bernhard Greiner and Christoph Schmidt, 227–48. Freiburg: Rombach Verlag, 2002.

———. *Kabbalah New Perspectives*. [in English] New Haven: Yale University Press, 1988.

———. *Messianic Mystics*. [in English] New Haven: Yale University Press, 1998.

Jacobs, Louis. "Hasidism and the Dogma of the Decline of the Generations." In *Hasidism Reappraised*, edited by Ada Rapoport-Albert. London: Littman Library of Jewish Civilization, 1996.

Jacobson, Eric. *Metaphysics of the Profane: The Political Theology of Walter Benjamin and Gershom Scholem*. [in English] New York: Columbia University Press, 2003.

Kelley, Theresa M. *Reinventing Allegory*. [in English] Cambridge: Cambridge University Press, 1997.

King, Richard. *Orientalism and Religion: Postcolonial Theory, India and "the Mystic East."* [in English] London; New York: Routledge, 1999.

Koselleck, Reinhart. *Critique and Crisis: Enlightenment and the Pathogenesis of Modern Society*. [in English] Cambridge, MA: MIT Press, 1988.

Lederhendler, Eli. *The Road to Modern Jewish Politics*. [in English] New York: Oxford University Press, 1989.

Levine, Hillel. "'Should Napoleon Be Victorious . . .': Politics and Spirituality in Early Modern Jewish Messianism." *Jerusalem Studies in Jewish Thought* 16–17 (2001): 65–83.

Lewis, Yitzhak. "Revealing and Concealing as Literary Devices in the Tales of Rabbi Nachman, or, the Case of the Missing Ending." MA Thesis, Columbia University, 2010.

———. "Writing the Margin: Rabbi Nachman of Braslav, Jorges Luis Borges and the Question of Jewish Writing." Doctoral Dissertation, Columbia University, 2016.

Leżajsk, Elimelech of. *Sefer No'am Elimelech*. [in Hebrew] Lemberg, 1787.

Liberman, Haim. "R. Nachman breslaver und die umener maskilim." [in Yiddish] *YIVO Bleter* 29 (1947): 201–19.

Liebes, Yehuda. "The Novelty of Rabi Nahman of Bratslav." [in Hebrew] *Daat: A Journal of Jewish Philosophy & Kabbalah* 45 (2000): 91–103.

———. "R. Nahman of Bratslav's "Hattikkun Hakkelali" and His Attitude towards Sabbatianism." *Zion* 45, no. 3 (1980): 201–45.

———. "Tendencies in the Research of Bratslav Hasidism: A Reply to Y. Mondshine." *Zion* 47, no. 2 (1982): 224–31.

Lurie, Ilia, ed. *History of the Jews of Russia*. Edited by Israel Bartal. 3 vols. Vol. 2. Jerusalem: Zalman Shazar Center for Jewish History, 2012.

Lyadi, Shneur Zalman of. *Tanya, Ve-Hu, Sefer Likute Amarim*. [in Hebrew] n.a.: Defus Dov Ber ben Yisrael ve Dov Ber ben Pesach, 1796.

Macherey, Pierre. *The Object of Literature*. [in translation of *ίA quoi pense la littíerature?*] Cambridge [England]; New York: Cambridge University Press, 1995.

Magid, Shaul. "Associative Midrash: Reflections on a Hermaneutical Theory in Rabbi Nachman of Braslav's Likkutei Moharan." In *God's Voice from the Void: Old and New Studies in Bratslav Hasidism*, edited by Shaul Magid, 15–66. Albany: State University of New York Press, 2002.

———. *Hasidism Incarnate: Hasidism, Christianity, and the Construction of Modern Judaism*. [in English] Stanford, CA: Stanford University Press, 2015.

———. "Through the Void: The Absence of God in R. Nahman of Bratzlav's 'Likkutei Moharan.'" *The Harvard Theological Review* 88, no. 4 (1995): 495–519.

Mahler, Refa'el. *Hasidism and the Jewish Enlightenment: Their Confrontation in Galicia and Poland in the First Half of the 19th Century*. [in English] Philadelphia, PA: Jewish Publication Society of America, 1985.

Malkiel, Eliezer. *Hokhmah U-Temimut: Perush Le-Khamah Torot Ve-Sipurim Shel Rabi Nahman Mi-Breslav*. [in Hebrew] Tel-Aviv: Yedi'ot aharonot: Sifre hemed, 2005.

Mamdani, Mahmood. *Define and Rule: Native as Political Identity*. [in English] Cambridge, MA: Harvard University Press, 2012.

Mark, Zvi. *Hitgalut Ve-Tikun: Bi-Khetavav Ha-Geluyim Veha-Sodiyim Shel R. Nahman Mi-Breslav*. [in Hebrew] Yerushalayim: Magnes Press, Hebrew University, 2011.

———. *Megilat Setarim: He-Hazon Ha-Meshihi Ha-Sodi Shel R. Nahman Mi-Braslav*. [in Hebrew] Ramat-Gan: Bar-Ilan University, 2006.

———. *Mistikah Ve-Shigaon Bi-Yetsirat R. Nahman Mi-Breslav*. [in Hebrew] Tel Aviv: Am Oved, 2003.

———. *Mysticism and Madness: The Religious Thought of Rabbi Nachman of Bratslav*. [in English] London; New York; [Jerusalem]: Continuum; Shalom Hartman Institute, 2009.

———. *The Scroll of Secrets: The Hidden Messianic Vision of R. Nachman of Breslav*. [in English] Translated by Naftali Moses. Brighton, MA: Academic Studies, 2010.

———. "Why Did R. Moses Zvi of Savran Persecute R. Nathan of Nemirov and Bratslav Hasidim?" [in Hebrew] *Zion* 69, no. 4 (2004): 487–500.

———, ed. *Kol Sipure Rabi Nahman Mi-Braslav: Ha-Ma'Asiyot, Ha-Sipurim Ha-Sodiyim, Ha-Halomot Veha-Hezyonot*. Edited by Dov Elbaum. Jerusalem, Israel: Mosad Bialik; Yedi'ot Sefarim; Bayit—Yetsirah Ivrit, 2014.

Masuzawa, Tomoko. *The Invention of World Religions: Or, How European Universalism Was Preserved in the Language of Pluralism*. [in English] Chicago: University of Chicago Press, 2007.

Meir, Jonatan. *Hasidut Medumah: 'Iyunim Bi-Khetavav Ha-Satiriyim Shel Yosef Perl [Imagined Hasidism: The Anti-Hasidic Writings of Joseph Perl]*. [in Hebrew] Jerusalem: Mosad Bialik, 2013.

———. *Imagined Hasidism: The Anti-Hasidic Writings of Joseph Perl*. [in Hebrew] Yerushalayim: Mosad Bialik, 2013.

Meir, Yonatan. *Literary Hasidism: The Life and Works of Michael Levi Rodkinson*. [in English] 2016.

Mendelssohn, Moses. *Jerusalem, or, on Religious Power and Judaism*. [translated from the German] Translated by Allan Arkush. Hanover: Published for Brandeis University Press by University Press of New England, 1983.

Mendes-Flohr, Paul. *Gershom Scholem: The Man and His Work*. [in English] Albany; Jerusalem: State University of New York Press; The Israel Academy of Sciences and Humanities, 1994.

Mendes-Flohr, Paul R. *Divided Passions: Jewish Intellectuals and the Experience of Modernity*. [in English] Detroit: Wayne State University Press, 1991.

Mendes-Flohr, Paul R., and Jehuda Reinharz. *Jew in the Modern World: Documentary History*. [in English] Oxford: Oxford University Press, 1995.

Miron, Dan. "Bodedim Be-Mo'Adam: Li-Deyoknah Shel Ha-Republikah Ha-Sifrutit Ha-'Ivrit Bi-Tehilat Ha-Meah Ha-'Esrim." [in Hebrew] (1987).

———. *From Continuity to Contiguity toward a New Jewish Literary Thinking*. [in English] Stanford, CA: Stanford University Press, 2010.

Miron, Dan, and Anita Norich. "The Politics of Benjamin the Third." In *The Field of Yiddish*, edited by Marvin I. Herzog et al. Philadelphia: Institute for the Study of Human Issues, 1980.

Mondshein, Yehosha. *Ha-Ma'asar Ha-Rishon*. [in Hebrew] Israel: Hish-Hafatsat ha-Ma'ayan, 2012.

———. "On 'R. Nahman of Bratzlav's "Hattikun Hakkelali" and His Attitude towards Sabbataianism.'" *Zion* 47, no. 2 (1982): 198–223.

Nachman, R. of Braslav. *Likkutei Moharan*. [in Hebrew] Vol. 1, Ostroh, 1808.

———. *Likkutei Moharan*. [in Hebrew] Vol. 2, Mohilev, 1811.

———. *Sippurei Maasiyot*. [in Hebrew, Yiddish] Lemberg, 1815.

Pannekoek, Anton. *A History of Astronomy*. [in English] New York: Dover, 1989.
Piekarz, Mendel. *Hasidut Braslav: Perakim Be-Haye Meholeleha Uvi-Khetaveha*. [in Hebrew] Yerushalayim: Mosad Byalik, 1972.
Pillai, Johann. "Irony, Romantic." In *Encyclopedia of the Romantic Era, 1760–1850*, edited by Christopher John Murray. London: Routledge, 2003.
Pitrushka, Sh. "Makor Polani Le-'Sippurei Ma'asiyot' Shel Rabi Nachman Mi-Braslav." [in Hebrew] *Ketuvim* 42, no. 91 (July 12, 1928): 3.
Polnoie, Jaakov Joseph of. *Sefer Toldot Ya'Akov Yosef*. [in Hebrew] 1780.
Propp, Vladimir. *Morphology of the Folktale*. [in English] Translated by Laurence Scott. Austin: University of Texas Press, 1968.
Raeff, Marc. *Michael Speransky: Statesman of Imperial Russia, 1772–1839*. [in English] Hague: M. Nijhoff, 1957.
Rancière, Jacques. *The Politics of Aesthetics: The Distribution of the Sensible*. [in English] London; New York: Continuum, 2006.
———. *Short Voyages to the Land of the People*. [in English] Stanford, CA: Stanford University Press, 2003.
Rapoport-Albert, Ada. "Concerning Y. Liebes' Article (Zion Xlv, 1980, Pp. 201–245)." *Zion* 46, no. 4 (1981): 346–51.
———. "Hasidism after 1772: Structural Continuity and Change." In *Hasidism Reappraised*, edited by Ada Rapoport-Albert. London: Littman Library of Jewish Civilization, 1996.
———. "'Katnut,' 'Pshitut' Ve-'Eini Yode'a' Shel Rabi Nachman Mi-Braslav." In *Studies in Jewish Religious and Intellectual History*, edited by Siegfried Stein and Raphael Loewe. Institute of Jewish Studies, London, and the University of Alabama Press, 1979.
———. "Shnei Mekorot Le-Te'ur Nesi'ato Shel Rabi Nachman Mi-Braslav Le-Eretz Yisrael." *Kiryat Sefer* 46 (1971): 147–53.
Rosenfeld, Sophia. "Writing the History of Censorship in the Age of Enlightenment." In *Postmodernism and the Enlightenment: New Perspectives in Eighteenth-Century French Intellectual History*, edited by Daniel Gordon. New York: Routledge, 2001.
Roskies, David G. *A Bridge of Longing: The Lost Art of Yiddish Storytelling*. [in English] Cambridge, MA: Harvard University Press, 1995.
Rosman, Murray Jay. *Founder of Hasidism: A Quest for the Historical Ba'al Shem Tov*. [in English] Berkeley: University of California Press, 1996.
Said, Edward W. *Beginnings: Intention and Method*. [in English] New York: Basic Books, 1975.
———. *Representations of the Intellectual: The 1993 Reith Lectures*. [in English] New York: Pantheon Books, 1994.

Salomon, Albert. "The Messianic Bohemians." In *The Intellectuals: A Controversial Portrait*, edited by George B. de Huszar. Glencoe, IL: Free Press, 1960.

Schechter, Ronald. *Obstinate Hebrews: Representations of Jews in France, 1715–1815*. [in English] Berkeley: University of California Press, 2003.

Schlegel, Friedrich. *Friedrich Schlegel's Lucinde and the Fragments.* [in English] Translated by Peter Firchow. Minneapolis: University of Minnesota Press, 1971.

Schleicher, Marianne. *Intertextuality in the Tales of Rabbi Nahman of Bratslav: A Close Reading of Sippurey Maasiyot.* [in English] Leiden; Boston: Brill, 2007.

Scholem, Gershom. "Martin Buber's Hasidism." *Commentary* 1961.

———. *On the Kabbalah and Its Symbolism.* [in English] New York: Schocken Books, 1965.

Scholem, Gershom Gerhard. *Major Trends in Jewish Mysticism.* [in English] New York: Schocken Books, 1961, 1995.

———. *The Messianic Idea in Judaism and Other Essays on Jewish Spirituality.* [in English] New York: Schocken Books, 1971.

———. *Sabbatai Sevi: The Mystical Messiah, 1626–1676.* [in English] Princeton, NJ: Princeton University Press, 1973.

Schwartz, Howard. "Rabbi Nachman of Bratslav: Forerunner of Modern Jewish Literature." *Judaism* 31, no. 2 (1982): 211–24.

Schwartz, Seth. *Imperialism and Jewish Society: 200 B.C.E. To 640 C.E.* [in English] Princeton: Princeton University Press, 2009.

Seeman, Don, and Shaul Magid. "Mystical Poetics: The Jewish Mystical Text as Literature." *Prooftexts* 29, no. 3 (2009): 317–23.

Seton-Watson, Hugh. "The Russian Intellectuals." In *The Intellectuals: A Controversial Portrait*, edited by George B. de Huszar. Glencoe, IL: Free Press, 1960.

Shait, Heddy. *The Evolution of Rootlessness in Twentieth Century Hebrew Literature.* [in Hebrew, table of contents also in English] Ramat-Gan: Bar-Ilan University Press, 2015.

Shmeruk, Chone. *Prokim fun der yidisher literatur-geshikhte.* [in Yiddish] Tel-Aviv; Yerusholaim: Farlag Y.L. Perets; Yidish-opteylung, der Hebraisher universitet in Yerusholaim, 1988.

Siff, David B. "Shifting Ideologies of Orality and Literacy in Their Historical Context: Rebbe Nahhman of Bratslav's Embrace of the Book as a Means for Redemption." *Profftexts* 30 (2010).

Silber, Michael. "The Emergence of Ultra-Orthodoxy: The Invention of a Tradition." In *The Uses of Tradition: Jewish Continuity in the Modern Era*, edited by Jack Wertheimer, 23–84. New York; Cambridge, MA: Jewish Theological Seminary of America; Distributed by Harvard University Press, 1992.

Sinkoff, Nancy. *Out of the Shtetl Making Jews Modern in the Polish Borderlands.* [in English] Providence, RI: Brown Judaic Studies, 2008.

Smith, Chani Haran. *Tuning the Soul: Music as a Spiritual Process in the Teachings of Rabbi Nahman of Bratzlav.* [in English] Leiden; Boston: Brill, 2010.

Sosnowski, Saúl. *Borges Y La Cábala: La Búsqueda Del Verbo.* [in Spanish] Buenos Aires: Ed. Hispamérica, 1976.

Speight, Allen. "Friedrich Schlegel." In *The Stanford Encyclopedia of Philosophy*, edited by Edward N. Zalta, 2011.

Spiegel, Yaakov Shmuel. *Chapters in the History of the Jewish Book.* [in Hebrew] 3 vols. Vol. 3—*BeSha'arei HaDefus*, Ramat-Gan: Bar-Ilan University, 2014.

Spivak, Gayatri Chakravorty. "Can the Subaltern Speak?" In *Marxism and the Interpretation of Culture*, edited by Cary Nelson and Lawrence Grossberg, 271–313. Urbana: University of Illinois Press, 1988.

Staël, Germaine de. *Politics, Literature, and National Character.* [in English] Translated by Morroe Berger. New Brunswick, NJ; London, UK: Transaction, 2000.

Stanislawski, Michael. *Tsar Nicholas I and the Jews: The Transformation of Jewish Society in Russia, 1825–1855.* [in English] Philadelphia: Jewish Publication Society of America, 1983.

Steinsaltz, Adin. *Beggars and Prayers: Adin Steinsaltz Retells the Tales of Rabbi Nachman of Bratslav.* [in English] Translated by Yehuda Hanegbi. New York: Basic Books, 1979.

Stern, Eliyahu. *The Genius Elijah of Vilna and the Making of Modern Judaism.* New Haven: Yale University Press, 2013.

Sternhartz, Nathan. *Chayey Moharan.* [in Hebrew] Lemberg 1874.

———. *Sefer Yemei Moharnat.* Lemberg, 1876.

———. *Shivchei Haran.* [in Hebrew] Ostroh, 1816.

———. *Sichot Haran.* [in Hebrew] Jerusalem: Even Shtiya, 2011 [1850].

Stieglitz, Robert R. "The Hebrew Names of the Seven Planets." *Journal of Near Eastern Studies* 40, no. 2 (1981): 135–37.

Sufrin, Claire. "On Myth, History, and the Study of Hasidism: Martin Buber and Gershom Scholem." In *Encountering the Medieval in Modern Jewish Thought*, edited by James Diamond and Aaron Hughes. Leiden and Boston: Brill, 2012.

Taylor, Dov, ed. *Joseph Perl's Revealer of Secrets: The First Hebrew Novel.* Boulder, CO: Westview, 1997.

Teller, Adam. *Money, Power, and Influence in Eighteenth-Century Lithuania: The Jews on the Radziwill Estates.* [in English] Stanford, CA: Stanford University Press, 2017.

Tocqueville, Alexis de. *The Old Regime and the French Revolution.* Garden City, NY: Doubleday, 1955.

Todorov, Tzvetan. *Theories of the Symbol.* Translated from the French by Catherine Porter. Ithaca, NY: Cornell University Press, 1984.
Travis, Yakov. "Adorning the Souls of the Dead." In *God's Voice from the Void Old and New Studies in Bratslav Hasidism*, edited by Shaul Magid, 155–92. Albany: State University of New York Press, 2002.
Tshingal, Avraham Eliezer, ed. *Sefer Siach Sarfei Kodesh.* Yerushalayim: Agudat Meshekh ha-Nachal, 1988.
Twersky, Isadore. *Introduction to the Code of Maimonides: (Mishneh Torah).* [in English] New Haven: Yale University Press, 2010.
Urban, Martina. *Aesthetics of Renewal: Martin Buber's Early Representation of Hasidism as Kulturkritik.* [in English] Chicago: University of Chicago Press, 2008.
Veblen, Thorstein. "The Intellectual Pre-Eminence of Jews in Modern Europe." *Political Science Quarterly* 34, no. 1 (March 1919): 33–42.
Weiss, Joseph. *Mehkarim Ba-Hasidut Braslav.* [in Hebrew] Yerushalayim: Mosad Byalik, 1974.
———. "Torat Ha-Dialektika Ve-Ha-Emuna Le-Rabi Nachman Mi-Braslav." Hebrew University of Jerusalem, 1951.
Wilensky, Mordecai. *Hasidim U-Mitnagdim: Le-Toldot Ha-Pulmus She-Benehem.* [in Hebrew] Yerushalayim: Mosad Byalik, 1970.
Williams, Raymond. *Culture and Society, 1780–1950.* [in English] New York: Columbia University Press, 1958.
———. *Writing in Society.* [in English] London: Verso, 1983.
Wiskind-Elper, Ora. *Tradition and Fantasy in the Tales of Reb Nahman of Bratslav.* [in English] Albany: State University of New York Press, 1998.
Wolfson, Elliot. *Through a Speculum That Shines: Vision and Imagination in Medieval Jewish Mysticism.* [in English] Princeton, NJ: Princeton University Press, 1994.
Yovel, Yirmiyahu. *The Other Within: The Marranos: Split Identity and Emerging Modernity.* [in English] Princeton, NJ: Princeton University Press, 2009.
Zadoff, Noam, and Jonathan Meir. "The Empty Space, Sabbateanism and Its Melodies—Joseph Weiss' Reading of Liqqutei Moharan 64." *Kabbalah: Journal for the Study of Jewish Mystical Texts* 15 (2006): 197–232.

Index

Abramovitsh, Sholem Yankev, 2, 162–63
Adam (biblical figure), 142, 204n24
alcohol licenses, 31, 43, 67, 183n14
Alexander I of Russia, 33, 35, 43; Committee for the Amelioration of the Jews and, 27; as enlightened despot, 34, 40; Hasidic view of, 177n13; Nachman and, 26. *See also* "Statute Concerning the Organization of Jews" of
Alexander II of Russia, 1
Alexander III of Russia, 1, 4, 6, 162
allegory, 120–28, 197n13, 198n16; Benjamin on, 120, 121; Caplan on, 124, 126, 142; Dan on, 124, 146–47, 199n36; interpretations of, 141, 143–47, 199n36
American Revolution, 23
Anidjar, Gil, 201n65, 202n79
antiphilosophy, 107–14
anusim (converts), 43–45, 48, 183n16; *gzerat shmad* and, 31, 43. See also *marranos*
astrology, 50–51, 54–56, 61–62, 64, 186n20
astronomy, 61–62, 67–68, 186n7

Austria, 21, 22

Baal Shem Tov, Yisra'el (the *baal shem tov*), 23; as founder of Hasidism, 10, 14, 174n25; hagiography of, 83, 157, 207n69; on innovation, 81; on Isaiah, 193n36; Mendelssohn and, 94; on Sabbatianism, 184n22; as storyteller, 138–39
Band, Arnold, 75–76, 80, 83, 117–18, 169n6; on Kabbalistic stories, 130, 185n45
Barsky, Shimshon, 11
Bartal, Israel, 5
Baruch of Medzhybizh, 14
bechina (aspect), 18, 38, 41, 56, 65–70; of disagreement, 70, 109; Shaul Magid on, 175n45; of Moses, 105, 108, 112, 196n76; of silence, 112; of withdrawal, 109
beginnings, 137–40, 156, 161; Said on, 137, 148–50, 154, 156
ben Eliezer, Yisra'el. See *baal shem tov*
Benda, Julian, 191n16
Benjamin, Walter, 120–22, 124, 198n16
Ber, Dov (magid of Mezhirech), 22
Ber, Dov (maskil of Uman), 174n27

Ber Hurwitz, Hirsch, 106, 194n55
Bialik, Haim Nachman, 1–2
Borges, Jorge Luis, 200n55
Bosteels, Bruno, 107–10
Bourdieu, Pierre, 163
Buber, Martin, 7, 132, 169n6; on detachment from past, 164; on Hasidism, 171n7, 208n2; *Tales of Rabbi Nachman*, 2–3, 133, 161

Caplan, Marc, 5, 12–13, 98; on Nachman's tales, 124, 126, 142
Catherine the Great of Russia, 24, 178n18
Chabad school of Hasidism, 24
Chayey Moharan, 27, 82
Chomsky, Noam, 131
Christianity, 202n79; Jewish converts to, 183n16, 194n55; mysticism tradition in, 132, 201n65. See also *marranos*
civil rights, 32
Council of the Four Lands, 22, 30, 32, 46, 99, 176n3

Dan, Joseph, 76, 83, 149–50, 169n6; on allegorical interpretations, 124, 146–47, 199n36; on Kabbalah, 130, 135; on Nachman's endings, 141–43, 145; Scholem and, 123
Daniel, Book of, 47, 51–55, 60
de Man, Paul, 120, 121, 147
Defoe, Daniel, 174n27
"demographic rule," 32, 179n38
Deuteronomy, 67, 68
diglossia (Hebrew/Yiddish), 173n19
Dinur, Ben-Zion, 4
dress codes, 39–40, 182n8; for higher education, 29, 39; under Nicholas I, 181n52; for travel, 30, 40. See also "Statute Concerning the Organization of Jews"
Dreyfus Affair (1894), 6, 34
Dubnow, Simon, 29, 31, 34
Durchslag, Audri, 145–46
Dynes, Ofer, 178n23
Dynner, Glen, 5

Ecclesiastes, 70, 186n13
Elimelech of Leżajsk, 176n6
Elisha ben Abuya, 97, 111
Elstein, Yoav, 121, 142, 204n13
emancipation ideology, 34
endings, 161; "missing," 140–47
Enlightenment ideology, 5, 24, 29–34, 88, 95–96; "madness" and, 158; modernization and, 150–51, 183n13; Nachman's views of, 102; religion and, 132–33, 194n54. See also Maskilim; rationalism
Ephraim of Sudilkov, 14
Esther, Book of, 45
Etkes, Immanuel, 4
Etz haChaim, 101
Ezekiel, Book of, 69–70

faith, 88–89, 97; doubt and, 103, 189n39; melody of, 112
Foucault, Michel, 151, 207n59
free will, 87–89, 189n35
Freemasons, 48, 177n11
French Revolution, 23, 34, 150
Frieden, Ken, 169n6, 171n9

Galicia, 21, 26, 176n9
"geographic rule," 32
George III of Great Britain, 151, 153
Gramsci, Antonio, 97–99, 191n16

Green, Arthur, 80–81, 122, 128, 130, 198n24; on allegorical interpretation, 146–47; on faith, 193n48; on Nachman's name, 169n6
Grimm brothers, 10–12, 80, 83, 122
gzerat shmad (decree of conversion), 31, 43

ha-rav (ordained rabbi), 168n6
Habermas, Jürgen, 172n13
Hasidism, 4–5; Buber on, 171n7, 208n2; Chabad school of, 24; "founder" of, 10, 14, 174n25; Green on, 80–81; innovation of, 189n24; Kabbalah and, 130–31; leaders of, 22, 168n6; Maskilim on, 93, 94; Mitnagdim conflicts with, 1, 21–24, 81; rationalism and, 190n5; romanticism and, 80, 83; Scholem on, 208n2
Haskalah. *See* Maskilim
Horowitz, Chaikel, 174n27
Hosea, Book of, 38
human flight, 11–12
Hundert, Gershon, 5
Huss, Boaz, 131, 133, 143, 202n71
Huszar, George, 93–94

Idel, Moshe, 198n16
in-between, the, 82, 89, 163; heresy and, 97, 165; intellectual's social position and, 95–98; as Vacant Space, 99, 100, 104–6, 111–13, 161–62, 165
"indirect rule," 179n38
innovation: definitions of, 77–78; of Hasidism, 189n24; Nachman on, 8, 75–89, 171n7
intellectuals, 176n6; definitions of, 191n16; Gramsci on, 97–99, 191n16; Maskilim as, 96–97; *zadiks* as, 94–95, 99
interdisciplinary approaches, 77
interpretive frameworks, 120–23
"intransitive beginning," 149–50, 154, 156
intransitivity, poetics of, 8, 137–40, 150–59
"invisibility of confessional differences," 16, 30–31, 38–42, 113–14; dress codes and, 182n8; limits of representation and, 69, 71, 75; in literature, 114, 137, 162; in "Tale of a King Who Decreed Conversion," 47–49, 52, 57, 60, 63, 64
irony, 147–48, 206n46

Jacobs, Louis, 81
Jewish family names, 31

Kabbalah, 130–31, 193n35; Huss on, 202n71; Nachman's stories and, 121, 128–36, 142–45, 200n56; redemption narrative in, 119–21, 130, 142–43; Safed, 173n21; Scholem's work on, 123; *shechina* in, 204n17; symbolism in, 141, 142, 199n36, 204n17. *See also* Lurianic Kabbalah; mysticism
Kafka, Franz, 200n55
Karo, Yosef, 44
King, Richard, 132, 201n70
Koselleck, Reinhart, 172n13

"language wars" (Hebrew versus Yiddish literature), 173n19
Lederhendler, Eli, 167n2
Lefin, Menachem Mendl, 178n19
Leib, Arye, 13, 14, 26
Leshem, Zvi, 199n32

Levi Yitzhak of Berditchev, 14, 28
Liberman, Hayim, 106
Liebes, Yehuda, 76, 80, 187n4
Likkutei Moharan (Nachman), 16, 38, 85, 99–100, 193n40. *See also* Teaching
literacy, 29, 66–67; print culture and, 38–39, 41, 56, 60, 69–71
Lithuania, Grand Duchy of, 21–24, 26–27. *See also* Polish-Lithuanian Commonwealth
Louis XVI of France, 11, 151, 153
Luria, Yitzhak, 44, 149, 173n21, 193n34
Lurianic Kabbalah, 10, 44, 92; redemption narrative in, 130, 143; on Withdrawal, 100–101, 193n35. *See also* Kabbalah

Macherey, Pierre, 79, 134, 188n9
madness, 151–59; as demonic possession, 157, 208n72; Foucault on, 151, 207n59; Nachman on, 151–52, 155–56, 163, 207nn70–71; Pinel on, 157, 158; in *Shivchei haBesht*, 157; social emancipation and, 153
Magid, Shaul, 105, 134, 169n6, 175n45, 193n48
Maimonides, Moses, 39
Mark, Zvi, 10, 36, 83; on madness, 157, 158; on Nachman's mystical experiences, 201n66
marranos, 45–46, 49, 53, 60, 64, 183n16, 191n18. See also *anusim*
Maskilim (Jewish Enlightenment scholars), 1, 14, 33, 35, 39; "heresy" of, 92, 190n5, 194n48194n54; as intellectuals, 96–97; of Uman, 174n27; *zadiks* and, 93, 94, 100, 105–6, 191n15; Zionism and, 133

"May Laws" (1882). *See* "Temporary Regulations Regarding the Jews"
Meir, Jonatan, 171n9
Mendelssohn, Moses, 39, 94, 183n13
Mendes-Flohr, Paul, 91, 92, 95, 96, 105, 113; on detachment, 163–64; on intellectuals, 191n16
meribah (quarrel), 70, 187n28
messianism, 83, 123–25, 142–43, 145–47
Mezhirech, magid of, 22–23, 28
Miron, Dan, 188n10, 202n74
mise-en-abyme, 127, 206n46
Mitnagdim, 35, 40; Hasidim conflicts with, 1, 21–24, 81; on innovation, 82; on Shneur Zalman of Lyadi, 24, 177n11
Mitnagdim of Vilna, 176n6
modernity, literary, 1–8, 139, 161–65; Band on, 118; "crisis" of, 5–6, 37; modernization and, 13
Mondshein, Yehoshua, 80
monolingual Jewish literature, 173n19
Montgolfier brothers, 11
mysticism, 132–33, 187n6, 202n71; Christian, 132, 201n65; Huss on, 143; Mark on, 201n66. *See also* Kabbalah

Nachman of Breslav, 8–15, 161, 167n2; biography of, 27; Buber on, 133, 161; as innovator, 8, 75–89, 171n7; Kabbalistic stories of, 121, 128–36, 142–43, 200n56; on madness, 151–52, 155–56, 163, 207nn70–71; as Messiah, 117–20, 124, 127–28; on music, 195n72

Nachman of Tscheherin, 204n16
Naftali (Nachman's disciple), 11
Napoleon Bonaparte, 3, 25–26,
    150, 177n13; as emperor, 28,
    34–35, 40
Nebuchadnezzar's dream, 51–54
"news of the world," 10–12, 26,
    174n27
Nicholas I of Russia, 181n52
Noah (biblical figure), 142, 204n24
Numbers, Book of, 70

oral culture, 38–39, 41, 56, 60,
    69–71

Pale of Settlement, 1–4, 9, 29–30,
    38, 140, 167n1; Committee for
    the Amelioration of the Jews
    and, 27; disintegration of, 162;
    dress codes in, 182n8; public
    education in, 29, 42–43
parabasis, 147–48, 150, 154, 206n46
"Parable of the Turkey," 17, 150,
    151, 154–59, 162–63
"Parable of the Wheat," 17, 150,
    151–54
parrhesia (free speech), 48,
    184nn26–27
Paul I of Russia, 24, 178n18
"the people," concept of, 150–54,
    207n62
Perl, Joseph, 192n26
phylacteries (*tefillin*), 49, 55, 63, 64,
    69, 154
Pinel, Philippe, 157, 158
Pinsker, Leon, 1
Pirkei Avot, 46
Pitrushka, Sh., 204n13
plagiarism, 83, 85
plugta (disagreement), 70, 187n29
poetics, 11, 120, 147; of
    intransitivity, 8, 137–40, 150–59

Poland, Kingdom of, 21–22;
    Russian annexation of, 24,
    26–27, 178n18
Polish-Lithuanian Commonwealth:
    Council of the Four Lands and,
    22, 30, 32, 99, 176n3; partitions
    of, 3, 6–7, 22, 150
print: culture of, 18, 38–39, 41, 56,
    60, 69–71; technology of, 23, 82,
    200n56, 203n7
Proverbs, Book of, 65, 71, 186n17
public sphere, 16, 40–42, 47–49,
    64, 114; establishment of, 6,
    29–30; Foucault on, 182n10;
    Habermas on, 172; Mendelssohn
    on, 183n13; *parrhesia* as, 48,
    184n26

Rabba bar bar Hanna, 85
rabbi, 32–33, 137; as honorific,
    167n6; "unfit," 65–68
rabi (Hasidic leader), 168n6
Rancière, Jacques, 151–52
Rapoport, Nachman-Nathan, 91,
    189n1
Rapoport-Albert, Ada, 5, 22, 28, 80
rationalism, 92, 102, 132;
    epistemology of, 110; of Hasidic
    movement, 190n5; limits of,
    107; Nachman on, 193n40;
    romanticism and, 198n28. *See
    also* Enlightenment ideology
reb (honorific), 167n6
romanticism: Benjamin on,
    120, 122; Hasidism and, 80,
    83; rationalism and, 198n28;
    Schlegel and, 147
Roskies, David, 12, 76, 80; on
    storytelling, 83, 144
Russia revolution (1905), 1
Russian Empire, 24, 26–27, 178n18.
    See also Pale of Settlement

Sabbatianism, 44, 184n22
Sadan, Dov, 117
Said, Edward, 134–35, 172n15, 203n80; on beginnings, 137, 148–50; on intellectuals, 191n16
Schechter, Ronald, 34
Schlegel, Friedrich, 147–48, 206n46
Schleicher, Marianne, 129
Shneur Zalman of Lyadi, 24, 34, 177n11
Scholem, Gershom, 120, 123, 131, 169n6; on Hasidism, 208n2; on mysticism, 132, 171n7, 202n71
"Scroll of Secrets," 143, 150, 206n53
Seeman, Don, 134
Sefer haZichronot, 45, 50, 51, 54
Sefer haZohar, 129, 130, 193n35, 201n65
Sefer Yetzirah, 195n63
shechina, 141, 142, 204n17
Shim'on (Nachman's disciple), 25–26
Shivchei haBesht, 10, 83, 157
Shmeruk, Chone, 10, 144
Siff, David, 82
sifrut (literature), 79
Sippurei Maasiyot (Nachman), 75–76, 129, 150
Spain, 47; expulsion of Jews from, 44–45, 47; *marranos* of, 45–46, 50, 53, 64, 183n16, 191n18
Speransky, Michael, 179n36
Spivak, Gayatri Chakravorty, 207n59
Staël, Madame de, 94, 188n9
"Statute Concerning the Organization of Jews" (1804), 4, 9, 24, 150, 162; modifications to, 181n52; provisions of, 28–33, 38–43, 182n8; reactions to, 33–36. *See also* Alexander I of Russia
Steinsaltz, Adin, 205n40
Sternhartz, Nathan, 9–10, 91, 128, 137; Band on, 75–76; Nachman's biography by, 27, 82; as Nachman's disciple, 172n17; on *punktin*, 28; on "Tale of the Lost Princess," 204n16; writing style of, 171n9
Swift, Jonathan, 11
symbolism, 120–23, 197n13, 198n16; Kabbalistic, 141, 142, 199n36, 204n17

"Tale of a Fly and Spider," 140, 142
"Tale of a King Who Decreed Conversion," 8, 16, 42–57, 59, 138–39; ending of, 145; wise man in, 60–64, 68–69, 154
"Tale of the Lost Princess," 120, 140–42, 144, 150, 204n16
"Tale of the Seven Beggars," 140, 142, 143
tallit (prayer shawl), 49, 55, 56, 63, 64, 69
talush (person detached from society), 163
Teaching I:21 (*Likkutei Moharan*), 86–87
Teaching I:61 (*Likkutei Moharan*), 16, 59, 64–65, 110
Teaching I:64 (*Likkutei Moharan*), 70, 92–93, 97–110, 113, 161–62, 190n7, 193n48
Teaching II:28 (*Likkutei Moharan*), 16, 38, 45, 56, 60, 63, 67–69, 71, 114
tefillin (phylacteries), 49, 55, 56, 63, 64, 69, 154

"Temporary Regulations Regarding the Jews" (1882), 4, 6, 162
Terhovitza, magid of, 82
theosophy, 122
Toqueville, Alexis de, 94
Torah, 70, 138; written versus oral, 38–39, 41, 56, 60, 69–71
Travis, Yakov, 9
tsin'ah, 44, 48–49
"turkey prince." See "Parable of the Turkey"

Urban, Martina, 2–3

Vacant Space, 100–113
Vittal, Chaim, 193n34

Weiss, Joseph, 91, 92, 122; on allegory, 126; on doubt, 103; on faith, 88–89; Scholem and, 123; on Vacant Space, 100–103

Wiesel, Naftali Hertz, 82
Williams, Raymond, 94, 135, 203n80
Wiskind-Elper, Ora, 50, 80, 83, 145, 169n6
Withdrawal of divinity (*tzimtzum*), 100–104, 109, 193n35
Wolfson, Elliot, 131

Yisroel of Rodzin, 189n31

zadik (righteous man), 23, 35, 108, 112; hierarchies of, 195n76; as intellectual, 94–95, 99; as intermediary, 176n6; Jacobs on, 81; Maskilim and, 93, 94, 100, 105–6, 191n15; Nachman as, 36, 57, 71; true versus false, 196n76
Zadikism, 23, 35, 195n76
Zionism, 3, 133
Zohar, 129, 130, 193n35, 201n65

www.ingramcontent.com/pod-product-compliance
Lightning Source LLC
Chambersburg PA
CBHW030647230426
43665CB00011B/993